The National Labor Relations Act

Health Systems Management

Edited by Samuel Levey, Ph.D. and Alan Sheldon, M.D.

Financial Management of Health Institutions

Personnel Administration in the Health Services Industry:
Theory & Practice
Norman Metzger

Organizational Issues in Health Care Management
Alan Sheldon

The National Labor Relations Act:
A Guidebook for Health Care Facility Administrators,
Dennis D. Pointer and Norman Metzger

The National Labor Relations Act

A Guidebook for Health Care Facility Administrators

Dennis D. Pointer
Association of American Medical Colleges, Washington, D.C.

and

Norman Metzger
The Mount Sinai Medical Center, New York

SP

S P Books Division of
SPECTRUM PUBLICATIONS, INC.
New York

Distributed by Halsted Press
A Division of John Wiley & Sons

New York Toronto London Sydney

To
Our
Parents

Spectrum Publications, Inc.
86-19 Sancho Street, Holliswood, New York 11423

Distributed solely by the Halsted Press Division of John Wiley & Sons, Inc., New York.

Third Printing, 1981

Library of Congress Cataloging in Publication Data

Pointer, Dennis Dale.
The National Labor Relations Act.

(Health Systems Management)
1. Health facilities—Law and legislation—United States. 2. Labor laws and legislation—United States.
I. Metzger, Norman, 1924- , joint author.
II. Title.
KF3580.H4P6 344'.73'041 74-34375
ISBN 0-470-69146-8

Printed in the United States of America
123456789

CONTENTS

FOREWORD

Although the jurisdiction of the Wagner Act of 1935 originally covered all private hospitals, the Taft-Hartley Act removed nonprofit hospitals from the scope of the law in 1947. The Taft-Hartley restriction had little effect on the real world of labor relations for many years; the National Labor Relations Board did not actively assert full-scale coverage in the health care field until 1967. Since that time, the Board has been covering private proprietary hospitals, and has also assumed jurisdiction over other types of health care facilities, both proprietary and nonprofit, such as nursing homes and clinics. Thus, nonprofit private hospitals, employing approximately one and a half million people, constituted the only employee segment in the health care field without NLRA coverage until Public Law 93-360 was enacted by President Richard M. Nixon on July 26, 1974.

Long before this historic date, I had come to the conclusion that there was no logical reason why employees engaged in the same industry should be treated differently. I sought the enactment of a bill that would eliminate the disparity of treatment while at the same time ensuring that the orderly procedures of the National Labor Relations Act would resolve the often bitter and wasteful confrontations which had resulted in prior disputes in the health care industry. For instance, I viewed the extension of the NLRA as a proper vehicle to alleviate one of the most serious problems in hospital labor relations today--the recognitional strike. In sum, I was convinced that the time had come to place private, nonprofit hospitals under the salutary provisions of the National Labor Relations Act.

While extension of the Act was manifestly appropriate, I was determined to work for carefully tailored legislation to treat the health care industry uniquely in certain important respects. Limited safeguards were necessary to protect the public interest in the delivery of health care services but which, at the same time, would not be unduly restrictive of either party's freedom of action in the collective bargaining setting. Therefore, I pressed for safeguards now embodied in the legislation which avoid mere mechanical application of the existing National Labor Relations Act procedures. Hopefully, these safeguard procedures will substantially help health care institutions and their employees to settle their disputes responsibly and peacefully and will further assure the greatest possible success of the collective bargaining process prior to the need to resort to strikes or other economic sanctions.

Over an extended period of time, the only thing that prevents strikes and disruptive labor disputes is the establishment and maintenance of a good collective bargaining climate. I believe this legislation should assure that kind of climate by covering employees in the private health care field under the National Labor Relations Act in essentially the same manner that employees in other industries are covered. To that end, and within the context of the safeguards that are embodied in the statute, I believe the legislation not only is in the best interests of the employees of nonprofit hospitals, but will also serve to reduce rather than increase the number and intensity of labor-management disputes in this industry.

Robert Taft, Jr.
U.S. Senator, Ohio

FOREWORD

I have been involved in labor relations, as an advocate or legislator, for more than 30 years. The enactment of P.L. 93-360 represents, in my opinion, the most significant and complex amendment to the National Labor Relations Act since the Landrum-Griffin Act of 1959.

The Congress not only extended the protection and coverage of the National Labor Relations Act to the largest segment of the health care industry, nonprofit hospitals, it provided separate treatment--for the first time--for a segment of the work force covered by the NLRA. The former is important for the first time tens of thousands of nonprofit hospital employees will have an opportunity for a living wage and job security. The latter is significant: it may set precedent for the extension of NLRA coverage in other areas.

Dennis Pointer and Norman Metzger share an intimate knowledge and understanding of this health care facility legislation. Dr. Pointer has studied and written extensively on the subject. Mr. Metzger testified in the 92d and 93d Congresses as an expert witness during legislative hearings held by my Special Subcommittee on Labor. Members of the Subcommittee found their earlier joint venture, Labor-Management Relations in the Health Services Industry, to be of invaluable assistance in their deliberations on this complex legislation.

I find their latest book, The National Labor Relations Act: A Guidebook for Health Care Facility Administrators, to be a timely and comprehensive analysis; it will be a necessary aid to the health care administrator as he attempts to understand the new law and deal with it in the arena of health care facility labor management relations.

I commend the authors on a superb presentation and recommend this book to all who share my interest in this vital field.

Frank Thompson, Jr.
U.S. Representative, New Jersey

AUTHORS' PREFACE

In our first book, Labor-Management Relations in the Health Services Industry: Theory and Practice, we attempted to provide the reader with a general overview of the conduct of the employer-employee relationship in health care facilities. This book, in every way, is a direct outgrowth of that previous effort, but in a substantive sense, it addresses a changed environment. Broad segments of the industry are now covered by federal labor relations statutes for the first time; those facilities previously covered by the Act are subject to amended guidelines. With the passage of the 1974 amendments (P.L. 93-360), labor relations in health care facilities is now subject to a complex body of statutory, administrative and case law. It is important to emphasize, however, that the basic principles and modes of approach outlined in our previous book remain unaltered if not enhanced. The need is critical, on the part of health care administrators, for a foundational knowledge of personnel administration, labor relations and labor law if the industry is to increase the productivity of human resources in the provision of patient-care services.

In a personal sense, this book has provided the authors with a vehicle to continue and enhance a collaborative relationship which began over five years ago. Debates over both message and medium, rather than placing strain on a friendship, have cemented a relationship that has been the greatest reward derived from the joint authorship of two books and numerous articles.

Few books are the sole product of the individuals fortunate enough to have their names displayed on the covers--this effort is no exception. The authors work in stimulating environments populated with individuals willing and able to encourage good ideas and bury many poor ones. During the gestation period of this book numerous colleagues checked upon the conditions of both the "mothers" and the "fetus." To these individuals we express our thanks; the project was made more enjoyable through demonstrated interest on the part of others.

Many people unselfishly assisted us in bringing this book to fruition. Gail Mather typed numerous rough and "final" drafts of the manuscript; she served admirably as a guardian of the syntax and her watchfulness infused readability into the final product.

Appreciation is expressed to Bob Moss, counsel for the House Special Labor Subcommittee, who was always responsive to our questions and was quick to provide us with needed documents. We thank Robert Stephens, the editor of Hospital Progress, for permission to borrow from previously published material in the preparation of Chapter II. We wish also to thank the Practising Law Institute for permission to quote extensively from Winning NLRB Elections, Management's Strategy and Preventive Programs by Louis Jackson and Robert Lewis.

Dennis Pointer would like to express his special thanks to Richard Knapp, director of the Department of Teaching Hospitals, Association of American Medical Colleges, who has, in every way, proved to be a most valued colleague and friend; and to his wife, Terri, who, through eight years of marriage, has had to constantly reorder her own schedule to the production of "just one more" article, book or paper, and without whose understanding he could not have initiated or completed this effort.

Norman Metzger would like to note the privilege of being associated with Howard Lichtenstein, Esq., of the firm of Proskauer, Rose, Goetz & Mendelsohn. During this period the more subtle implications and multifaceted nature of labor law were brought to his attention by this outstanding practitioner. He is indeed indebted to S. David Pomrinse, M.D., director of The Mount Sinai Hospital and chairman of the Department of Administrative Medicine of the Mount Sinai School of Medicine, for his encouragement and support. He would like to make special note of his relationship with William Abelow, Esq., executive director and counsel for the League of Voluntary Hospitals and Homes of New York, whose wise counsel and expert knowledge of the law have always been extremely valuable. Of course, he continues to be deeply indebted to Marlin "Bud" Cruse, who has labored with him through three books, and whose energies are boundless, his advice invaluable. He also proudly acknowledges his wife Marcia's role in giving unlimited support and encouragement to his endless need for time to write.

What approbation this book receives, if any, must be shared with those named here and the many others who have contributed both directly and indirectly to its production. The errors, both of commission and omission, are the responsibility of the authors alone.

Dennis D. Pointer
Washington, D.C.

Norman Metzger
New York, New York

I
Introduction

In one of his last official acts before resigning the presidency of the United States, Richard M. Nixon signed into law P.L. 93-360, the 1974 amendments to the National Labor Relations Act. For the first time all nongovernmental health care facilities (hospitals, clinics, HMO's, nursing homes, as well as homes for the aged) are uniformly covered by federal labor law. The passage of the 1974 amendments to the Act causes two immediate and significant problems for the health services industry.

First, union organizational activity will increase drastically. Labor union attempts to represent health workers are not a recent phenomenon. Unions were active in California hospitals immediately prior to World War I; several Seattle, Washington, hospitals had collective bargaining contracts in the late 1920's and a large number of Minnesota hospitals were subject to union organizational drives in the late 1930's and early 1940's. Although organizing attempts have been conducted for the last sixty years (some with significant success), concerted union activity in the industry extends back only a little more than one decade. To date, approximately 15 to 20 percent of the nation's hospitals have collective bargaining contracts with at least some segment of their employees (no comparable data are available for nursing homes, clinics, homes for the aged, etc.). Most observers expect this figure to increase drastically in the decade ahead. Union efforts to organize health workers have been hampered by the lack of labor law coverage. This barrier has now been removed. Union membership relative to industrial-sector employment has been declining for the last eight years. Unions are eyeing the health services industry (one of the fastest growing segments of the U.S. economy) as a lucrative avenue of needed membership growth.

Second, health care facility administrators will be required to operate under a complex body of statutory, administrative and case law. Health facility administrators have had little experience with or exposure to this body of law. Labor law is a topic that most administrators have had little acquaintance with during their formal training or through specialized course work. Most educational programs in hospitals, health or nursing home administration offer no instruction in personnel administration, labor relations or labor law.

Undoubtedly this will change in the future. Similarly, few administrators have had any long-term practical experience with operating under the guidelines provided in federal labor laws because the greatest segment of the industry has not been covered by them.

It is the objective of this book to provide the health care facility administrator and his management team with a general familiarity with the structure and function of the National Labor Relations Act as amended and to discuss its impact upon the industry. The book is specifically aimed at the practicing administrator and his/her assistants, departmental heads and supervisors. Hopefully, the book will also have value for students in both undergraduate and graduate programs in health services administration.

The book is not meant to be a comprehensive treatment of health facility labor law. Labor law is a complex blend of statutory law, administrative rulings and court decisions. The intent here is to provide the reader with an introductory knowledge of the National Labor Relations Act as amended. The Act is applied in specific circumstances and interpreted through rulings of the National Labor Relations Board and decisions of the federal courts. To understand the functioning and requirements of the Act, pertinent rulings and decisions will be examined in passing. The treatment will, however, be indicative rather than exhaustive. Additionally, many federal statutes that affect the labor relations of health care facilities (such as the Federal Fair Labor Standards and the Occupational Health and Safety Acts) will be completely ignored. This is not to imply that these statutes are unimportant--they clearly are; however, their discussion is best left to other volumes.

It must be noted that the subject matter of labor cannot be separated from personnel administration and labor relations. It has been our experience that often the relationship between management and unions is both studied and conducted from a narrow legalistic perspective. We feel strongly that this is detrimental. Knowledge of one's legal rights and responsibilities is critically important, but managers must be ever cognizant that the employer-employee relationship has aspects that are social, psychological and cultural as well as legal-economic. The topics of health-facility labor relations and personnel administration have been covered in our previous book; thus they will be addressed here only in reference to requirements of the law.

Provided below is a brief synopsis of the chapters that follow.

Chapter II discusses the development of health-facility labor law. Since both the statutory and common law treatment of health-facility labor relations have their foundation in the industrial sector, the development of labor law in the broader economic environment is briefly covered. Emphasis is placed upon describing the evolution of labor statutes in England and the United States prior to 1930. The chapter discusses the status of health care facilities under the Wagner Act, passed in 1935, and the Taft-Hartley Act, enacted in 1947. The intent here is to highlight the fragmented, constantly changing and often conflicting labor law guidelines applied to health care facilities. It is this environment that eventually stimulated the passage of the 1974 amendments to the National Labor Relations Act.

Chapter III provides the reader with a "walking tour" of the National Labor Relations Act. Labor law is multifaceted; its foundation stems from such diverse sources as the United States Constitution, the National Labor Relations Act, decisions of the National Labor Relations Board, rulings of the federal courts, labor-management collective bargaining contracts and arbitration awards. Each of these sources of labor law is reviewed. The chapter also provides a section-by-section description of the National Labor Relations Act as amended. Key provisions, as they apply to health care facilities, are outlined and briefly discussed. The intent is to offer the reader a general overview of the Act prior to examining selected provisions in some detail.

Chapter IV details the events leading up to the passage of the 1974 amendments to the Act. The introduction, consideration and eventual passage of any bill is a complex and often interesting procedure. The chapter seeks to give the reader a feel for the legislative process. "Health facility" amendments to the National Labor Relations Act were first proposed in 1971; the bills containing the amendments to the Act were finally passed in 1974. The intervening three years saw struggles for influence, changes in position, political bargaining and eventually compromise. The chapter also discusses each provision of the amendments as enacted and analyzes relevant committee reports attached to the law.

Chapter V describes guidelines regarding bargaining-unit determination and the conduct of representation elections. The chapter discusses the type of bargaining units that can be certified by the National Labor Relations Board, the criteria employed for bargaining-unit delineations, the establishment of craft and industrial units, and the status of professional, supervisory, guard and confidential employees. The chapter describes the manner in which elections are conducted to select employee representatives. The selection of observers, challenges, voter eligibility, ballot tallying and the filing of unfair labor practice charges are discussed. Forms employed by the NLRB in certifying bargaining units and conducting elections are included as exhibit items.

Chapters VI and VII discuss employer and union unfair labor practices respectively. Those practices when committed by management that are deemed to be illegal were included in the original Wagner Act passed in 1935; the delineation of union unfair labor practices was added to the law in 1947 with the passage of the Taft-Hartley amendments to the National Labor Relations Act. Each employer and union unfair labor practice is described with regard to applicable statutory and case law; examples of prohibited practices are provided where meaningful.

Chapter VIII discusses labor-management disputes. Alterations made by the 1974 amendments to the sections of the Act pertaining to disputes settlement procedures are described in detail. Health care facilities are now treated differently than other employers covered by the Act regarding reporting requirements. The Act was amended to make mandatory the engagement of the Federal Mediation and Conciliation Service in collective bargaining disputes involving health care facilities. Health care facilities and unions dealing with them are also required to provide the other party with ten days' notice prior to a job action or a lockout. The chapter describes the emergency disputes settlement procedure applicable to health care facilities. Different categories of "illegal strikes" are discussed; special attention is accorded the job status of strikers and the ramifications of the violation of "no strike" clauses in collective bargaining agreements.

Chapter IX describes the five major forms of union security arrangements: closed shop (defined as illegal under the Act), union shop, modified union shop, maintenance of membership shop and agency shop. Examples of various union security collective bargaining contract clauses are provided. Argument supporting and refuting the inclusion of a union security arrangement in collective bargaining contracts are discussed. The chapter also describes the manner in which union security discharges are executed, the establishment of checkoff procedures, and provisions of the 1974 amendment to the Act allowing religious exemption from the payment of dues and fees under a union security agreement.

The Labor-Management Reporting and Disclosure Act (LMRDA) is the topic of Chapter X. The LMRDA amended the Taft-Hartley Act in 1959 and was an outgrowth of the McClellan committee chartered by the Senate to investigate alleged improper activities of managements and labor unions. The chapter describes the Labor-Management Reporting and Disclosure Act's provisions regarding 1) labor-organization and labor-official reporting requirements; 2) reports required of employers and labor relation consultants when engaged in certain activities; 3) union members' bill of rights; and 4) the creation of trusteeships and the conduct of union elections.

Chapter XI addresses the mechanism through which the National Labor Relations Act is administered; the functions and structure of the National Labor Relations Board are described. Particular emphasis is placed upon the Board's functions of certifying collective bargaining units, conducting representation elections and ruling on unfair labor practice cases. The duties of the Board itself and of the General Counsel and trial examiners are discussed. An exhibit is included that lists the NLRB regional offices, their directors and chief attorneys.

Chapter XII focuses upon many legal and nonlegal points not covered elsewhere in this book. "Labor relations" is defined as the arena where labor law meets the practical test of application. The chapter describes and discusses the vulnerability of health care facilities to unionization; a checklist details the factors labor organizations consider in selecting a health care facility for a representational campaign. Supervisors are the critical link to employees during an organizational drive and throughout the life of the collective bargaining contract; the role of the supervisor along with the guidelines for allowed and prohibited behavior is described. During a union representational effort, management strategy and tactics are critical to election outcome. However, the employment atmosphere that management has created in past years is probably the single most important determinant of whether or not a union will be successful in its bid to represent employees; the "preventive medicine" approach to preparing unfertile ground for union activity is discussed. The chapter also describes statutory provisions, NLRB decisions and court rulings regarding management "free speech," campaign buttons, and distribution and solicitation rules. The contract negotiation process is analyzed and some sample contract clauses are provided.

A series of appendices are provided to assist the reader in his study of health facility labor law. Appendix A contains the complete text of the National Labor Relations Act as amended. The Act should be consulted by the reader as specific portions are discussed in the various chapters; it is suggested that after completing the book the reader gain a general familiarity of the Act by reviewing it in total. Appendix B provides the full text of P. L. 93-360, the 1974 amendments to the National Labor Relations Act. Appendices C and D contain the reports of the Senate Committee on Labor and Public Welfare and the Joint House-Senate Conference Committee on the bill amending the Act. The reports contain language that specifies the intent of Congress in enacting the amendment critical to the law's interpretation by the National Labor Relations Board and the federal courts. Appendix E contains three current National Labor Relations Board rulings on bargaining-unit determinations in health care facilities cited with approval in the committee reports.

Passage of the 1974 amendments to the National Labor Relations Act provides a unique challenge to health care administrators. P. L. 93-360 will likely have an impact upon health facilities equaled only by the implementation of Medicare and Medicaid in 1966. This book is designed to provide the reader with a foundational knowledge of the structure and functions of federal labor law as it applies to the health services industry. Before delving into the substantive material of this book, several observations deserve particular emphasis.

1. Labor law is a complex body of statutory law, administrative rulings and court decisions that is applied to variable situations over time. The application and interpretation of this body of law in specific circumstances require competent legal assistance. Hopefully, after completing this book the reader will be better able to appreciate the need for the advice provided by counsel and/or labor relations consultants and will be better able to seek, implement and subsequently evaluate such advice.

2. The relationship between employers and employees is social, psychological, cultural and economic as well as legal. Labor law

is much like the frame of a picture--essential because it establishes the boundaries for behavior (both actions and reactions). However, the subject of labor relations can be compared to the picture itself--the frame has no meaning in its absence. In dealing with the conduct of the labor-management relationship there is often a tendency to overemphasize legal issues. The law is critically important, but the administrator must be ever sensitive to the dynamics of interpersonal and intergroup relations.

3. As discussed here, amendments to the National Labor Relations Act open up the health industry to a concerted effort on the part of labor organizations to seek to represent the employees of health facilities not previously covered by the Act. Passage of the amendments, or for that matter the direct efforts of unions, will not automatically organize employees. Management practices, policies and attitudes are generally the primary factors that establish fertile ground for union representational efforts. Health facility administrators seeking to continue to operate in a union-free environment must reassess and often redesign or initiate wage and salary administration plans, grievance procedures, overtime scheduling and personnel policies. In the face of a union organizational effort, management can and must wage an effective "counter-representation" campaign. However, no amount of effort will overcome a pattern of poor personnel-relations performance. The time to initiate a program to overcome union organization efforts is long before the union enters the facility.

4. Supervisors are the key link in the development and execution of personnel administration and labor relations programs; to underestimate their importance is fatal. Every facility should have a structured program to enhance the skills of supervisory personnel. Remember: during a union election more workers vote for or against their immediate supervisor than for or against the health facility or the union. During a union organization drive, supervisors should receive training in the rudiments of labor law, for it is their actions that have the potential to be the most harmful or helpful. Hopefully, this book will assist the supervisory staff of health care facilities in developing a feel for the basics.

5. One of the more common faults of administrators during union organizational campaigns is that they underestimate the opposition. What is unfamiliar territory for the administrator and his staff is often traveled terrain for the labor organizer. Most organizers (especially those associated with unions active in the health industry) understand health facilities far better than the administrators comprehend the dynamics of unions. It is a common tactic for organizers to play down their knowledge, technical sophistication and perceptiveness. Don't make the mistake of being lulled into unwarranted self-confidence.

6. If a labor organization is successful in organization, management will be required to adopt a new perspective toward unions and their participation in the health care facility. It is not suggested

that administrators stop viewing the union as a threat to management--especially management prerogatives. However, to believe that labor union weakness means management strength is delusionary! One may deplore unionization, but a weak union without an established role, function and authority and without strong, secure and effective leadership will mean strife, demogoguery, irresponsible demands and increasing bitterness and tension. The result will not be management effectiveness but, rather, management frustration.

II
The Development of Health Facility Labor Law

THE LEGAL FRAMEWORK

Law is a body of rules, both implicit and explicit, that guides conduct and serves as an instrument of social control. America is becoming more legalistic in nature; this increase in legalism is due to the increasing complexity of interpersonal and intergroup relations and the accelerated pace of social and technological change. For example, in America's early period, a single craftsman and his several workers had a well-defined relationship even though it was primarily personal in nature. As the number of employees in a working unit increased and technology advanced, the relationships among the workers, between the workers and the employer, and between workers and the technology became more structured--increasing size and complexity being the primary stimulants.

The legal framework provides boundaries within which union leaders and health facility administrators must act and react. It is the purpose of Chapters II and III to provide the reader with a basic understanding of the development of labor law both generally and specifically with regard to health care facilities. While the thrust of this book is to examine health facility labor law, the assumption is made that to comprehend legal relationships in this specific sector one must be familiar with the general aspects of labor law as it has developed and as it is applied in the broader economic environment. Both the common law and statute treatment of health facility labor-management relations have their foundations in the industrial sector.

LABOR LAW FOUNDATIONS: ROME TO THE DEPRESSION

The genesis of labor law is not distinct. A body of law was developed by the Roman city-states to insure the collective rights of slaves. During the feudal period in England the serf was considered to be property (chattel) subject to the complete will of the overlord; property rights thus governed the master-subject relationship. The first "system" of labor law emerged after the demise of feudalism.

In the mid-fourteenth century, the plague engulfed Europe and, according to some estimates, killed between one-third and one-half of the continent's population. In the aftermath of the plague (which had killed many workers), the English enacted the first restrictive labor laws. The Statute of Laborers Act bound workers to their jobs and fixed wages; criminal action was provided for violators. A subsequent statute placed severe restrictions on the mobility of laborers--and attempted to halt the large migration of people from rural to urban areas. In addition to statutes, the English legal system developed common law guidelines regarding labor. In Rex v. Journeyman Taylors, the court developed the doctrine of criminal conspiracy, which held that worker combination was in and of itself criminal, regardless of the consequences of such action. Later this doctrine was modified: worker combinations themselves were not criminal, but the ends of those combinations were held to be the determining factor regarding legality. If the combination had legal ends, the combination was legal.

Early American labor law generally paralleled the English experience. In what has been described as the first American labor case, Philadelphia Cordwainers (Commonwealth v. Pullis), decided in 1806, the court addressed the problem of whether a strike of shoemakers was legal. The court held that actions which might legally be performed individually (e.g., stopping work) became illegal when exercised in concert if such actions were harmful to the public interest. This logic was applied widely in the 1820's and 1830's to mitigate the power of unions (at that time known as "combinations," "collectives," or "the group"). The generally accepted concept of laissez-faire economics was, however, being modified in the mid-1800's as impetus developed to apply the concept to labor as well as to capital organization. Along with the increase in permissible monopolization by business, the corollary right of worker combination was becoming more accepted.

In Commonwealth v. Hunt the Massachusetts Supreme Court expressed the opinion that the legality of worker combination depended upon both the objective of the combination and the means used for its accomplishment. Since this decision, the right of workers to combine for their own mutual benefit has not been seriously questioned by the courts in the United States--the means by which the combination is achieved, however, has been subject to much litigation.

In 1890 the Sherman Anti-Trust Act was passed with the intent of prohibiting certain monopolies. The Act stated in Section 1 that "Every contract, combination in the form of a trust or otherwise, or conspiracy, in restraint of trade or commerce among the several states, or with foreign countries, is hereby declared to be illegal." The Attorney General was allowed to seek injunctions in the federal courts to prevent and restrain violations of the Act. Although it appeared that the Sherman Act was directed at business combinations, the Supreme Court used statutory guidelines of the Act to allow an injunction of a union attempting to organize workers of hat manufacturers in several states (Lawlor v. Lowe, the "Danbury Hatters Case"). The Court reasoned that although the legislation was designed to combat monopolistic combinations of business enterprises, labor organizations were not specifically excluded from coverage.

The Clayton Anti-Trust Act, passed in 1914, was designed to eliminate the abuses of the injunction remedy by removing unions from the coverage of the Sherman Act. Section 6 of the Act stated that "the labor of a human being is not a commodity or article of commerce...nor shall labor organizations be held to be illegal combinations or conspiracies in the restraint of trade under the anti-trust laws." Section 20 of the Clayton Act provided that no injunction could be issued in a dispute between employees and employers unless irreparable damage to property or property rights had been threatened or committed. However, the courts chose to ignore completely what unions had hailed as their "bill of rights." In Duplex v. Deering, the Supreme Court stated that

> There is nothing in...[Section 6 of the Clayton Act] to exempt...[a union] or its members from accountability where it or its members depart from its normal and legitimate objectives and engage in an actual combination or conspiracy in restraint of trade.

In this and several other cases, the courts reduced the intent of the Clayton Act to impotence by declaring that the Act 1) did not actually change the Sherman Anti-Trust Act; 2) did not apply when a union was engaged in a secondary boycott (i.e., an illegal objective); 3) did not protect nonemployees, such as union organizers; 4) did not apply where a union's objective was organizational or recognitional; 5) did not apply to strikers, since they are not considered employees; and 6) did not apply where a "yellow-dog contract" was in effect (a "yellow-dog contract" is an agreement signed by an employee at the time of initial employment stating he will not join a union).

The injunction proved to be an effective weapon against labor unions. The labor injunction is a legal order issued by a court of equity in which it can forbid an individual or group of individuals from committing an act that would result in irreparable damage under circumstances where there are no adequate remedies at law (e.g., the award of monetary damages). The violator of an injunction could be held in contempt of court. Injunctions issued in labor disputes could usually be obtained ex parte (granted immediately without a formal hearing and although technically temporary in nature, many orders existed indefinitely).

In response to widespread criticism regarding the abuse of the labor injunction, the Norris-La Guardia Act was passed in 1932. The Act succeeded in doing the job for which the Clayton Act was designed in 1914. The legislation stated in Section 2 that it was the policy of the Act to foster labor union growth and development without employer interference. The Act divested the federal courts of the jurisdiction to grant injunctions in labor disputes except in cases where 1) unlawful acts were threatened or committed; 2) irreparable damage to property was clearly indicated; 3) the injury to the complainant was greater than the injury to the defendant unless the action was enjoined; 4) the complainant had no adequate remedy at law; and 5) the police were unable or unwilling to furnish protection to the complainant's property. The Norris-La Guardia Act also prevented the use of ex parte and omnibus injunctions, outlawed the "yellow-dog contract" and based its definition of labor dispute on the notion that the parties to the action need not stand in the relationship of employer and employee. Defendants in an injunction action could now demand a trial and cross-examine witnesses.

It is significant to note that this legislation was passed during the height of the Depression. John Maynard Keynes, economic adviser to President Roosevelt, advocated the implementation of a national wage policy to establish an income floor. The Congress, hesitant to enter the market directly, perceived that the encouragement of union organization and subsequent collective bargaining efforts would positively affect wage stability and stimulate a sagging national income.

In 1933 the Congress passed the National Industrial Recovery Act (NIRA). This was the first of a series of laws designed to aid the nation in its recovery from the Depression. Although not specifically labor legislation, it did provide a code of fair competition. Section 7(a) of the Act stated:

> ...employees shall have the right to organize and bargain collectively through representatives of their own choosing, and shall be free from the interference, restraint or coercion of employers of labor, or their agents, in the designation of such representatives or in self organization or in other concerted activities for the purpose of collective bargaining or other mutual aid or protection;...

This in effect provided broad segments of American labor the right, for the first time, to organize and collectively bargain with their respective employers. To adjudicate disputes and provide interpretation of the Act, the President established the National Labor Board; the NLB was replaced in 1934 with the National Labor Relations Board (NLRB), which functioned much like its current-day counterpart.

The NIRA was declared unconstitutional in 1935. The Supreme Court ruled that the Congress illegally delegated its lawmaking responsibility and that federal authority to regulate commerce among the several states did not extend to the particular firm involved in the litigation. The case seriously questioned the authority of Congress to initiate legislation regulating labor-management relations.

In the face of this decision, however, Congress passed the National Labor Relations Act (Wagner Act) in 1935, which stands as the foundation of the United States' labor code. The Act was comprehensive in nature--its full scope need not be described here--but several aspects of the Act are pertinent to the later discussion of the labor law status of health care facilities. Section 1 of the code noted that the purpose of the Act was

> ...to remove obstructions to commerce and restore equality of bargaining power arising out of employers' general denial to labor of the right to bargain collectively with them from which denial resulted a number of detrimental consequences...

The most significant portions of the legislation were Sections 7 and 8, which enumerated general employee rights under the Act and prohibited certain management behavior deemed as unfair. The unfair practices listed in Section 8 were as follows: 1) to interfere with employees in their rights to organize and bargain collectively; 2) to dominate a labor organization as to its management or control (e.g., setting up company unions); 3) discrimination with regard to hire or tenure because of union activity; 4) discrimination for filing charges under the Act; and 5) refusing to bargain in good faith. The constitutionality of the Wagner Act was affirmed in NLRB v. Jones and Laughlin Steel Corporation. The major point of the case, which refuted the decision rendered in the case declaring the National Industrial Recovery Act as unconstitutional, was that Congress had the right to pass legislation regarding the labor-management relations of organizations "affecting commerce;" the organizations need not necessarily be in commerce per se.

THE WAGNER ACT AND HEALTH CARE FACILITIES

The Wagner Act did not specifically exempt charitable, religious or educational institutions. Generally speaking, the courts in several cases also found no implied exemption. For example, NLRB v. Polish National Alliance (332 U.S. 643) established that the mere fact that a fraternal benefit insurance plan was not organized for profit did not exempt the organization from coverage under the Wagner Act if the organization had an impact on interstate commerce. The same conclusion was reached in Christian Board of Publication v. NLRB (113 F.2d 753, D.C. Cir. 1942), in which the court noted that the jurisdictional touchstone of the Wagner Act was its impact on interstate commerce rather than the question of whether or not the organization was formed for the purpose of making a profit. Both of these cases dealt with nonprofit organizations per se, rather than those considered to be eleemosynary in character.

The question concerning the applicability of the Wagner Act to voluntary hospitals was raised for the first time in regard to the request of two unions to be recognized as the bargaining agent of workers employed at Central Dispensary and Emergency Hospital in Washington, D.C. In a hearing before the NLRB, the hospital moved to dismiss the proceedings on the grounds that 1) the Wagner Act did not apply to hospitals because they were not engaged in "trade, traffic, or commerce" within the meaning of the Act; and 2) the hospital should be exempt from jurisdiction because it was a non-profit institution.

The NLRB found no merit in the contention that the jurisdictional words of the Act were inappropriate in describing a hospital's activities. The Board noted that each month the facility did import material and supplies valued at $5,000 from points outside the District of Columbia. Thus, its dealings were deemed interstate in nature. Furthermore, the NLRB ruled that the hospital's activities could be considered "trade" based on the precedent established in U.S. v. American Medical Association (App. D.C. 110 F.2d 703). In this case a federal court of appeals ruled that the AMA violated the Sherman Anti-Trust Act because it restrained trade among hospitals located in several states (by limiting hospital privileges). In the AMA decision the court noted that the word "trade" had developed meaning which covered any occupation in which men were engaged to earn a livelihood. Since workers employed by a hospital were engaged in earning a livelihood, the hospital itself was engaged in trade as defined in the Wagner Act.

Counsel for the hospital stressed as a reason for exemption from the Act the fact that the facility was not organized for profit. However, no cases were cited which held that the power conferred on Congress by the commerce clause of the U.S. Constitution was in any way limited to interstate transactions entered into with a motive of financial gain. It was observed that the hospital was entering into contracts with firms whose activities were commercial in every sense. Observing that transactions with such organizations did not lose their commercial character even though the hospital had a motive other than profit, the NLRB said: "The commerce clause looks to the activities carried on, rather than to the motives. The jurisdiction conferring words of the National Labor Relations Act, trade, traffic, commerce, transportation, or communication are words of activity, and when used together do not give a connotation of essential motive" (44 NLRB at 540, 1942).

The Central Dispensary and Emergency Hospital case was later appealed to a federal court, which enforced the NLRB decision to include the nonprofit hospital under the jurisdiction of the Wagner Act. In its ruling, the federal court stated:

> ...the hospital argues that the spirit or policy of the Act is such that we should read into it an exemption of charitable hospitals.... We cannot understand what considerations of public policy deprive

> hospital employees of the privilege granted to the employees of other institutions. The opinions..., holding that charitable hospitals and their nonprofessional employees are subject to the labor relations acts of those states, present what seems to us the only tenable view....[1]

The labor law status of health care facilities, other than for nonprofit voluntary hospitals, was not directly considered by the courts during this period. Given the ruling in the Central Dispensary case it was assumed that proprietary hospitals and nursing homes, regardless of ownership, were considered to be included under the jurisdiction of the Wagner Act "in principle" if their operation could be demonstrated to have an impact upon interstate commerce. In fact, however, such institutions would have probably been considered "local in character" had the National Labor Relations Board been required to make a ruling. State, municipal and federal hospitals were specifically exempted from jurisdiction through Section 2(2) of the Act (governments were not considered to be employers).

CHANGING PUBLIC SENTIMENT

Since the Wagner Act neither specifically included nor excluded nonprofit hospitals, interpretation of the legislative intent of the Act was left to the discretion of the courts. The Central Dispensary and Emergency Hospital case proved to be the exception to the majority of court rulings that dealt with the applicability of comprehensive labor legislation to nonprofit hospitals.

Immediately after the passage of the Wagner Act, several states enacted labor legislation that incorporated provisions similar to those contained in the federal statutes. Public sentiment toward the acceptability of hospital unionism can be perceived by examining several state court cases that considered whether or not nonprofit hospitals should be treated like other business enterprises with regard to the regulation of labor-management relations.

A New York court ruled that a nonprofit hospital, in caring for the indigent sick, was in fact, if not in name, a government agency that performed a governmental function that would become a responsibility of the state if not successfully discharged by the hospital. The court decided that the same doctrine that exempted the state and its political subdivisions from the statute required that a charitable institution such as a voluntary hospital also be excluded.[2]

In considering whether nonprofit hospitals could be included under the jurisdiction of a state labor law modeled after the Wagner Act, a Pennsylvania court noted that

> ...[the operation of such facilities] would be

> impossible should we hold the Labor Act applicable with all its attending ramifications, interruptions, and possible cessations of service due to labor disputes and attending financial inability to function. Surely the legislature had no such intention...[3]

During this period, the great majority of court decisions followed the general line of reasoning developed in the preceding two cases. The courts concluded that 1) the Wagner Act (as well as associated state labor laws modeled after it) was not intended to extend coverage to the workers of nonprofit hospitals; 2) the delivery of health care was essentially a governmental function, thus, hospitals--like governments and their political subdivisions--were excluded from labor law coverages; and 3) making voluntary hospitals subject to the provisions of comprehensive labor statutes was not in the public interest. In addition, the rationale for excluding charitable institutions from labor legislation coverage centered on a distinction between those organizations created for gain and those whose goal was eleemosynary. A New York court stated that "...the character of such employers [nonprofit charitable institutions]...was sufficient assurance of fair dealing with their employees to render unnecessary the protection of the Labor Relations Act."[4] There also seemed to be some concern that if nonprofit institutions were required to bargain collectively, much charitable contribution would be withdrawn.

Neil Chamberlain and James Kuhn state that "...labor law can best be understood if one thinks of the courts as an instrument of society adjusting to changed social conditions."[5] Courts base their rulings not only on precedent but also on the perceived mood of the public at a given time. The environment created by the preceding court decisions formed the foundation for a statutory enactment that embodied the prevailing mood of the public regarding the control of labor-management relations in health care facilities.

THE TAFT-HARTLEY ACT OF 1947

Stimulated by the provisions of the Wagner Act, the expansion of union membership in the industrial sector gave rise to new problems regarding the regulation of union-management relations. Jurisdictional strikes (disputes over which union should do what), abuses of the secondary boycott, the refusal of some unions to bargain in good faith, and the sharp increase in industrial conflict in the immediate postwar period created widespread public demand for remedial action. In this environment, Congress passed the Labor-Management Relations (Taft-Hartley) Act of 1947. Today, this statute stands as the nation's major piece of labor legislation.

The Taft-Hartley Act amended the Wagner Act and maintained that it was unfair labor practice for a union to 1) coerce employees in the execution of their rights; 2) cause an employer to discriminate against his employees; 3) refuse to bargain in good faith with an employer; 4) engage in certain strikes and boycotts deemed unlawful in their objectives; 5) require the payment of excessive or discriminatory fees under a union security agreement; and 6) engage in "featherbedding" practices (these practices will be discussed in Chapter VII). In addition, the legislation expanded management's rights of free speech, excluded supervisors from the provisions of the Act, and gave the President the power to enjoin a strike if it would imperil the national health or safety. The major provisions of the Taft-Hartley Act will be discussed in Chapter III.

Of particular interest regarding the status of health care facilities is Section 2(2) of the Act, which delineated those employers considered to be exempt from the legislation's provisions. This section states that the Act "...shall not include the United States or any wholly owned government corporation..., or any state or political subdivision thereof, or any corporation or association operating a hospital, if no part of the net earnings inures to the benefit of any private shareholder or individual..."

This statutory directive reflected the climate of opinion created by the courts prior to 1947 regarding health care facilities. Under the Taft-Hartley Act, nonprofit hospitals were specifically excluded from the provisions of the legislation. Federal, state and municipal government hospitals were also exempt because they were operated by governments or recognized political subdivisions thereof. Proprietary hospitals and nursing homes were not specifically excluded from coverage, and it appeared that if their operations had impact on interstate commerce, federal labor law would be applicable.

VOLUNTARY HOSPITALS UNDER THE 1947 TAFT-HARTLEY ACT

The original bill to amend the National Labor Relations (Wagner) Act was reported out of Congressman Hartley's Committee on Education and Labor, and Senator Taft's Committee on Labor and Public Welfare. The House bill recommended exemption of all employers considered to be religious, charitable, scientific or educational institutions not organized for profit. The rationale governing the exemption focused on the fact that these facilities frequently assisted local government units in carrying out their essential functions and thus should be left to exclusive local jurisdiction. The Senate bill mentioned no exemptions other than those that had been incorporated in the original Wagner Act. However, when the proposed bill reached the Senate floor, Senator Tydings of Maryland offered an amendment exempting nonprofit hospitals which was eventually incorporated into Section 2(2) of the Taft-Hartley Act. In introducing the amendment, Senator Tydings commented:

> ...this amendment is designed merely to help a

> great number of hospitals which are having very difficult times. They are eleemosynary institutions; no profit is involved in their operation; and I understand from the Hospital Association that this amendment would be very helpful in their efforts to serve those who have not the means to pay for hospital service, enable them to keep the doors open, and operate the hospitals.[6]

An examination of the record makes it obvious that the hospital exemption amendment was consciously considered and later enacted on the premise that only charitable nonprofit hospitals should not be deemed as employers under the Act. Nonprofit hospitals that were not charitable in nature, as well as for-profit hospitals, were included in the coverage. The exemption of nonprofit hospitals hinged neither on their nonprofit status nor on their functions as hospitals, but rather on their "charitable" character.

The implications of the exemption of nonprofit hospitals from the provisions of the Taft-Hartley Act were clear. In the absence of any state statute which specifically included nonprofit hospitals, such hospitals had no obligation under the law to recognize or deal with their employees on a collective basis. Additionally, hospital management could engage in direct action to halt or limit union activity (e.g., discharging union organizers or limiting promotions of those employees sympathetic to the union cause). Phillip Taft, in his widely acclaimed book on the history of American unionism, notes that when a particular employee group is denied the protection of labor legislation, union recognition and subsequent collective bargaining are essentially impossible to achieve.[7]

PROPRIETARY HOSPITALS UNDER THE 1947 TAFT-HARTLEY ACT

In the early years following the passage of the Taft-Hartley Act, the federal labor law status of for-profit health care facilities was uncertain. A literal reading of the legislation tended to indicate that since proprietary hospitals and nursing homes were not specifically excluded from the provisions of the Act (as were nonprofit hospitals), jurisdiction would be granted if impact on interstate commerce could be demonstrated.

In a 1959 ruling, the National Labor Relations Board asserted jurisdiction over a hospital operated by Kennecott Copper Corporation. The company operated a hospital and branch dispensary in connection with a copper-mining operation in Santa Ria, N.M. The NLRB determined that the company was engaged in interstate commerce and that the hospital and dispensary were operated primarily to provide security to the employer against on-the-job injuries. During the four years preceding the hearing 86 percent of the patients of the facility were employed by the company. In addition, it was noted that the health care facility had no separate legal identity apart from the company.

Kennecott Copper Corporation had moved that a petition for union recognition election in the hospital be dismissed on the grounds that 1) the hospital's operation was exempted from the Act by Section 2(2), i.e., it was a voluntary nonprofit hospital; and 2) the operation of the hospital was not involved in interstate commerce and did not affect interstate commerce. In deciding that the hospital and dispensary should be included in the coverage of the Taft-Hartley Act, the NLRB noted:

> We find no merit to the employer's first contention because the Board has held that a hospital is exempt by Section 2(2) of the Act only if the corporation operating the hospital is, itself, operated on a nonprofit basis.... We reject the employer's second contention, and in accord with the petitioners [the union seeking recognition], find...that the hospital is clearly an integral part of the employer's operations and thus in and affecting interstate commerce...[8]

A 1955 NLRB hearing asserted that a proprietary hospital operated at Hato Tejas, Puerto Rico, was subject to the jurisdiction of the Wagner Act. The hospital had a gross business of $431,000 per year, 98 percent of which was realized from the treatment of veterans pursuant to a contract with the United States Veterans Administration. In asserting jurisdiction, the NLRB noted that the operation of the proprietary hospital, by reason of its contract with the Veterans Administration, was directly related to the national defense and thus should be covered by the provisions of the Taft-Hartley Act.[9]

On January 13, 1960, the NLRB received a petition for an election and bargaining-unit determination at Flatbush General Hospital, located in Brooklyn, New York. This case raised for the first time the question of whether or not the NLRB had legal jurisdiction over proprietary hospitals other than those in which 1) the facility was located in the District of Columbia; 2) the proprietary hospital was directly related to national defense; or 3) the hospital was integrated with an organizational unit over which the NLRB had jurisdiction.

The NLRB recorded the following as statement of fact. Flatbush General Hospital was a 111-bed proprietary facility which employed 140 employees. The facility had an estimated yearly gross income of $1 million, and approximately two-thirds of its purchase of supplies came directly or indirectly from outside the state. Most of the hospital's patients were residents of New York State. The union had reportedly been engaged in recognitional picketing at the hospital for a period of forty days. This action would have been an unfair labor practice under Section 8(b)(7)(c) of the

Taft-Hartley Act if indeed the hospital could be considered under the coverage of the Act (this unfair labor practice will be discussed in Chapter VII).

The union moved to dismiss the hospital's petition for an election (thus allowing it to maintain the recognitional picket) on the grounds that the employer was a proprietary hospital not engaged in interstate commerce. The union held that even if statutory jurisdiction were found to exist, the impact of the operation of a proprietary hospital such as the employer's was insufficient in dollar volume to warrant NLRB jurisdiction. The employer, on the other hand, opposed the motion for dismissal (thus allowing jurisdiction to be granted, whereby the picket would be declared unfair) on the grounds that the New York State Labor Relations Board had decided in three earlier cases that the operation of proprietary hospitals affected interstate commerce to such an extent that they should fall under federal control.

The NLRB, in declining to assert jurisdiction, stated:

> We are satisfied that the employer has sufficient inflow of goods from out-of-state to meet the requirements for a finding of legal jurisdiction [e.g., the employer was in interstate commerce]. However, we are of the opinion that the operation of this class of proprietary hospitals, although not wholly unrelated to commerce, are (sic) essentially local in nature and, therefore, the effect on commerce of labor disputes involving such hospitals is not substantial enough to warrant the exercise of the Board's jurisdiction. Our conclusion that such hospitals are local in character rests primarily on the facts that they service local residents and that their operations are subject to close regulation by the states for the protection of the health and safety of their residents.[10]

Thus it appeared that as of 1960 the NLRB would decline jurisdiction over proprietary hospitals unless they were in the District of Columbia, had an impact on national defense, or were integrated with an organization over which it had jurisdiction.

However, several cases decided by the NLRB in 1967 reversed the ruling handed down in the Flatbush General Hospital decision. The NLRB announced that it would assert jurisdiction over proprietary hospitals having at least $250,000 gross annual revenue.[11]

NURSING HOMES AND HOMES FOR THE AGED UNDER THE 1947 TAFT-HARTLEY ACT

As with proprietary hospitals, it appeared that the labor law status of nursing homes (regardless of control) was not considered when the Taft-Hartley Act was passed in 1947. Since they were not specifically excluded, as were voluntary nonprofit hospitals, one could assume that such facilities would be included within the provisions of the Act if impact upon interstate commerce could have been demonstrated.

In 1967 the labor law status of a proprietary nursing home was considered in University Nursing Home, Inc. (168 NLRB at 53). Paralleling the decision made with regard to proprietary hospitals, the National Labor Relations Board held that it would assert jurisdiction over for-profit nursing homes having a gross annual revenue exceeding $100,000. This guideline was devised by the Board to separate those facilities that were deemed to have a significant impact upon interstate commerce from those enterprises that were considered to be local in character.

The Board later extended jurisdiction of the Act to voluntary nursing homes and homes for the aged regardless of ownership.[12] Such facilities were held to have a significant impact on interstate commerce if gross annual revenue exceeded $100,000.

GOVERNMENTAL HOSPITALS UNDER THE 1947 TAFT-HARTLEY ACT

Governmental hospitals (federal, state, municipal and district) were specifically exempted from the provisions of the Taft-Hartley Act by Section 2(2). However, the labor relations of such facilities have been subject to increasing control since 1947.

In each session of Congress between 1949 and 1961, legislation was introduced requiring agencies and departments of the federal government to recognize and negotiate collectively with their employees. However, the realization of federal employees' demands had to await John F. Kennedy's assumption of the presidency in 1961. In June of 1961, Kennedy issued a memorandum creating a task force to study the issues of union recognition and collective negotiation in the federal civil service. The task force made its recommendations to the President in November. As an outgrowth of the task force report, President Kennedy, on January 17, 1962, issued Executive Order 10988 which outlined for the first time the government's policy on union recognition and collective bargaining and established mandatory regulation regarding these matters. Essentially, E.O. 10988 gave all federal employees the right to join or not to join organizations of their own choosing that would represent them regarding terms of employment. Three types of union or association recognition were established, depending upon the proportion of organization membership in the appropriate unit: exclusive, formal and informal.

A supplementary order, issued by the President in May 1963, was roughly equivalent to the unfair labor practices contained in Sections 8(a) and 8(b) of the Taft-Hartley Act, with two major exceptions: 1) strikes and picketing by government employees were prohibited; and 2) employee organizations were forbidden to discriminate against any employee with regard to terms or conditions of membership because of race, creed, color or national origin.

In October 1969 President Nixon issued Executive Order 11491 which replaced E.O. 10988. The order created a central authority, the Federal Labor Relations Council (FLRC), to administer the government's labor program and to serve as the final arbitrator of policy questions and disputed matters. The Federal Service Impasse Panel was also created; it was given the authority to settle deadlocks in contract negotiation if voluntary negotiations failed.

Although specifically excluded from the Taft-Hartley Act of 1947, state and state governmental subdivision (local, municipal, district) hospitals have been subject to regulation by an increasing number of public employee labor laws enacted by individual states. Until 1959, when Wisconsin enacted a public employee collective bargaining bill, no jurisdiction placed an obligation on state or local governmental management to deal collectively with employees. In the decade following the adoption of the Wisconsin statute, a wide variety of legislation, court decisions, attorney generals' opinions and executive orders were generated to deal with this issue. At present, over three-quarters of the states have labor laws that in some way regulate the recognitional and collective bargaining activities of public employees. These labor laws differ considerably with regard to their treatment of 1) the basic right to organize collectively; 2) the right to meet and confer with management regarding terms and conditions of employment; 3) the right to bargain collectively; 4) the establishment of dispute settlement mechanisms; and 5) the prohibition and/or prevention of strikes.

LABOR LAW QUAGMIRE

Such was the status of health care facilities under the Taft-Hartley Act of 1947. Voluntary nonprofit hospitals were specifically excluded from the Act by Section 2(2) although covered by some state labor laws (by the early 1970's, over a dozen jurisdictions had labor laws that covered voluntary hospitals). Proprietary hospitals were neither specifically excluded nor included under the Act. Between 1947 and 1974 their status changed several times as a result of rulings of the National Labor Relations Board. The latest ruling held that for-profit hospitals would be covered by the Act if their gross annual revenue exceeded $250,000. By the 1970's the NLRB had held that nursing homes and homes for the aged, regardless of ownership, would be included under the provisions of the Act if their gross annual revenue exceeded $100,000. Governmental hospitals (federal, state, municipal, district, etc.) were specifically excluded from coverage under the Taft-Hartley Act, although their labor relations have come under increasing control within the last decade. The employees of federal hospitals (as well as workers in other federal governmental agencies) have been extended organizational and collective bargaining rights through a series of executive orders. State hospitals have been increasingly covered by public employee bargaining legislation.

To say that the labor law status of the health care industry was fragmented often proved to be the classic understatement. During the late 1960's and early 1970's, considerable sentiment began to build for a consolidation of health facility labor law status. For an industry as large and interstate in nature to remain under such fragmented (and often conflicting) labor regulations appeared both inequitable and unfunctional. The following chapter will provide the reader with a general overview of the structure and functions of the National Labor Relations Act. Chapter IV will describe events leading up to the passage of the 1974 amendments to the Taft-Hartley Act and will discuss the major provisions of the legislation.

Footnotes

1. Central Dispensary and Emergency Hospital v. NLRB, 145 F.2d 852 (D.C. Cir., 1944), cert. denied 342 U.S. 847, 65 Sup. Ct. 684 (1945).
2. Jewish Hospital of Brooklyn v. Doe, 252 App. Div. 581 at 584 (1938)
3. Western Pennsylvania Hospital v. Lichliter, 340 Pa. 382, 17A 2d 206 (1941). Cited in 6 LRRM at 1133.
4. Trustees of Columbia University v. Herzog, 269 App. Div. 24 aff'd., 295 N.Y.S. 605 (1945). Subquoted from Judith Valadeck, "Collective Bargaining in Voluntary Hospitals and Other Non-Profit Institutions," Proceedings of New York 19th Annual Conference on Labor, ed. Thomas G.S. Christensen, Washington, D.C., Bureau of National Affairs, Inc., 1965, p. 279.
5. Neil W. Chamberlain and James W. Kuhn, Collective Bargaining, 2nd ed., New York, McGraw-Hill Book Co., 1965, p. 279.
6. Comments of Senator Tydings, 92 Congressional Record, May 12, 1947.
7. Phillip Taft, Organized Labor and American History, New York, Harper & Row, Publishers, 1964, p. 579.
8. Kennecott Copper Corporation, cited in 99 NLRB at 110 (1952).
9. Hospital Hato Tejas, Inc., cited in 111 NLRB at 155 (1955).
10. Flatbush General Hospital, cited in 126 NLRB at 145 (1960).
11. Medical Center Hospital, cited in 169 NLRB at 52.
12. See for example: Drexel Homes, cited in 194 NLRB at 63, and Glen Manor Home for the Jewish Aged v. NLRB (6th Cir., case no. 72-1537; February 1973).

III
The Nation's Labor Law: A Walking Tour

INTRODUCTION: THE SOURCES OF LABOR LAW

Labor law is multifaceted; its foundation stems from many sources. Among some of the more important bases for the regulation of labor-management relationships in the United States are the following:

1. the United States Constitution;
2. the National Labor Relations Act (NLRA), as amended;
3. decisions of the National Labor Relations Board;
4. rulings of the federal (district, appellate and Supreme) courts;
5. labor-management collective bargaining agreements; and
6. arbitration awards.

Each of these sources will be briefly discussed in this section.

U.S. Constitution

The Constitution of the United States serves as both the foundational and supreme law of the land. All governmental powers derive directly from it and must be interpreted in light of its provisions. All federal labor legislation (the National Labor Relations Act, the Labor-Management Reporting and Disclosure Act and the Fair Labor Standards Act, to mention only a few examples) has been enacted by Congress under the delegated powers as provided for in the Constitution. Particularly important in the development of labor law is the commerce clause specified in Article I, Section 8. This provision of the Constitution holds that "the Congress shall have power to regulate commerce with foreign nations, among the several states, and with Indian tribes..." Thus, Congress can enact labor laws designed to regulate the activities of employers (and their employees) who are deemed to participate in commerce among the states--i.e., those enterprises engaged in interstate commerce. The several major challenges to the constitutionality of the NLRA have been argued from the perspective that the enterprises over whom the Act sought jurisdiction could not reasonably be defined as being engaged in interstate commerce. The Supreme Court has viewed the commerce clause as being broadly constructed. Indeed, in one case the Court argued that to be subject to federal labor law an enterprise need not be directly involved in interstate commerce but merely have impact on it.

In 1947 the decision to exclude voluntary nonprofit hospitals from coverage of the Act was, in part, based upon the argument that such facilities were local enterprises having no substantial impact on commerce between states. In the 1950's and early 1960's certain classes of health care facilities (proprietary hospitals and nursing homes) were deemed to be excluded from coverage of the NLRA because the National Labor Relations Board had ruled that they did not have an impact on interstate commerce significant enough to warrant jurisdiction. In the mid-1960's the National Labor Relations Board modified its rulings and held that facilities exceeding a specified gross annual revenue could be considered to be engaged in and have impact upon interstate commerce to the extent that their inclusion under the Act was justified.

The NLRA

The National Labor Relations Act (NLRA) and its amendments enacted in 1947, 1959 and 1974 serve as the nation's primary mechanism for regulating the relationship between employers and employees with respect to union recognition and collective bargaining issues. The legislation guarantees the rights of labor organizations, employees and employers; restricts certain behavior; makes available certain remedies; and establishes mechanisms to carry out the intent of the Act. The Act is comprehensive in that it addresses many facets of the labor-management relationship. The NLRA is complemented by other statutes that govern specific aspects of employee, union and employer behavior; the Norris-La Guardia Anti-Injunction, Federal Fair Labor Standards and Civil Rights Acts are three examples of such laws.

The largest portion of this chapter will be devoted to providing a brief section-by-section description of the National Labor Relations Act as amended. It is significant to note here, however, that the NLRA as a statute must be interpreted within a framework of other sources of labor law discussed in this section.

NLRB Rulings

The National Labor Relations Board (NLRB) was established to administer the National Labor Relations Act. The Act itself sets up only the bare bones of a regulation and control mechanism. The statute must be both applied to specific situations and interpreted in light of constantly changing circumstances. Although the Board is charged with numerous responsibilities, two duties are primary. First, the Board delineates and designates collective bargaining units and conducts elections of employee representatives. The process of unit determination and election procedures are discussed fully in Chapter V. Second, the Board adjudicates unfair labor practice cases arising out of Sections 8(a) and 8(b) of the Act. The substance of employer and employee unfair labor practices are discussed in Chapters VI and VII; the workings of the NLRB are covered in Chapter XI.

Rulings of the NLRB form a body of administrative law. Decisions of the Board are written, certified and form the frame of reference for the establishment of precedent in future cases. In Board hearings, rules of evidence employed in the federal courts are utilized, witnesses are called and subpoenas can be issued. The Board has the authority to grant awards (e.g., worker reinstatement, payment of back wages) and can seek injunctions from the courts. In one sense the courts have been divested of some of their powers in this area. The rationale for establishing quasi-judicial administrative bodies like the NLRB is twofold. First, the courts are slow to act because of crowded schedules; expeditious action on labor matters is deemed desirable. Second, courts of general jurisdiction are thought not to have the focused competence and experience necessary to handle labor issues.

The Courts

Rulings issued by the NLRB--essentially administrative decisions--are subject to court review in the enforcement process. Under the National Labor Relations Act, only the federal courts have complete jurisdiction. Rulings of the NLRB can either be observed or ignored. In and of itself a ruling of the Board carries no compulsion--it is not self-enforcing. A Board ruling becomes binding on participants only when it is enforced by a federal court. Subsequent to the NLRB ruling, the case can be appealed to a federal court on the basis of a petition for enforcement filed by the Board itself or by a petition for review presented by any party to the case. Cases generally enter the federal system at the district court level; they may be appealed all the way to the Supreme Court. In considering an NLRB ruling on appeal the courts determine whether 1) findings of fact are substantiated by evidence submitted; 2) the ruling is in accordance with the evidence; 3) a fair hearing has been conducted; and 4) whether the NLRB order advances the policy of the Act.

Court review ensures that the nation's labor law as delineated in legislative statutes is, while stable, not static. Divergent situations and the passage of time itself require that laws be interpreted and reinterpreted. Court review of administrative decisions formulated by the NLRB checks the conduct of the law's administrators and breathes life into the statute itself.

Collective Bargaining Agreements

Collective bargaining agreements are the intra-facility statutory law of the employer-employee relationship. A negotiated collective bargaining agreement specifies both the relationship and responsibilities of the employees, through their elected representatives, and the employer. The collective bargaining agreement must meet requirements established in the National Labor Relations Act (in addition to other statutes) as interpreted by rulings of the National Labor Relations Board and as reviewed by the courts.

Collective bargaining agreements specify the structure within which the union and management deal with each other. Much attention has been accorded the role of the contract in delineating job classification levels, pay rates and fringe benefits--these issues indeed lie at the heart of any negotiating process and the contract that results from it. However, collective bargaining contracts do far more than define the economic terms of employment. Such agreements specify the extent of management's prerogatives, the mechanisms through which the union can maintain its membership in the bargaining units; procedures for granting seniority, layoff and callback; characteristics of the grievance procedure; the issues over which employees cannot strike during the term of the contract; and many other conditions of employment. The collective bargaining agreement permeates most aspects of the way an employer deals with his employees.

Historically, the collective bargaining agreement has been viewed as a statement of the terms under which a firm's employees are collectively willing to work. Legally, the collective bargaining agreement does not bind any individual to provide service; rather, it assures that when service is provided it will be provided pursuant to provisions of the agreement. It states the terms upon which labor will be provided. As will be discussed later, the NLRA provides the mechanism whereby parties to a collective bargaining agreement can file damage suits for its violation, thus insuring their status "at law." While collective bargaining agreements are legally enforceable, thus creating an intra-facility statutory law, such agreements may also be viewed as constitutions that establish a governance structure. There is increasing acceptance in the labor relations field to view the collective bargaining agreement from this latter perspective. Such a perspective accentuates the continuity of the labor-management relationship.

Arbitration Awards

Whether the collective bargaining agreement is viewed as an intra-facility statutory law or as a constitution that establishes a system of governance, the grievance procedure and arbitration awards stemming from it are significant sources of labor law. Fully 85 percent of the collective bargaining agreements now in existence have implemented a grievance procedure ending in binding arbitration through which disputes occurring under the agreement are resolved. The grievance procedure can be viewed as the machinery that is established to interpret the meaning of the collective bargaining agreement. Justice William O. Douglas, in United Steelworkers of America v. Warrior and Gulf Navigation Co., wrote in this famous decision that

> The collective agreement...calls into being a new common law of a particular industry or of a particular plant...arbitration is the means of solving the unforeseeable by molding a system of private law for all the problems which may arise and to provide for their solutions in a way which will generally accord with the variant needs and desires of the parties.

THE NATIONAL LABOR RELATIONS ACT

The National Labor Relations Act is the keystone of federal labor policy governing the employment relationships of managements and collectively organized workers. As noted previously, the Act flows from Article I, Section 8, of the United States Constitution, is applied in specific situations by the National Labor Relations Board and the federal courts, and lays the foundation for intra-facility labor law specified in collective bargaining contracts as interpreted through arbitration awards. The NLRA is a broadly framed complex statute that has evolved through amendments to the original Act (which became law in 1935) passed in 1947, 1959 and, most recently, 1974.

Before delving into the development of the 1974 amendments and documenting the impact of the Act upon health care facilities specifically, the remainder of this chapter will provide the reader with a walking tour of the NLRA. Like any walking tour, the orientation is meant to be general. All major structures will be examined, but few will be entered. Subsequent chapters of this book will examine particularly relevant provisions in some detail. The full text of the Act is provided in Appendix A. The reader is encouraged to refer to specific sections in process and to familiarize himself with both the structure and content of the full Act after completing this book.

The National Labor Relations Act is subdivided into six major sections: a short identification and declaration of purpose and five titles (three of which will be discussed here). Each title is subdivided into numerous sections. These titles and their sections are discussed below.

Preamble

The preamble to the National Labor Relations Act, as amended, states that industrial strife can be avoided or substantially minimized if employers, employees and unions each recognize, under the law, one another's legitimate rights with regard to their relationships.

In order to promote the full flow of commerce, it is the purpose and policy of the Act to

1. prescribe the legitimate rights of both employees and employers in their relations affecting commerce;
2. provide orderly and peaceful procedures for preventing the interference by either employees or employers with the legitimate rights of the other;
3. protect the rights of individual employees in their relations with labor organizations;
4. define and prescribe practices on the part of labor and managements which affect commerce and are detrimental to the general public welfare; and to
5. guard the rights of the public in connection with labor disputes affecting commerce.

Title I of the NLRA

Title I is the longest title of the National Labor Relations Act; it will be the primary focus of the remaining chapters of this book. Title I delineates general findings and policies of the Act, defines terms employed in the Act, specifies the structure and functions of the National Labor Relations Board, states the rights of employees, denotes unfair labor practices, specifies the manner in which employee representatives are chosen, empowers the Board to prevent unfair labor practices, describes investigatory powers under the Act and lists limitations.

Sections 1 and 2: Findings and Definitions

Section 1 of the Act delineates the general findings and principles that underlie the formulation of specific provisions. In part, the section notes that

> The denial by some employers of the right of employees to organize and the refusal by some employers to accept the procedure of collective bargaining lead to strikes and other forms of industrial strife or unrest, which have the intent or the necessary effect of burdening or obstructing commerce by (a) impairing the efficiency, safety, or operation of the instrumentalities of commerce; (b) occurring in the current of commerce; (c) materially affecting, restraining or controlling the flow of raw materials or manufactured or processed goods from or into the channels of commerce, or the prices of such materials or goods in commerce; or (d) causing diminution of employment and wages in such volume as substantially to impair or disrupt the market for goods flowing from or into the channels of commerce.

The section goes on to note that certain practices engaged in by labor organizations also have been found to detrimentally affect the unrestricted flow of commerce. It is the stated purpose of the Act to eliminate and/or mitigate these obstructions.

Section 2 defines terms employed elsewhere in the Act. Some of the more important definitions are discussed briefly below.

1. The term employer (i.e., those covered by the Act), does not include United States or wholly owned government corporations, the Federal Reserve Bank, any state or political subdivision thereof, any person subject to the Railway Labor Act or any labor organization other than when acting as an employer. Thus, this definition excludes from the Act federal hospitals (veterans, military and public health service) and state and local governmental (city, county and hospital district) health care facilities.

2. The term "labor organization" means any organization in which employees participate and which exists for the purpose (in whole or in part) of dealing with employers concerning grievances, labor disputes, wages, rates of pay, hours of employment or conditions of employment. It is important to note that the term is defined in light of behavior rather than in name alone--that is, a group may not perceive itself to be a labor organization, but nonetheless may be found to be acting as such under the Act.

3. As will be noted later, supervisors are not covered by the Act (supervisors are not defined as employees). A supervisor is defined as

> ...any individual having authority, in the interest of the employer, to hire, transfer, suspend, lay off, recall, promote, discharge, assign, reward, or discipline other employees, or responsibility to direct them, or to adjust their grievances, or effectively to recommend such action, if in con-

> nection with the foregoing the exercise of such authority is not of a merely routine or clerical nature, but requires the use of independent judgment.

4. While "professionals" are considered to be employees within the meaning of the Act and are included under its provisions, such persons are accorded special rights regarding their inclusion in bargaining units containing nonprofessionals (see Chapter V). A professional is defined as

> ...(a) any employee engaged in work (i) predominantly intellectual and varied in character as opposed to routine mental, manual, mechanical, or physical work; (ii) involving the consistent exercise of discretion and judgment in its performance; (iii) of such a character that the output produced or the result accomplished cannot be standardized in relation to a given period of time; (iv) requiring knowledge of an advanced type in a field of science or learning customarily acquired by a prolonged course of specialized intellectual instruction and study in an institution of higher learning or a hospital, as distinguished from a general academic education or from an apprenticeship or from training in the performance of routine mental, manual or physical processes; or (b) any employee, who (i) has completed the courses of specialized intellectual instruction and study described in clause (iv) of paragraph (a), and (ii) is performing related work under the supervision of a professional person to qualify himself to become a professional employee as defined in paragraph (a).

Sections 3 through 6: The NLRB

Section 3 of the NLRA delineates the structure and functions of the National Labor Relations Board (operation of the Board is discussed in Chapter XI). The NLRB is empowered to delineate bargaining units, conduct union certification elections and make rulings regarding unfair labor practices. The conduct of the elections is governed by Section 9 of the Act and is described in Chapter V.

The National Labor Relations Board is comprised of five members appointed by the President with the advice and consent of the Senate; members serve a term of five years. The general counsel of the Board, who is also appointed by the President with the advice and consent of the Senate, has final authority with regard to the investigation of charges, the issuance of complaints and the prosecution of such complaints before the Board.

Section 7: Employee Rights

Section 7 delineates the rights of employees under the Act. It states that

> Employees shall have the right to self-organization, to form, join, or assist labor organizations, to bargain collectively through representatives of their own choosing, and to engage in other concerted activities for the purpose of collective bargaining or other mutual aid or protection, and shall also have the right to refrain from any or all of such activities except to the extent that such right may be affected by an agreement requiring membership in a labor organization as a condition of employment as authorized in Section 8(a)(3).

Section 8: Unfair Labor Practices

Section 8 delineates practices that if engaged in by either labor or management are deemed to be unfair. Unfair labor practices are given a more comprehensive treatment in Chapters VI and VII.

It is an unfair labor practice for management to

1. interfere with rights guaranteed in Section 7;
2. dominate or interfere with the formation or administration of a labor organization or contribute financially to it;
3. discriminate with regard to hire or tenure of employment or to encourage or discourage membership in a labor organization;
4. discharge or otherwise discriminate against an employee for filing charges or giving testimony under the Act; or to
5. refuse to bargain collectively with the duly elected representatives of employees belonging to a recognized bargaining unit.

It is an unfair labor practice for a labor organization to:

1. coerce or restrain employees in the exercise of their rights guaranteed in Section 7 or employers in the selection of their bargaining representatives;
2. discriminate under a union shop agreement for any reason other than for the nonpayment of uniform dues and fees;

3. refuse to bargain in good faith;
4. engage in certain strikes, secondary boycotts or other coercion for specified illegal purposes;
5. charge excessive or discriminatory dues or fees under a legal union security agreement;
6. cause (or attempt to cause) an employer to deliver anything of value for work not actually performed or work not to be performed; or to
7. engage in or threaten recognitional picketing unless certain conditions have been met.

This section also specifies certain actions that must be undertaken by both labor organizations and management to ensure that good-faith bargaining does, in fact, take place. Notification requirements regarding labor disputes in health care facilities are also provided for, along with specifications regarding the mandatory involvement of the Federal Mediation and Conciliation Service in health facility labor disputes.

Section 9: Representatives and Elections

Section 9 delineates the responsibilities of the Board in certifying bargaining units and conducting elections. The provision notes that

> (a) Representatives designated or selected for the purpose of collective bargaining by the majority of the employees in a unit appropriate for such purposes shall be the exclusive representatives of all the employees in such unit for the purposes of collective bargaining in respect to rates of pay, wages, hours of employment, or other conditions of employment... (b) The Board shall decide in each case whether, in order to assure to employees the fullest freedom in exercising the rights guaranteed by this Act, the unit appropriate for the purposes of collective bargaining shall be the employer unit, craft unit, plant unit, or subdivision thereof...

The section notes the procedures under which elections must be undertaken. These procedures in addition to the factors considered in forming bargaining units are discussed in Chapter V.

Section 10: The Prevention of Unfair Labor Practices

Section 10 details the authority and powers available to the

Board in preventing unfair labor practices. The Board can

1. issue a complaint regarding an unfair labor practice and hold hearings to examine such allegations;
2. order such parties to cease and desist from engaging in unfair labor practices;
3. take affirmative action to remedy the effects of an unfair labor practice (e.g., ordering reinstatement or the payment of back wages);
4. petition the federal courts for temporary relief or a restraining order;
5. adjudicate jurisdictional disputes unless such a dispute has been solved by the participating parties (or procedures have been agreed to whereby the dispute can be resolved) within ten days after a notice has been filed; and
6. take certain unfair labor practice allegations and provide expedited relief and priority case handling.

Section 11: Investigatory Powers

Section 11 establishes the investigatory powers of the National Labor Relations Board. The Board has the right to subpoena evidence it deems necessary to execute its duties under the Act. The Board and its agents can administer oaths and affirmations, examine witnesses and receive evidence. The Board can go to the federal courts to enforce issued subpoenas; parties refusing to obey such orders can be found in contempt of court. No person can be excused from testifying or producing evidence in obedience to a subpoena of the Board on the ground that the testimony or evidence presented may tend to incriminate him. However, no individual can be prosecuted or be subject to any penalty for an account of any transaction for which he is compelled to testify after claiming his privilege against self-incrimination.

Any person found guilty of willfully impeding, resisting, preventing or interfering with a member of the Board or any of its agents in the conduct of their official duties can be punished by a fine of not more than $5,000 or by imprisonment for not more than one year, or both.

Sections 13 through 18: Limitations

Sections 13 through 18 of the Act delineate certain limitations and provisions. The most important are the following:

> 1. Nothing in the Act, except as specifically provided for, can be construed so as either to interfere with or impede or diminish in any way the right to strike, or to affect the limitations or qualifications on that right.
> 2. Nothing contained in the Act can prohibit any individual employed as a supervisor from becoming or remaining a member of a labor organization, but no employer subject to the Act shall be compelled to deem individuals defined as supervisors therein as employees for the purpose of any law, either national or local, relating to collective bargaining.
> 3. Nothing in the Act shall be construed as authorizing the execution or application of agreements requiring membership in a labor organization as a condition of employment in any state or territory in which such execution or application is prohibited by state or territorial law.

Title II of the NLRA

Title II of the National Labor Relations Act establishes the structure and functions of the Federal Mediation and Conciliation Service and specifies procedures that are to be invoked in the occurrence of a labor dispute that imperils the national health or safety. Section 201(b) states that

> The settlement of issues between employers and employees through collective bargaining may be advanced by making available full and adequate governmental facilities for conciliation, mediation, and voluntary arbitration to aid and encourage employers and the representatives of their employees to reach and maintain agreements concerning rates of pay, hours, and working conditions, and to make all reasonable efforts to settle their differences by mutual agreement reached through conferences and collective bargaining or by such methods as may be provided for in any applicable agreement for the settlement of disputes.

Federal Mediation and Conciliation Service

Under the Act, the Federal Mediation and Conciliation Service (FMCS) is charged with preventing or minimizing interruptions of the free flow of commerce growing out of labor disputes, to assist parties to labor disputes in settling such disputes through mediation and conciliation. In economic sectors other than the health facility industry, the Federal Mediation and Conciliation Service may proffer its services either upon its own motion or upon the request of one or more parties to the dispute. Prior to involving itself in a dispute the director of the FMCS is charged with determining that the dispute has the potential of substantially disrupting commerce. Under the Act (and as a result of the 1974 amendments) the FMCS is required to participate in mediation and conciliation in the case of collective bargaining involving a health care facility thirty days prior to the termination of agreement and at the point of initial agreement negotiation. Failure of either party to the negotiation to participate in mediation and conciliation as directed by the FMCS may be ruled an unfair labor practice.

As required by Section 204, employers, employees and their representatives are required to

> 1. exert every reasonable effort to make and maintain agreements concerning rates of pay, hours, and working conditions, including provision for adequate notice for any proposed change in the terms of such agreement;
> 2. whenever a dispute arises over the terms or application of a collective bargaining agreement and a conference is requested by a party or prospective party thereto, arrange promptly for such a conference to be held and endeavor in such conference to settle such dispute expeditiously; and
> 3. in case such dispute is not settled by conference, participate fully and promptly in such meetings as may be undertaken by the Service under the Act for the purpose of aiding in a settlement of the dispute.

The Act establishes a National Labor-Management Panel comprised of six labor and six management representatives noted in their fields. The panel is charged with advising the director of the FMCS regarding the avoidance of industrial controversies and the manner in which mediation and voluntary adjustment of labor disputes shall be administered.

National Emergencies

Section 206 of the NLRA states that

> Whenever in the opinion of the President of the United States, a threatened or actual strike or lock-out affecting an entire industry or a substantial part thereof engaged in trade, commerce,

> transportation, transmission, or communication among the several States, or with foreign nations, or engaged in the production of goods for commerce, will, if permitted to occur or to continue, imperil the national health or safety, he may appoint a board of inquiry to inquire into the issues involved in the dispute and to make a written report to him within such time as he shall prescribe. Such report shall include a statement of the facts with respect to the dispute, including each party's statement of its position but shall not contain any recommendations. The President shall file a copy of such report with the Service and shall make its contents available to the public.

The composition of the board of inquiry is a prerogative of the President; it may sit anywhere in the United States. Sections 9 and 10 (Title I) of the Act--discussed earlier, regarding the taking of evidence--apply to activities of the Board.

Upon receiving the report of the board of inquiry, the President may direct the Attorney General to petition a district court having jurisdiction to enjoin such a strike or lockout, and if the court finds that such threatened or actual dispute

> (i) affects an entire industry or a substantial part thereof engaged in trade, commerce, transportation, transmission, or communication among the several States or with foreign nations, or engaged in the production of goods for commerce; and (ii) if permitted to occur or to continue, will imperil the national health or safety, it shall have jurisdiction to enjoin any such strike or lock-out, or the continuing thereof, and to make such other orders as may be appropriate.

During the period of the injunction, the President is required to reconvene the board of inquiry. At the end of a sixty-day period (unless the dispute has been settled), the board reports to the President regarding the position of the parties and their efforts toward reaching a settlement. During the succeeding fifteen days, the National Labor Relations Board is required to take a vote to determine if the employees are willing to accept the final offer of settlement made by the employer. After the results are known, the Attorney General must move to discharge the injunction. Under the Act, the President is required to report to Congress and may make such recommendations regarding the matter that he deems appropriate.

Hospital Emergency Disputes Provision

Section 213 of Title II, which was added to the Act by the 1974 amendments, specifies the procedures to be undertaken in helping to resolve "emergency labor disputes" in health care facilities. The substance of this provision is more thoroughly discussed in Chapter VIII.

Under Section 213, a special procedure is added to the Act to assist in the settlement of threatened or actual strikes and lockouts that have the capability of substantially interrupting the delivery of health care services in the locality concerned. Under this provision (if an emergency is deemed to exist as defined above), the director of the Federal Mediation and Conciliation Service would establish a board of inquiry thirty days after it received a notice of contract termination under Section 8(d) of the Act (parties to a contract must notify the FMCS sixty days prior to termination if such a contract involves a health care facility). The board of inquiry would have fifteen days to report its findings and recommendations to the parties; the parties would then have fifteen days to engage in continued negotiations before a work stoppage or lockout could take place. In the case of initial contract negotiations, the provision requires that after union certification the FMCS must be given thirty days' prior notice of a dispute. If, in the opinion of the director of the FMCS, an emergency exists or is threatened, the board of inquiry must be convened no less than ten days after receiving a notice of dispute. After the emergency procedure has been implemented, the process is the same as under agreement renegotiation.

Title III of the NLRA

Title III of the Act addresses 1) suits by and against labor organizations; 2) restrictions on payments to employee representatives; 3) boycotts and other unlawful combinations; and 4) restrictions on political contributions. Title III's consideration of payments to employee representatives is covered more comprehensively in the Labor-Management Reporting and Disclosure (Landrum-Griffin) Act (see Chapter X) and thus will not be discussed here.

Suits for violation of a contract between an employer and a labor organization covered by the Act may be brought in any district court without regard to the amount in controversy (usually $10,000 in damages must be demonstrated) or without respect to the citizenship of the parties. Additionally, any labor organization may sue or be sued as an entity and in behalf of the employees whom it represents. The Act also notes that enterprises injured through boycotts and other combinations prohibited in Section 8(b)(4) may bring suit against a labor organization for damages in a district court of the United States.

Section 304 of the NLRA amends Section 313 of the Federal

Corrupt Practices Act. This provision makes it illegal for any corporation or labor organization to make certain political contributions.

Given this background, the next chapter addresses the events leading up to the passage of the 1974 amendments to the National Labor Relations Act. The provisions of the amendments as they have impact upon health care facilities will be discussed.

IV
The 1974 Amendments to the Taft-Hartley Act

ANTECEDENTS TO CHANGE

As noted in Chapter II, the health facility industry was subject to a fragmented (and often changing) federal labor law structure in the years that followed the passage of the Taft-Hartley amendments to the National Labor Relations Act in 1947. At the outset, virtually the entire industry was excluded from coverage of the Act (either specifically, as in the case of voluntary hospitals, or through its application, as in the case of proprietary hospitals). As union activity in the industry increased, labor law policy was modified to adjust to this development. Proprietary hospitals, nursing homes and homes for the aged were brought under the National Labor Relations Act along certain guidelines; federal governmental hospitals were subject to increasing control of their labor relations through the proclamation of several executive orders; and increasingly the employees of state and municipal governmental hospitals were granted collective bargaining rights through the enactment of numerous public employee bargaining bills.

Public policy regarding the labor-management relations of voluntary nonprofit hospitals was far less developed. The employees of such facilities were specifically excluded from the coverage of the Taft-Hartley Act. Although eighteen states had enacted comprehensive labor legislation, less than twelve jurisdictions protected and regulated the collective organizational and contract negotiation activity of at least some segment of the employees of voluntary hospitals. Therefore, in approximately thirty-eight states, voluntary nonprofit hospitals were not required to recognize or bargain collectively with their employees. Voluntary hospitals constituted the largest single sector of the health services industry, representing 48 percent of the total number of hospitals, 66 percent of the admissions, and 54 percent of the total industry payroll expense. Thus, structured public policy regarding labor relations was virtually nonexistent in that sector of the industry which was the largest and by all indications appeared to be attracting the greatest amount of union organizational attention.

The employees of voluntary nonprofit hospitals were excluded from the provisions of labor legislation (at both the state and federal level) on the basis of the following arguments:

> 1. the continued and uninterrupted operation of hospitals is of such importance that their exemption is indicated;
> 2. the organization is nonprofit in character;
> 3. the facility is semipublic in nature and engages in functions that if not executed would have to be assumed by the government; and
> 4. the charitable character of such organizations is sufficient assurance of fair dealing with employees to make the regulation of labor relations unnecessary.

During the late 1960's, the logic which formed the foundation for these arguments began to be questioned. For the first time, those involved in the development of public policy, the public and health care professionals themselves began to assess the rationale underlying the exemption of voluntary nonprofit hospitals from the Taft-Hartley Act. It is this consideration of the status of voluntary hospitals under the Act that directly precipitated the move toward the 1974 amendments. In view of this, a brief discussion of the arguments underlying voluntary hospital exclusion appears warranted.

Organizational Importance

The first argument contends that hospitals are unusual institutions providing critical services that if curtailed or seriously disrupted, would be deleterious to the general public health and safety; few indeed would deny the plausibility of this statement. However, the right to organize collectively was extended to the employees of proprietary, state and federal hospitals as well as to an increasing proportion of firemen, policemen and public school teachers. The question was asked: Are the services provided by these individuals and the institutions in which they are employed any less critical than the functions performed by voluntary hospitals?

Nonprofit Character

Nonprofit hospitals were excluded from the National Labor Relations Act through Section 2(2), which stated that the Act "...shall not include...any corporation or association operating a hospital if no part of the net earnings inures to the benefit of any private shareholder or individual..." Thus, it appeared that the basis for the exemption was clearly the nonprofit character of the hospital. One could suggest, however, that the nonprofit nature of the voluntary hospital appeared to be a strange criterion upon which to establish the exclusion of these facilities from the jurisdiction of the Act. Indeed, in several decisions, the National Labor Relations Board held that the nonprofit character of an enterprise was not sufficient grounds to warrant exclusion from the Taft-Hartley Act. One could ask the question: Since the Act covered other types of hospitals and other types of nonprofit institutions, why should nonprofit hospitals be excluded?

Semipublic Character

A third argument utilized to justify the exemption of voluntary hospitals from labor legislation was that such facilities were actually semipublic in character in that if for some reason their functions were curtailed or eliminated completely, these functions would have to be carried out by the state. Most state constitutions note that it is the duty of the political subdivision to protect the "public health and safety." Unions contended that while voluntary hospital employees were considered to be providing a quasi-governmental service, they possessed none of the benefits that consideration warranted. Labor organizations argued that employees of voluntary hospitals excluded from the Act through the quasi-governmental-function argument were provided with no benefits that would "subsidize" them for that exclusion. Such employees were often not covered by guaranteed tenure, promotion review boards, grievance appeal panels, job security provisions or adequately developed pension plans common among civil and state service employment.

Charitable Nature Assures Fairness

It was also argued that voluntary hospitals should be excluded from labor legislation through the rationale that they were charitable institutions and that because of this fact they would treat their employees equitably as a matter of course. Unions argued that this had not been the case. They contended that hospital employees were underpaid, overworked and often treated unfairly as a rule, rather than as an exception. Unions suggested that employees of voluntary hospitals were expected to share in their employers' charitable purpose. They held that hospital employees should not have been expected to subsidize the health care bill of the community which they served while the charitable nature of that institution was often used as a justification for withholding collective bargaining rights.

Whatever the validity of these arguments, they nonetheless stimulated a reexamination of the labor law status of health care facilities. During the 1960's, unions had been extremely active in their attempts to organize health care facility employees: strikes in the industry--some lasting months and closing multiple facilities in the same locality--had increased. With the exception of the agricultural industry, health care facilities remained the only major sector of the American economy not covered by the National Labor Relations Act. Indeed, the NLRA had asserted jurisdiction over a broad array of other nonprofit and charitable institutions.

Pressure to open the consideration of amendments to the NLRA were being actively advocated by labor organizations. As noted earlier, union membership had dropped relative to total employment. Unions were eyeing the health care industry as a source of critically needed membership growth. Organization efforts were being hampered by the fact that significant portions of the industry were not covered by federal labor law.

By late 1971 these divergent forces had consolidated, and a bill was introduced in Congress to amend the National Labor Relations Act in order to alter the labor law status of health care facilities. The next three years would witness much debate, pressure and maneuvering regarding this issue--the "Dance of Legislation" had begun.

A FIRST ATTEMPT--THE NINETY-SECOND CONGRESS

H.R. 11357 was introduced in the Ninety-second Congress on October 21, 1971, by Congressman Frank Thompson, Jr. (Dem., N.J.). The purpose of the bill was "...to restore to the employees of nonprofit hospitals the rights guaranteed to most all other employees by Section 7 of the National Labor Relations Act." The bill proposed a simple amendment to the NLRA. It would strike out the clause "...or any corporation or association operating a hospital, if no part of the net earning inures to the benefit of any private shareholder or individual" from Section 2(2) of the Act. It is this clause that defines hospitals as "nonemployers" for the purpose of the NLRA.

The bill was referred to the House Special Subcommittee on Labor (of the full Committee on Education and Labor), chaired by the bill's author, Frank Thompson, Jr. The subcommittee held hearings on H.R. 11357 in Washington, D.C., on November 9, 10, and 16, 1971, and January 18, 1972; the subcommittee also conducted hearings in Los Angeles, California, on December 10, 1971, and in San Francisco on December 13. Congressman Thompson set the tone of and the reasons behind the hearings when he noted, on the first day of testimony, in his opening remarks that

> [voluntary hospital] employees were initially covered by the NLRA when it was passed in 1935, but then were excluded from coverage in 1947 when the Taft-Hartley Amendments were passed. The legislative history sheds little light on the reasons for their exclusion, and we intend to re-examine the

> wisdom of that decision.
>
> We will also be looking at the problems of employees in publicly operated hospitals and private, for-profit hospitals, and nursing homes during these hearings.
>
> Hospitals and nursing homes employ well in excess of 2 million people in this country. In the past several years we have witnessed a series of bitter labor disputes, some of which we are going to hear about today, and we want to examine the underlying causes of this unrest and determine whether a legislative remedy is called for.

A letter from the Secretary of Labor James Hodgson (representing the position of the Nixon Administration on the measure) stated that

> In many instances, lack of ground rules for union recognition and collective bargaining in this sector has resulted in uncontrolled tests of strength in which the public as well as the parties suffer heavily. These issues will continue to arise, probably with increasing frequency. It is far better that they should be resolved through the orderly procedures of the National Labor Relations Act than through bitter and wasteful confrontations.

The subcommittee received testimony from numerous provider representatives. The American Medical Association, the Catholic Hospital Association and the Federation of American Hospitals (representing proprietary facilities) neither supported nor opposed the legislation. The American Hospital Association (AHA) was the only national organization of providers that initially opposed H.R. 11357; however, the New York and Massachusetts state AHA affiliates favored passage. Testimony was taken from most unions that represented substantial numbers of health care employees. They uniformly endorsed the bill, although the American Nurses Association urged the subcommittee to better define the term "supervisor" in the legislation so that nurses with only minimal supervisory duties would not be denied protection of the Act (supervisors are excluded from coverage of the NLRA).

H.R. 11357 was reported to the full House Committee on Education and Labor on June 8, 1972, without amendment. The bill was unanimously ordered, by voice vote, to the floor of the House by the Committee on Education and Labor on July 18, 1972. The bill passed the full House on August 7, 1972, by an overwhelming vote of 295 to 85 on a suspension of the rules. Events had moved quickly in the House--so quickly, in fact, that well-organized resistance to the measure could not be formed. It was presumed that even if the bill was approved by the Special Labor Subcommittee, there was little chance that the full committee would report the measure or that a rule would be granted by the House Rules Committee--which is necessary before a bill is debated on the floor of Congress. The movement of events had shown this logic disastrously optimistic: the labor amendment had now gone half the distance.

Given the wide margin by which the bill passed the House, blockage in the Senate appeared doubtful at best; the measure had gained momentum, which is critical to the passage of any legislation. The bill went to the Senate Committee on Labor and Public Welfare, whose chairman, Harrison Williams, Jr. (Dem., N.J.) strongly favored the bill's passage. The original strategy was to send the measure directly to the floor without committee hearings. Strong provider representative pressure resulted in the scheduling of a hearing on August 16, 1972. This session was intended to be only a formality; indeed, the committee had planned to "mark up" the bill on the next day and forward it to the floor for a vote on the eighteenth. However, Senator Robert Taft (Rep., Oh.), influential in labor affairs (the 1947 amendments bear his father's name), requested a subsequent hearing that was scheduled for September 6, 1972. At this session the AHA mustered its forces and strenuously opposed passage of the legislation along with proposing a series of amendments to the bill that would provide safeguards for the continuity of patient care during labor disputes. With this hearing, concerted support evaported for reporting the bill before the end of the session. Taft's efforts to slow down the process should not be underestimated; however, organized labor was becoming less enthusiastic. Unions were afraid that the consideration of an amendment to the NLRA, no matter how narrow in scope, would cause an avalanche of proposals to change the law from anti-labor legislators.

In the latter part of 1972, after the second hearing on the bill, attention in Washington turned to other matters. It was an election year; members of Congress were spending increasing amounts of time in their home states. Action on the Taft-Hartley amendments would have to await the Ninety-third Congress. The process would begin again, however, the cast of characters and the primary issues would remain the same.

ROUND TWO: THE NINETY-THIRD CONGRESS

On the first day of the Ninety-third Congress, Representatives Frank Thompson and John Ashbrook (Rep., Oh.) introduced H.R. 1236. This measure was identical to the bill introduced by Congressman Thompson during the second session of the Ninety-second Congress that passed the House by an overwhelming margin. In submitting the bill, Thompson stated:

> ...during the 92nd Congress, the House passed a bill which would have placed employees of non-profit hospitals under the coverage of the National Labor Relations Act...the exclusion [of voluntary hospitals from the Act] has created acrimonious labor situations, and has worked to the disadvantage of the hospitals, their employees--and has certainly not helped their patients.

A companion bill (identical to the House measure) was introduced in the Senate on February 7, 1973, as S. 794 by Alan Cranston (Dem., Cal.) and Jacob Javits (Rep., N.Y.) Senator Cranston said:

> ...I introduce today a bill which I believe is vitally needed to remedy the denial of collective bargaining rights to employees of non-profit hospitals which are guaranteed to other American workers under the National Labor Relations Act... I have always supported the rights of workers to bargain collectively through a union they choose, with their employers. Without such protections, workers have little recourse but to depend on the benevolence of their employers to provide adequate pay.

Hearings on H.R. 1236 were held by the House Special Labor Subcommittee on April 12 and 19, 1973. Debate on the bill followed the same pattern as in the second session of the Ninety-second Congress, although the battle lines had firmed. The AHA strongly opposed H.R. 1236, noting that the bill would bring voluntary hospitals under the Act without providing mechanisms that would facilitate the continuance of patient care during threatened or actual labor disputes. The AHA submitted a series of proposed amendments to the existing NLRA that it deemed would be needed if hospitals were to be included under the Act. Organized labor maintained its staunch support for the measure.

The Senate held three days of hearings on S. 794--July 31, August 1 and 2, 1973; the Senate bill, a duplicate of H.R. 1236, proposed to strike the exemption of voluntary hospitals under the Act while making no other substantive changes in the law. On the first day of hearings, Senator Taft introduced S. 2292, which encompassed the suggested amendments to the Act offered by the American Hospital Association during their testimony in the House.

The Taft bill contained the following features:

1. It eliminated the exemption for not-for-profit hospitals.
2. It defined "health care institution" broadly so

that all nonpublic health facilities would be included under the Act.
3. It provided an impasse resolution procedure for health care facilities which included a ninety-day notice of agreement termination to the other party; a thirty-day notice to the Federal Mediation and Conciliation Service--the FMCS would engage in mediation with the parties thirty days prior to agreement termination; a sixty-day "cooling-off period" following the termination of agreement--fact finding would take place during this time unless the parties agreed to a binding procedure for resolving the dispute.
4. It required that strike notice be given thirty days prior to planning job action. The strike could not be instigated until workers had expressed their concurrence through a secret-ballot strike vote supervised by the Federal Mediation and Conciliation Service.
5. It provided that strikes or picketing of health care facilities not conducted under procedures specified above would be deemed an unfair labor practice.
6. It limited the number of broad bargaining units in health care facilities to no more than four: professional employees, technical employees, clerical employees, and service and maintenance employees.
7. It provided for priority NLRB case handling for situations involving strikes, picketing or lockouts in health care facilities.
8. It would allow a health care institution to seek injunctive relief to prevent an unlawful strike or picketing.

The Senate hearings produced another surprise. Richard F. Schubert (Under Secretary of Labor) testified for the Administration, saying that it had changed its position since 1972, when it favored blanket inclusion of voluntary hospitals under the Act without any other changes in the law. Probably as a result of Taft's efforts, the Administration backed off from its previous position. Using language that clouded rather than clarified the issues, Schubert said:

> This Department supported legislation identical to S. 794 last year, and we support the concept of S. 794 this year... We favor the concept of extending the proven benefits of NLRA to non-profit hospitals. We also favor some limited safeguards to protect the public interest in the

delivery of health care services. [emphasis added]

In the House, Representative John Erlenborn (Rep., Ill.) introduced H.R. 10086, roughly similar to the Taft bill. H.R. 10086 differed from S. 2292 in that 1) it would not limit the number of permissible bargaining units; 2) it would not allow unions to sue for certain types of damages; and 3) it would permit persons with certain religious convictions to be excluded from paying dues and fees under union security agreements.

By September, the issues had become muddy. First, the Thompson/Cranston (H.R. 1236/S. 794) and the Taft/Erlenborn (S. 2292/H.R. 10086) measures were far apart. The former measures proposed to include voluntary hospitals under the NLRA as it was. The latter measures proposed a major restructuring of the Act. Second, the Administration had shifted gears. Initially it supported blanket inclusion of voluntary hospitals under the existing NLRA; now it appeared to lean toward the need for some amendments to "safeguard hospitals." Third, Representative Thompson (chairman of the House Special Labor Subcommittee) wanted to hold up action on any measure until the Senate passed a bill. Thompson felt that he could deliver passage of H.R. 1236 (remember that an identical measure passed the House during the Ninety-second Congress by a vote of 295 to 85), and that the removal of the major stumbling block--Senate approval--should be attempted first.

Thus, active Congressional consideration of health care facility labor amendments again stalled. Senator Cranston held "quickie hearings" on S. 794 on October 4, 1973. The hearings lasted only fifty minutes. They were scheduled to receive testimony from Andrew J. Biemiller, legislative director of the AFL-CIO; Biemiller, the "dean of Washington lobbyists," testified that labor supported S. 794 and felt that hospitals should be subject to the same labor regulations as other industries. He stated:

> It is important, we think, that S. 794 be reported favorably without encumbering amendments or additions which would have the purpose of establishing different procedures for non-profit hospitals than for other business establishments, including proprietary hospitals. Other industries now subject to the National Labor Relations Act have their own special characteristics upon which claims for special treatment could just as logically have been made. Yet such claims have usually been rejected by Congress. The Act's framework is broad enough and flexible enough to encompass the special characteristics which distinguish the hospital industry from other industries. We would strongly urge the Subcommittee, therefore, to apply the National Labor Relations Act to non-

> profit hospitals without substantial change and without establishing special rules of procedures for this industry.

It appeared that Cranston was looking for some "give" in the labor position--he didn't find it.

Maneuvering room was needed if any measure was to be given even the slightest chance of enactment into law. The solidification of positions set the stage for background debate and discussion between the major players that would lead to the development of a compromise.

TOWARD A COMPROMISE

In late December 1973, through Senator Robert Taft's efforts, staff members of the Senate Labor Subcommittee, the personal staff of Senator Taft, hospital association representatives and representatives of organized labor held five meetings that struck a compromise between H.R. 1236/S. 794 (the "blanket inclusion" measure) and S. 2292/H.R. 10296 (the "safeguard" measure). Organized labor was represented in the negotiation process by the Service Employees' International Union and the Laborers' International Union. Officials of the AFL-CIO were involved, and George Meany was said to have reviewed draft proposals.

The House Special Labor Subcommittee avoided direct involvement in the compromise negotiations. Representative Frank Thompson, chairman of the committee, favored blanket inclusion of voluntary hospitals under the NLRA. Thompson wanted the option of accepting or rejecting the compromise package outright--an option that could not be maintained if he or his staff participated in the negotiations.

The final blessing of the compromise measure was conferred by the AFL-CIO Executive Council at its meeting in Miami, Florida, during January 1974. Senator Taft introduced S. 3088, which encompassed provisions of the compromise on February 28, 1974. In introducing the measure, Taft stated:

> I am today introducing legislation that is the result of protracted negotiations on the issue of extension of coverage of the National Labor Relations Act to the health care field. This legislation contains elements of a proposal I advanced earlier on this subject, S. 2292, and like any proposed compromise, it is not precisely what parties in interest would view as an optimum solution. I do believe, however, the statutory language I present today when combined with meaningful legislative report language...will provide a constructive basis for resolution of this issue.

An identifical bill (H.R. 13678) was introduced in the House by Representatives Frank Thompson and John Ashbrook.

The primary provisions of the compromise measures were as follows:

1. The exemption of voluntary hospitals under the NLRA would be removed. All nonpublic health care facilities would be subject to existing provisions of the Act plus specific amendments provided for in the bill. A health care facility would be defined as a nongovernmental hospital, convalescent hospital, health maintenance organization, health clinic, nursing home, extended care facility, or other institution devoted to the care of sick, infirm or aged persons.

2. Parties to a negotiation would be required to give each other ninety days' notice of the expiration of a collective bargaining contract involving a health care facility (HCF).

3. Sixty days' notice of collective bargaining agreement termination would have to be provided to the Federal Mediation and Conciliation Service (FMCS). The FMCS would have to be informed thirty days prior to a dispute involving the negotiation of an initial collective bargaining agreement involving the HCF.

4. Thirty days prior to agreement termination the FMCS would be required to become involved in mediation with the parties.

5. The bill required that a ten-day notice be given before the conduct of a strike, picketing or any other concerted job action.

6. The number of bargaining units in HCF's were not specifically limited in the bill; however, the committee reports (attached to the bill and expressing Congressional intent) suggested that limitation under existing rules of the NLRB would be advisable.

7. The committee reports stated that it would be permissible for another HCF to accept patients transferred from a struck institution or provide critical specialized personnel for lifesaving functions. This was an exception to previous NLRB rulings which allowed a union to picket an employer aiding another employer who was being struck.

8. The committee reports recommended that the NLRB give priority to handling unfair labor practice charges involving HCF's. Additionally it was suggested that the NLRB act in less than thirty days (then the standard practice) in cases involving recognitional picketing at an HCF.

On March 13, 1974 (less than two weeks after Senator Taft had introduced S. 3088), the full Senate Committee on Labor and Public Welfare discharged the Labor Subcommittee from considering S. 794 and S. 2292. On March 20, 1974, S. 3203 was introduced and ordered to the floor by voice vote; S. 3203 was identical to S. 3088 (the original compromise bill submitted by Senator Taft). Reintroduction of the Taft bill under a different file number allowed Senator Harrison Williams, Jr. (Dem., N.J.), chairman of the full committee, to be the primary sponsor of the bill and permitted the entire committee membership (except Senator Dominick) to act as co-sponsors. H.R. 13678 (the companion bill to S. 3202) was reported to the floor of the House by the full Committee on Education and Labor, by a unanimous voice vote, on May 14, 1974.

Two and a half years had elapsed since Representative Frank Thompson had introduced H.R. 11357 "for purposes of amending the Taft-Hartley Act to include within its coverage the employees of voluntary hospitals." Numerous days of hearings had been held; various pressure groups had striven to have their desires incorporated into a host of legislative proposals; a Congressional staff had drawn a series of working papers and committee members had completed their deliberations. Comparable bills were now on the floor of both chambers. Passage of the bills, as submitted, was a certainty, the "Dance of Legislation" was drawing to a close--or was it?

SENATE DELIBERATIONS ON THE COMPROMISE BILL

The Senate held debate on S. 3203 on May 2 and May 7, 1974. Senator Alan Cranston (Dem., Cal.), co-sponsor and floor manager of the bill, stated:

> The National Labor Relations Act basically provides two avenues for the peaceful resolution of labor-management disputes. First it establishes a recognized machinery for workers' desires by means of representation elections. Second it seeks to protect both labor and management from unfair labor practices.
>
> Under S. 3202, we will have one set of rules applicable to all health care institutions. The bill contains several special provisions designed to facilitate collective bargaining settlements and to provide advance notice of any strike or picketing involving a health care institution.

Seven amendments to S. 3203 were offered during the floor debate. Six of the proposed amendments were either defeated or tabled:

1. An amendment supported by the Seventh Day Adventist Church was introduced by Senator Samuel Ervin (Dem., S.C.) to exclude church operated and controlled hospitals from the provisions of the bill. The amendment was defeated by a vote of 50 to 36.

2. A sixty-day cooling-off period amendment was offered by Senator Peter Dominick (Rep., Colo.). The amendment would have allowed implementation of the emergency disputes provision of the existing Act in instances where a dispute involving a health care facility would substantially affect the provision of health services in the locality. The amendment was defeated by a vote of 49 to 37.

3. An amendment was introduced by Senator John Tower (Rep., Tex.) that would vest the federal courts rather than the National Labor Relations Board with jurisdiction over unfair labor practices; the amendment was tabled by a vote of 60 to 23.

4. An amendment offered by Senator Dominick to make discrimination regarding union membership an unfair labor practice was tabled by a vote of 54 to 26.

5. An amendment was proposed by Senator Dominick to exempt individuals from either joining or financially supporting a labor organization under a union security agreement if they held religious or conscientious objections regarding such membership or support. The amendment was tabled on a vote of 50 to 37.

6. A nongermane (not related to the scope of the bill under consideration) amendment to the Occupational Health and Safety Act was tabled by a vote of 47 to 41.

The Senate did accept (through a voice vote) an amendment that would delay the effective date of the bill thirty days after the date of enactment.

S. 3203 was passed by the Senate on May 7, 1974, on a vote of 63 to 25. Other than for the delay-in-implementation amendment, the Senate-passed version of the bill was identical to measures that had been voted out of both the House and Senate committees. All was going according to plan. The bill would now move to the House, where a much more stringent measure (blanket inclusion of voluntary hospitals with no safeguards) passed in 1972 by an overwhelming margin.

HOUSE DEBATE AND AMENDMENT OF THE COMPROMISE BILL

H.R. 13678 (identical to the bill passed in the Senate), introduced by Representatives Frank Thompson (Dem., N.J.) and John Ashbrook (Rep., Oh.), was favorably forwarded to the full House by the Committee on Education and Labor on May 14, 1974, and was subject to floor debate on May 30, 1974.

Although the American Hospital Association had participated in the negotiations that led to the development of the compromise health facility measures (S. 3203 and H.R. 13678), it now pressed to have an emergency disputes provisions in any legislation. The AHA designed and executed a massive campaign to have H.R. 13678 amended so that it would include such a provision. The staff of the AHA Washington Office personally visited most members of the House and sent letters to all of them; the association urged all state affiliates and individual hospitals to forward telegrams outlining support for the amendment. The AHA arranged meetings between Congressmen and individual hospital and state hospital association representatives.

The AHA strategy and efforts worked; the emergency disputes amendment, introduced by Representative John Erlenborn (Rep., Ill.), passed by a vote of 168 to 137. The amendment provided that a sixty-day cooling-off period could be implemented after agreement termination at the discretion of the director of the Federal Mediation and Conciliation Service in cases where a labor dispute involved a health care facility. The amendment provided that the cooling-off period should be applied selectively, and only where the dispute had the potential to seriously affect the delivery of health services in a given locality. At the onset of the cooling-off period the FMCS director would appoint a board to investigate the dispute. During the sixty-day period the status quo would be maintained; no strikes, picketing or lockouts could be undertaken, and the parties would be expected to engage in good-faith collective bargaining.

An amendment was introduced by Representative Albert Quie (Rep., Minn.) that would have allowed the NLRB to cede jurisdiction over the representational and collective bargaining relationship involving any health care facility to states that had a labor law in effect prior to the passage of the Taft-Hartley Act in 1947. The amendment was designed to allow the continued existence of the Minnesota Charitable Hospitals Act. The measure would have provided that the NLRB could have allowed certain state labor laws affecting health care facilities to supersede federal statutes. It failed on a tally vote of 152 to 161.

In a surprise move the House passed an amendment introduced by Representative John Erlenborn providing that

> An employee of a health care institution who is a member of, and adheres to tenets or teachings of a bonafide religion, body or sect which has historically held conscientious objections to joining or financially supporting labor organizations shall not be required to join or financially support any labor organization as a condition of employment.

The amendment was actively supported by the Seventh Day Adventist Church; a similar measure failed in the Senate.

Early in the evening on May 30, 1974, the House passed H.R. 13678, with the amendments noted above, on a vote of 240 to 58. The addition by the House of amendments not found in the Senate-passed version of the bill threw the measure to a joint conference committee so that differences could be worked out. For the first time in fifteen years, bills to significantly amend the National Labor Relations Act had passed both chambers of Congress.

CONFERENCE REPORT AND FINAL PASSAGE

The conference committee is a mechanism designed by Congress to adjudicate differences between the House and the Senate when each chamber passes a different version of the same bill. The objective of the process is to negotiate differences in the separate versions of the bill and to report an identical measure to both chambers. The conference committee on S. 3203 and H.R. 13678 was comprised of thirteen Senate and seven House members.

The conference committee had two major tasks. First, it had to resolve differences regarding the emergency disputes "cooling-off period" provision passed by the House and rejected by the Senate. Second, it had to address the conscientious objection amendment.

In the conference, Representative Frank Thompson introduced an alternative to the sixty-day cooling-off period amendment passed by the House (the Thompson alternative was actively supported by organized labor). The measure provided that a thirty-day cooling-off period could be implemented prior to termination of the agreement (rather than for sixty days after termination, as provided for in the House-passed bill) in those instances where the director of the FMCS felt that a dispute would significantly affect the provision of health care services in the locality. A board of inquiry would be appointed, which would have the authority to forward recommendations to the parties along with their recommendations for resolving the dispute. (This provision, along with others, will be described briefly in the final section of this chapter.) This compromise amendment to the bill was adopted by the conferees.

In addition, the conference committee favorably considered Representative John Erlenborn's amendment to allow exemption from paying union dues or fees for those individuals having bona fide religious objections to belonging to or supporting a labor organization. An additional provision was added in conference, however, that would require workers so excluded to pay sums equivalent to union dues and fees to a nonreligious charitable organization exempt from taxation under Section 501(c)(3) of the Internal Revenue Code.

The conference version of the bill was reported to the House and Senate. The Senate passed the bill (conference version of S. 3203) on July 10, 1974, by a vote of 64 to 29. The House passed the conference measure by an extremely close vote of 205 to 193 on July 11, 1974. President Nixon signed P.L. 93-360 into law on Friday, July 26, 1974, and it became effective thirty days thereafter.

MAJOR PROVISIONS OF P.L. 93-360: A BRIEF REVIEW

P.L. 93-360 is a simple law: it extends the coverage of the NLRA to a broad spectrum of the health care industry, changes certain provisions and adds others to the existing Act to better accommodate the labor relations needs of the industry. Although the detailed specifics of the law's provisions will be discussed more thoroughly in the remaining chapters of the book, here is a brief review of its major provisions.

Coverage

The existing exemption of voluntary nonprofit hospitals was repealed. The Act will now cover all health care facilities under nonpublic ownership and control (i.e., federal, state and municipally owned institutions continue to be excluded from the Act's provisions). A health care facility (HCF) is defined as "...any hospital, convalescent hospital, health maintenance organization, health clinic, nursing home, extended care facility, or other institution devoted to the care of sick, infirm or aged persons."

Strike Notice

A new section is added to the Act whereby a labor organization is prohibited from striking or picketing a health care facility without first providing at least ten days' notice. The notice requirement is intended to provide health care facilities with advance warning of pending job actions so that arrangements for the continuity of patient care can be made. When an employer engages in an unfair labor practice, the union would be under no requirement to provide notice prior to engaging in a strike or a picket.

Contract Notice

Health care facilities and unions are required to provide the other party with ninety days' notice prior to modification or termination of an existing collective bargaining agreement; the Federal Mediation and Conciliation Service (FMCS) must be notified sixty days prior to modification or termination. Where a new contract is negotiated, the FMCS must be provided with thirty days' notice. During the notice period the status quo must be maintained, and strikes and lockouts are prohibited.

Mediation

Prior to the 1974 amendments to the Act, there was no requirement for parties to engage in mediation. The law now provides for mandatory mediation between the parties of the Federal Mediation and Conciliation Service in the case of collective bargaining involving health care facilities. The process of mediation seeks to facilitate an agreement between the union and the health care facility; it is a process for lubricating collecting bargaining. The parties to the negotiation need not come to an agreement. They are free to accept or reject substantive suggestions forwarded by the mediator; however, under the provisions of the Act, they must participate in the process of mediation.

Religious Exemption

A new section is added to the Act whereby employees of a health care facility with religious and conscientious objections against joining or financially supporting a union may not be required to pay dues or fees to a labor organization as a condition of employment under a union security agreement. To be eligible for the exclusion, the employee must be a member of a bona fide religion, body or sect that adheres to established and traditional tenets or teachings which have historically held conscientious objections to joining or financially supporting labor organizations. Employees may be required to pay sums equivalent to the exempted dues and fees to one of three nonreligious charitable organizations (excluded from federal taxation under Section 501(c)(3) of the Internal Revenue Code) selected by the parties to the contract.

Emergency Disputes

A special procedure is added to the Act to assist in the settlement of threatened or actual strikes and lockouts that have the capability of substantially interrupting the delivery of health care services in the locality concerned. Under this provision (if an emergency is deemed to exist as defined above), the director of the Federal Mediation and Conciliation Service would establish a board of inquiry thirty days after it received a notice of contract termination under Section 8(d) of the Act (parties to a contract must notify the FMCS sixty days prior to termination, if such a contract involves a health care facility). The board of inquiry would have fifteen days to report its findings and recommendations to the parties; the parties would then have fifteen days to engage in continued negotiations before a work stoppage or lockout could take place. In the case of initial contract negotiations, the provision requires that after union certification the FMCS must be given thirty days' prior notice of a dispute. If, in the opinion of the director of the FMCS, an emergency exists or is threatened, the board of inquiry must be convened no less than ten days after receiving a notice of dispute. After the emergency procedure has been implemented, the process is the same as under agreement renegotiation.

In recommending various pieces of legislation to the House and Senate for consideration on the floor, Congressional committees send a committee report along with the particular bill. These reports discuss the purpose of the bill and describe its legislative history. More important, such reports seek to clarify and/or expand on the scope and meaning of the particular legislative proposal. When a bill is enacted into law, the committee reports are viewed by the courts and administrative bodies as expressing the intent of Congress. Such reports do not carry the weight of law; however, they are accorded important status when provisions of a given Act are interpreted.

The reports of the House Committee on Education and Labor and the Senate Committee on Labor and Public Welfare in forwarding the respective bills that were eventually enacted as P.L. 93-360 have particular importance in defining the responsibilities of health care facilities and unions under the Act. Described below are the more important provisions of the House and Senate committee reports (the reports of both bodies are substantively identical).

Bargaining Units

The reports noted that there has been a tendency for bargaining units to proliferate in health care facilities. Such enterprises are complex service institutions employing a wide variety of manpower and having a divergent mix of skills. Conceivably, each skill category could seek to establish a separate bargaining unit and be represented by a different union. Such a situation would be highly detrimental to the efficient operation of the facility. The committee reports state that "due consideration should be given by the [National Labor Relations] Board to prevent the proliferation of bargaining units in the health care industry." The reports cite with approval several Board rulings that establish a limited and workable number of HCF bargaining units.

Supervisors

Supervisors are specifically excluded from the provisions of the NLRA through Section 14(a). Section 2(11) states that

> The term "supervisor" means any individual having authority, in the interest of the employer, to hire, transfer, suspend, lay off, recall, promote, discharge, assign, reward, or discipline other employees, or responsibility to direct them, or to adjust their grievances, or effectively to recommend such action, if in connection with the foregoing, the exercise of such authority is not of a merely routine or clerical nature, but requires the use of independent judgment.

The committee reports note that during hearings various groups of health professionals urged adoption of legislative language that would specifically exclude professionals from the definition of "supervisor." The committees found that such language was unnecessary because of existing Board rulings.

> The Board has carefully avoided applying the

> definition of "supervisor" to a health care professional who gives direction to other employees in exercise of professional judgment, which direction is incidental to the professional's treatment of patients and thus is not the exercise of supervisory authority in the interest of the employer.

Recognitional Picketing

Under the NLRA, unions are allowed to picket an employer for recognition for a period up to thirty days, in the absence of unusual circumstances such as violence. The committee reports note that recognitional picketing of a health care facility is, in and of itself, an unusual circumstance. The NLRB is encouraged to limit the period allowed for recognitional picketing in health care facilities.

Priority Case Handling

Because of the potentially serious impact of strikes in the health care industry, the committee reports state that the NLRB is expected to accord special attention and priority to all charges of employee, employer and union unfair labor practice involving health care facilities. Unfair labor practice strikes in such institutions are expected to be investigated expeditiously so that if relief is warranted it can be sought quickly.

Ally Doctrine

The NLRB has ruled that during the course of a labor dispute where a secondary employer performs work that would have been executed by the striking workers of the primary employer, the secondary employer loses status as a neutral. In such a circumstance the union can extend job action activity (e.g., picketing) to the secondary employer. The committees have realized, however, that during a labor dispute patients must be transferred to other facilities and life-sustaining activities at the struck hospital must be maintained. Therefore,

> It is the sense of the Committee that where such secondary institutions accept the patients of a primary employer or otherwise provide life-sustaining services to the primary employer, by providing the primary employer with an employee or employees who possess critical skills, such as an EKG technician, such conduct shall not be sufficient to cause the secondary employer to lose its neutral status.

> It should be clear, however, that where a secondary employer enmeshes itself into the primary dispute by providing supervisors, nurses or staff other than those described, it loses its status of neutrality.

The full text of P.L. 93-360, the Senate Committee on Labor and Public Welfare report on S. 3202 (which does not differ in substances from the House Committee on Education and Labor report on H.R. 13678) and the conference committee report on S. 3203 are reproduced in Appendices B, C and D, respectively.

V
Collective Bargaining & Bargaining Rights

THE DUTY TO BARGAIN

Section 8(d) of the Taft-Hartley Act requires an employer and the union designated as the representative of a majority of the employees in a specific bargaining unit to meet at reasonable times, to confer in good faith and, finally, to reduce to writing the agreement reached if either party requests such written agreement. Section 8(d) provides that

> For the purpose of this section, to bargain collectively is the performance of the mutual obligation of the employer and the representatives of the employees to meet at reasonable times and confer in good faith with respect to wages, hours and other terms and conditions of employment, or the negotiation of an agreement or any question arising thereunder, and the execution of a written contract incorporating any agreement reached if requested by either party to agree to a proposal or require the making of a concession...

As will be discussed in Chapter VI, it is an unfair labor practice for an employer "to refuse to bargain collectively with representatives of his employees subject to the provisions of Section 9(a)..." It is well to note that it is an unfair labor practice for either party to refuse to bargain collectively with the other, but as stated above, this obligation in no way compels either party to agree to a proposal by the other. Neither is there a requirement under the law for either party to make a concession to the other.

The duty to bargain does not arise simply because a labor organization represents a majority of employees in a specific bargaining unit; rather, it flows from the request by the representative to bargain collectively. The Supreme Court in NLRB v. Columbia Enameling and Stamping Company (306 US 292, 59 S. Ct. 501, 83 L. Ed. 660, 1939) stated

> Since there must be at least two parties to a bargain and to any negotiations for a bargain, it follows that there can be no breach of the statutory duty by the employer--when he has not refused to receive communications from his employees--without some indication given to him by them or their representatives of their desire or willingness to bargain.

Therefore, the duty to bargain develops legally when the representative of an appropriate bargaining unit requests the employer to do so.

BARGAINING UNIT DETERMINATIONS

Section 9(a) provides that the employee representative that has been designated or selected for the purposes of collective bargaining by the majority of the employees in a unit appropriate for such purposes shall be the exclusive representative of all the employees in such unit for the purposes of collective bargaining. The National Labor Relations Board is delegated the responsibility to determine the appropriate bargaining unit. This is the initial element which is one of the most significant aspects of union organization.

Section 9(b) states that "the Board shall decide in each case whether, in order to assure to employees the fullest freedom in exercising the rights guaranteed by this Act, the unit appropriate for the purposes of collective bargaining shall be the employer unit, craft unit, plant unit or subdivision thereof..." In determining the appropriate collective bargaining unit, the Board can select from among the following types of arrangements:

1. multi-employer units
2. multi-plant units
3. plant-wide units
4. craft units
5. departmental units
6. professional units
7. clerical units
8. plant guard units

One can readily see that a unit may cover employees in one division of an institution or it may cover employees in multidivisions of the same employer. If the employer is a member of a multiemployer association the Board can include employees of two or more employers within the same unit.

There are certain limitations on the establishment of appropriate bargaining units. Section 9(b)(1) provides that the Board shall not approve a unit that includes both professional and nonprofessional employees unless a majority of the professional employees involved vote to be included in the mixed unit. This is often termed the right of self-determination. Section 9(b)(2) provides that the Board shall not hold a proposed craft unit to be inappropriate simply because a different unit was previously approved by the Board unless a majority of the employees in the proposed craft unit vote against being represented separately. Section 9(b)(3) prohibits the Board from including plant guards in the same unit with other employees. This section goes even further in dealing with plant guards. The Board may not certify a labor organization seeking to represent guards which has members who are nonguard employees if it is "affiliated directly or indirectly" with an organization that has members who are nonguard employees.

Supervisors are excluded by two provisions of the Act. In defining an "employee," Section 2 excludes supervisors. Under Section 2(11), a supervisor is defined as any person "having authority in the interest of the employer to hire, transfer, suspend, lay off, recall, promote, discharge, assign, reward or discipline other employees or responsibility to direct them or to adjust their grievances or effectively to recommend such action if...such authority is not of a merely routine or clerical nature, but requires the use of independent judgment." Through Section 14(a), employers are exempt from the duty to consider supervisors as employees under any law relating to collective bargaining. It is well to note that the Board cannot include supervisors in bargaining units with other employees or establish any collective bargaining unit composed entirely of supervisory personnel. Notwithstanding these two provisions, employers may voluntarily recognize a union of supervisors.

Under Section 2(12), the term "professional employee" is defined to mean any employee engaged in work 1) predominantly intellectual and varied in character as opposed to routine mental, manual, mechanical or physical work; 2) involving the consistent exercise of discretion and judgment in its performance; 3) of such a character that the output produced or the result accomplished cannot be standardized in relation to a given period of time; and/or 4) requiring knowledge of an advanced type in a field of science or learning customarily required by a prolonged course of specialized intellectual study in an institution of higher learning or a hospital as distinguished from a general academic education or from an apprenticeship or from training in the performance of routine mental, manual, or physical processes. The term "professional" also includes any employee who 1) has completed courses of specialized intellectual instruction and study described in 4, above; or 2) is performing related work under the supervision of a professional person in order to qualify himself to become a professional employee.

In <u>NLRB v. Bell Aerospace Company Division of Textron, Inc.</u> (72-1598, 83 LRRM 2945), the Supreme Court ruled that all employees properly classified as "managerial," and not merely those in positions susceptible to conflicts of interest, are excluded from protections of the NLRA. The Court concluded that Congress had intended to exclude all true managerial employees from the protection of the Act and stated that this "...exclusion embraced not only an employee so closely related to or aligned with management as to place the employee in a position of conflict of interest between his employer on the one hand and his fellow workers on the other, but also who is formulating, determining and effectuating his employer's policies or his discretion independent of an employer's established policy in the performance of his duties."

In its decision the Supreme Court held that all managerial employees are excluded from the National Labor Relations Act. With reference to the scope of this exclusion the Court stated:

> A major company, for example, may have scores of executive officers who formulate and effectuate management policies, yet have no supervisory responsibility or identifiable "conflict of interest in labor relations." If Congress intended the unionization of such executives, it most certainly would have made its design plain.

Moreover, the Court held that

> [T]he specific job title of the employees involved is not in itself controlling. Rather, the question whether particular employees are "managerial" must be answered in terms of the employees' actual job responsibilities, authority, and relationship to management.

Among many cases cited by the Supreme Court in handing down the majority ruling in this case were two important decisions, one of which was Palace Laundry Dry Cleaning Corporation (75 NLRB 320, 323 n4, 21 LRRM 1039, 1947) which stated that

> The determination of "managerial" like the determination of "supervisory" is to some extent necessarily a matter of the degree of authority exercised. We have in the past and before the passage of the recent amendments to the Act recognized and defined as managerial employees executives who formulate and effectuate management policies by expressing and making the operative decisions of their employer and have excluded such managerial employees from bargaining units. We believe this Act, as amended, contemplates the continuation of this practice.

In the second case, Swift and Company (115 NLRB 752, 7530754, 37 LRRM 1391, 1956) the Supreme Court noted that "It was the clear intent of Congress to exclude from the coverage of the Act all individuals allied with management. Such individuals cannot be deemed to be employees for the purposes of the Act. Accordingly we reaffirm the Board's position that representatives of management may not be accorded bargaining rights under the Act...."

In Minneapolis-Moline Company (85 NLRB 597, 24 LRRM 1443, 1949) and in B. F. Goodrich Company (115 NLRB 722, 37 LRRM 1383, 1956), the Board established an implied exclusion of confidential employees which was deemed necessary in order to make the Act function. Only confidential employees whose employment involves labor relations are excluded. Confidential employees, who assist in the formulation and execution of the employer's labor policies, are excluded from coverage under the law. It is not enough for an employee to have access to confidential information to be exempt from coverage. If such exemption is to be established, the information available to the employee must relate to critical matters concerning labor or personnel relations.

PRINCIPAL CRITERIA USED BY THE NLRB IN UNIT DETERMINATION

The Board has formulated a set of criteria in selecting the appropriate bargaining unit based upon the following statement as specified in the Fifteenth Annual Report of the NLRB (Vol. 39, 1950): "...the Board's primary concern is to group together only employees who have substantial mutual interests in wages, hours and other conditions of employment." The most important of these criteria are

1. community of interest among employees;
2. bargaining history;
3. the desires of the employees;
4. the extent of union organization; and
5. the organizational structure of the institution.

Each of these criteria are examined more closely below.

Community of Interest Among Employees

The Board has expressed its concern that an appropriate bargaining unit should group together only those employees who have substantial mutual interests in wages, hours and other conditions of employment. The factors it considers in determining this community of interest were enumerated in Kalamazoo Paper Box Corporation (136 NLRB 134, 49 LRRM 1715, 1962). Although this case specifically involved truckdrivers who sought to sever themselves from a plantwide unit of production workers, the principles stated by the Board are basic to the community-of-interest doctrine. The Board considered the following factors in determining community of interest: 1) differences in wages or compensation; 2) different hours of work; 3) different employment benefits; 4) separate supervision; 5) the degree of dissimilar qualifications, training and skills; 6) difference in job functions and amount of working time spent away from the place of employment or plant; 7) the infrequency or lack of contact with other employees; 8) lack of integration with the work functions of other employees or interchange with them; and 9) the history of collective bargaining. The Board carefully weighs all facts relating to the interest and activities of the workers in a potential bargaining unit.

Bargaining History

The Board is reluctant to disturb or change units which have been established in the past and within which, over a substantial period of time, collective bargaining has been carried on. The stability of labor relations is not quickly or lightly disturbed by the Board. Bargaining history is an important factor in the Board's consideration for determining an appropriate bargaining unit. On the other hand, the Board has often concluded that rigid adherence to this doctrine (bargaining history) must not stand in the way if this standard will interfere with employees' fullest freedom of choice. The Board may determine that bargaining history should be disregarded if such history is inconsistent with the purpose of the Act.

Desires of the Employees

In applying the Globe Doctrine--Globe Machine and Stamping Company (3 NLRB 294, 1-A LRRM 122, 1937)--the Board will give weight to the wishes of employees to be included in a separate unit. For example, the doctrine permits employees in a craft or skill unit the choice of voting to be in a separate unit or to be included in a broader unit of industrial employees. This is accomplished by an election of the members of the craft or skill unit to determine whether they wish to be a separate unit by voting for the union which has petitioned for the smaller unit. If, however, they wish to be included in a broader unit they can vote for the union seeking such representation. This can be accomplished by using two or more ballots in the same election, or by using one ballot specially constructed to offer these choices.

The Extent of Union Organization

Section 9(c)(5) of the Act provides that "In determining whether a unit is appropriate...the extent to which the employees have organized shall not be controlling." The Board may consider organizational penetration, but not as the sole determinant. The Board will give some weight to the extent that the union has organized a specific group of employees in determining whether the group is an appropriate unit. It is, however, only one of several criteria that the Board may consider.

The Organizational Structure of the Institution

The Board will consider similarity of working conditions among employees; similarity of supervision over such employees; the degree of integration of the employer's operation; the similarity in personnel policies for such employees; and the interchangeability of employees.

CRAFT VERSUS INDUSTRIAL UNITS

Industrial units or plant units include all employees of an employer in a single location, with the exception of those excluded from the unit either by union-management agreement or by law. Where employees perform work of a recognized skill in a bona fide craft, the Board may establish a craft unit. The Board has found craft units appropriate for such employees as carpenters, electricians, plumbers, steam engineers and machinists. The present Board policy on craft severance flows from the Mallinckrodt decision (162 NLRB 387, 64 LRRM 1011, 1016, 1966). In Mallinckrodt the Board listed six factors which it deemed relevant in considering craft severance petitions:

1. the distinctiveness of the craftsmen's group and the skilled nonrepetitive nature of their work;
2. the history of bargaining of the employees who wish to form a craft unit (this history includes experience at the institution involved, the stability of labor relations of the institution and whether such stability will be disrupted by the proposed change);
3. the extent to which the employees in the proposed craft unit have retained their identity while being included in a broader unit, and the extent that members of this proposed craft unit are integrated with other workers in the institution;
4. the history and pattern of bargaining in the industry involved;
5. the degree of integration of the craftsmen's work with that of other workers in the institution; and
6. the qualifications of the unions seeking to represent a severed unit.

The Board uses these standards not only in considering petitions for craft severances (the relatively unusual situation where a craft group has been organized as part of a broader unit and now wants its own independent unit), but also applies these standards to the initial formation of a craft unit in an institution which has previously been unorganized or where such employees have previously been unorganized.

In enacting the 1974 amendments to the National Labor Relations Act, Congress suggested that "...due consideration should be given by the Board toward preventing proliferation of bargaining units in the health care industry." In this connection, the House and Senate committees noted with approval the recent Board decision in Four Seasons Nursing Center (208 NLRB 50, 85 LRRM 1093, 1974), and Woodland Park Hospital (205 NLRB 144, 84 LRRM 1975, 1973) as well as the trend toward broader units enunciated in Extended Care of West Virginia (203 NLRB 170, 83 LRRM 1242, 1973). The full text of these rulings can be found in Appendix E.

In the Woodland Park Hospital case, the Board ruled that a unit of X-ray technicians did not have a community of interest that is any more separately identifiable than that of certain other employees in other technical departments. The Board stated, "To establish a separate unit for X-ray technicians in circumstances such as these would in our opinion lead to severe fragmentation of the units in the health care industry. As we see no basis for concluding that the X-ray technicians here involved, although separately supervised, constitute a separate appropriate unit, we shall dismiss the petition..."

In the Extended Care of West Virginia case, the Board found that the technical employees and service and maintenance workers share a substantial community of interest. They stated:

> We further note that the petitioner primarily seeks to represent in separate units a total of approximately 62 service and maintenance employees and only 7 technical employees. In this situation given the appropriateness of a separate unit of LPN's, where the technical employees are relatively few in number, a finding that two separate units are appropriate for bargaining would create unwarranted unit fragmentation. Accordingly, and as the petitioner has indicated a willingness to represent the technical employees and service and maintenance employees in one unit, we find that the technical employees and service and maintenance unit employees together constitute a unit appropriate for bargaining.

REPRESENTATION SELECTION

The Board is empowered to conduct representation elections by secret ballot. Section 9(c) of the Act provides that

> Representatives designated or selected for the purposes of collective bargaining by the majority of the employees in a unit appropriate for such purposes shall be the exclusive representatives of all the employees in such unit for the purpose of collective bargaining in respect to rates of pay, wages, hours of employment or other conditions of employment...

A petition can be filed by an employee or group of employees or any individual or labor organization acting in their behalf when a "question concerning representation" has arisen. An election can also be requested by an employer alleging that a labor organization has claimed to be a representative of his employees. Once the petition is filed, the Board conducts an investigation and holds a hearing, if necessary, in order to determine whether

1. the Board has jurisdiction to conduct an election;
2. there is sufficient showing of employee interest to justify an election;
3. a question of representation exists;
4. the election is sought in an appropriate unit of employees;
5. the representative named in the petition is qualified; and
6. whether there are any barriers to an election in the form of existing contracts or prior elections.

The Question of Board Jurisdiction

The Board's jurisdiction in the health care industry stems from the inclusion of the term "health care institution" in Section 2(14) of the Act and includes any nongovernmental hospital, convalescent hospital, health maintenance organization, health clinic, nursing home, extended care facility or other institution devoted to the care of sick, infirm or aged persons.

Showing of Interest

Section 9(c)(1)(4) of the Act provides that any petition for a Board-conducted election must be supported by a "substantial number of employees." In the Board's rules and regulations a "substantial number of employees" is defined as at least 30 percent. This showing of interest is established by the submission to the

Board of union authorization cards (membership cards) properly signed and dated. An intervening union (one that also claims interest in the same employees) need not display the 30 percent showing. The Board will accept a show of minimum interest (10 percent) in the case of intervening unions. In determining the validity of the cards presented by the union, the Board often requests a current roster of employees--normally a payroll listing from the employer. The employer is not permitted to inspect the cards.

Question of Representation

The Board's legal imposition in representation cases must flow from the existence of a question of representation. If the union claims to represent a majority, it must produce evidence that there is a question concerning representation. There must be a demand for recognition followed by a refusal by the employer. It is also raised by a petition to decertify a present representative previously certified or currently recognized by the employer.

Appropriateness of Unit

The Board must determine whether the petitioner is seeking certification for an appropriate bargaining unit. The Board's determination in this area is based upon the factors discussed earlier in this chapter.

Qualification of Petitioner

Section 2(4) of the Act states that an employee representative for purposes of collective bargaining can be "any individual or labor organization." The Board must determine whether the "labor organization" meets the definition under the Act. Section 2(5) of the Act defines a labor organization as

> ...any organization of any kind, or any agency or employee representation committee, or plan, in which employees participate and which exists for the purpose, in whole or in part, of dealing with employers, concerning grievances, labor disputes, wages, rates of pay, hours of employment, or conditions of work.

It is the union's willingness to represent the employees rather than its ability to do so that is the controlling factor in the NLRB's determination whether it qualifies as a bona fide representative of the employees. The Board's jurisdiction to certify a labor organization as the collective bargaining agent is limited by Section 9(b)(3), which prohibits certification of a union as a representative of a unit of plant guards if the union "admits to membership or is affiliated directly or indirectly with an organization which admits to membership employees other than guards." A supervisor or any other management representative may not be an employee representative. Board policy is to direct an election and to issue a certification unless the proposed bargaining agent fails to qualify as a bona fide representative of the employees.

Decertification

The Act provides a method for employees to withdraw the union's authorization to act as their bargaining representative. Employees or someone acting on their behalf can file a petition with the Board for a "decertification"; the petition must contain the signatures of at least 30 percent of the employees covered by an expiring collective bargaining agreement. An election similar to the certification election is then held by the Board. If a majority of the employees in the bargaining unit cast their ballots to decertify the union, the Board will issue such a decertification.

Barriers to an Election

The Board established a "contract bar" doctrine which states that an existing contract between a union and an employer will ordinarily stand in the way of an election. A valid contract for a period of three years or less has been determined to be a bar to an election for the period covered by that contract. A contract must be in writing and have a specific duration in order to be a bar to an election. The petition of the union seeking to replace the present union must be timely. If a union seeks an election where the bargaining unit is currently represented by another union, it must file a petition at least sixty but not more than ninety days before the expiration of the contract. A contract which has been prematurely extended cannot act as a bar in an election. A premature extension will not be a bar to the election if a contract is executed during the sixty-day period preceding the terminal date of the old contract. A contract is not a bar to an election if there is a requirement that the membership ratify such a contract and, indeed, the membership did not ratify that contract. A contract containing an illegal union security clause has also been deemed not to be a bar to an election. A contract covering an inappropriate bargaining unit is not a bar to an election. If a valid election has been held less than one year from the time a petition is submitted for another election, the Board has ruled to bar such an election. A labor organization must wait at least one year after an election has been held before the Board will conduct another election in a similar unit.

REPRESENTATION ELECTIONS

The Board, once establishing its jurisdiction and ascertaining that there is a question regarding representation, will attempt to obtain from the parties an agreement to a consent election. This agreement outlines the time and place of the election, choices availalbe to the employees on the ballot and, most important, the definition of the bargaining unit and a list of employees eligible to vote. There are two basic types of consent elections. In the agreement for consent election the regional director will make the final determination of any dispute regarding conduct of election. In the stipulation for certification on consent election the Board will be the final determinator of any dispute. If the parties are unable to reach an agreement, the Board is authorized to order the election after holding a formal hearing. The Board can designate the regional director as the determiner on any disputes arising from the election.

Date of the Election

The Board will not set an election less than ten days after the date the regional director receives the list of eligible voters. The Board will consider setting the election date on which the largest number of eligible voters may be present and able to vote.

Time and Place of the Election

If the employer agrees, the Board will set the election during working time, but in the face of employer objection, it can schedule the election on the employees' own time. The Board will give careful consideration in setting the time permissible for employees to vote in order to give all eligible employees full opportunity to exercise their right to vote. The election is generally held on the employer's premises whenever possible.

Eligibility to Vote

The Board requires the employer to submit a roster of eligible voters within seven days of its direction of an election. This list is made available to all parties. Generally the eligibility period is the employer's payroll period immediately prior to the date on which the election is directed. Such employees are eligible to vote who are in the employ of the employer at the time of the election. Section 9(c)(3) provides that employees who are engaged in an economic strike and have been permanently replaced are still eligible to vote if the election is held within twelve months from the time of the strike. Employees who are on layoff status and who have a "reasonable expectation of reemployment" in the near future have been deemed eligible to vote. Those who have been discharged for cause or who have quit between the date of the Board's setting of the election and the election date are ineligible, unless such employees have been discriminatorily discharged.

The Ballot: Observers and Challengers

The Act provides that an election by secret ballot shall be held under the supervision of the regional director. The ballot itself is provided by the Board. The question on the ballot which is addressed to all employees eligible to vote is either determined through the consent agreement signed by the employer and the petitioning labor organization or by direction of the Board. Generally, where one union is involved in the election, the employees are offered the choice whether or not to be represented by that union. Where more than one union is involved, the employee is given the choice of selecting one of the unions or no union. The employee is asked to mark an "X" in the box of his choice. A representative of the Board is present to supervise the election. The voting is by secret ballot. Each employee who presents himself at the voting place must be identified and a check is made against the eligibility roster. Each of the parties involved in the election may appoint an observer of his own selection who will receive printed instructions as to his behavior in fulfilling his responsibilities at the polling place. The employer may not appoint a supervisory employee as his observer. The observer assists in identifying voters, but, more important, is responsible for challenging individuals who present themselves to vote if he believes that they are not eligible to vote. The Board agent, the employer or the union(s) may challenge for good or reasonable cause the eligibility of any individual presenting himself to vote. Such an individual is permitted to cast his ballot, but the challenged ballot is impounded. Challenged ballots are reviewed and assume importance only if their number is sufficient to affect the outcome of the election. In that event, the regional director will investigate the challenges. Anyone whose name does not appear on the eligibility roster will be challenged by the Board's agent. An employee who is not in a classification specifically included in the Board's definition of the appropriate unit will not be permitted to receive a ballot unless the reason for his voting is deemed plausible. In such cases, or where there is a question concerning one's eligibility, the individual will be permitted to vote, but a challenge will be noted. Challenges must be identified before an individual casts his ballot. Challenge procedures employed by the Board are reproduced in

Exhibit 5.1 following this chapter.

Tallying of Ballots

As soon after the election as feasible, the votes are tallied by the Board's agent. The process is conducted in the presence of management and union observers, and the ballots are carefully reviewed for defects. Those ballots revealing the identification of the voter, unmarked ballots and improperly marked ballots are invalid. The Board agent then counts the valid ballots. The union must win a majority of the valid votes cast to be certified as the exclusive bargaining agent. It is not necessary for a union to receive the votes of a majority of the eligible voters; it is only necessary that it receive a majority of those valid votes cast. A union cannot be certified on the basis of a tie vote. If none of the choices in an election involving more than one union receives a majority, a runoff election is held as soon as possible. In the case of an election involving only one union, there can be no runoff if the election results in a tie. The runoff election is held between the choice receiving the most votes and the choice receiving the next highest number of votes.

Objections

Within five days after the issuance of the tally of ballots, any party may serve upon all other parties and file with the Board any objections to the election. The objections must be complete and concise with regard to the grounds; objections filed with the Board cannot merely make general allegations of interference with the election, but must contain facts supported by affidavit which prima facie raise an issue that the election does not represent the free choice of the voters. The key grounds for objections revolve around the compromising of "laboratory conditions" which are necessary to permit employees an absolutely free choice in the election. Misrepresentation by either party or promises, threats or inflammatory propaganda during the preelection period would void the results of an election. In general, an election will be set aside if the Board considers any action by either party as a cause of establishing an atmosphere of confusion or fear of reprisals and, therefore, affecting the employees' free choice of their representative. If the Board believes that the conduct under question tended to interfere with the free expression of the employees' choice, the election will be set aside. The Board in rulings regarding elections has provided that

1. An employer is prohibited from making speeches on company time and property to mass assemblies of employees within twenty-four hours before the time scheduled for an election.

2. Parties are prohibited from using reproductions of the official ballot as campaign propaganda.
3. The employer may not try to influence the voting by means of interviewing employees individually or in small groups away from their work stations and in a place of management authority.

After investigation, the regional director will issue a report on the objections; exceptions to the regional director's rulings on these objections may be filed with the Board for decision except in the case of elections that are held by consent of the parties. In the latter instance the regional director's ruling on an objection is final.

Organizational Picketing

Section 8(b)(7) of the Act will be discussed more comprehensively in Chapter VII; however, the relevant requirements are worth noting here:

> It shall be an unfair labor practice for a labor organization or its agents to picket or cause to be picketed, or threaten to picket or cause to be picketed, any employer where an object thereof is forcing or requiring an employer to recognize or bargain with a labor organization as the representative of his employees, or forcing or requiring the employees of an employer to accept or select such labor organization as their collective bargaining representative, unless such labor organization is currently certified as the representative of such employees:
> (A) where the employer has lawfully recognized in accordance with this Act any other labor organization and a question concerning representation may not appropriately be raised under Section 9(c) of this Act,
> (B) where within the preceding twelve months a valid election under Section 9(c) of this Act has been conducted, or
> (C) where such picketing has been conducted without a petition under Section 9(c) being filed within a reasonable period of time not to exceed thirty days from the commencement of such picketing: Provided, that when such a petition has been filed the Board shall forthwith, without regard to the provisions of Section 9(c)(1) or the absence of a showing of a substantial interest

> on the part of the labor organization, direct an election in such unit as the Board finds to be appropriate and shall certify the results thereof: Provided further, that nothing in this subparagraph (C) shall be construed to prohibit any picketing or other publicity for the purpose of truthfully advising the public (including consumers) that an employer does not employ members of, or have a contract with, a labor organization, unless an effect of such picketing is to induce any individual employed by any other person in the course of his employment, not to pick up, deliver or transport any goods or not to perform any services...

In recognition picketing cases, the Board has ruled that a reasonable period of time is thirty days, in the absence of unusual circumstances such as violence or intimidation. Picketing of a health care institution would in itself constitute an unusual circumstance justifying the application of a period of time less than thirty days.

Expedited Elections

When an unfair labor practice charge arising out of recognitional picketing has been filed pursuant to Section 8(b)(7), discussed in Chapter VII, an expedited election procedure is provided. The expedited procedure may be used only when the filing of a representation petition constitutes a defense to picketing otherwise in violation of the aforementioned section. Charges involving unfair labor practices must be disposed of prior to an expedited election by the Board.

Judicial Review of Election Results

The Board's administration of its procedures involving the determination of bargaining units and the conduct of elections is ordinarily not subject to judicial review. The Supreme Court has, however, permitted such review in cases involving "extraordinary circumstances." An employer desiring to contest a certification must first refuse to bargain and then raise such issues as a defense to an unfair labor practice proceeding.

FORMS EMPLOYED BY THE NLRB

The certification procedure is initiated by the filing of a petition (see Exhibit 5.2, NLRA-502). Such a petition may be filed for the investigation of a question concerning representation of employees.

As noted earlier in this chapter, it may be filed by an employee or group of employees or any individual or labor organization acting in their behalf or by an employer. To be appropriate, the petition must contain the following information:

1. the name of the employer;
2. the address of the establishment involved;
3. the general nature of the employer's business;
4. a description of the bargaining unit which the petitioner claims to be appropriate;
5. the names and addresses of any other persons or labor organizations who claim to represent any employees in the alleged appropriate unit and brief descriptions of the contracts, if any, covering the employees in such unit;
6. the number of employees in the alleged appropriate unit;
7. a statement that the employer declines to recognize the petitioner as the representative; and
8. the name, the affiliation, if any, and the address of the petitioner.

The Board will then send a letter to the parties bringing their attention to the filing of the petition. (See Exhibit 5.3, Regional Office 29-R-70.)

At the same time a poster will be forwarded to the employer with the suggestion that the employer post this notice to all employees. (See Exhibit 5.4, NLRB-666.) This poster outlines the rights of employees under federal law to 1) self-organization; 2) form joint or assist labor organizations; 3) bargain collectively through representatives of their own choosing; 4) act together for the purpose of collective bargaining or other mutual aid or protection; and 5) refuse to do any or all of these things unless the union and employer in a state where such agreements are permitted enter into a lawful union security clause requiring employees to join the union. The employer need not post this notice. Along with this notice, the Board will forward to the employer a commerce questionnaire (see Exhibit 5.5, Regional Office 29-C-5A). This questionnaire is needed to establish whether or not the Board can assert jurisdiction.

As has been noted above, the Board will attempt to obtain an agreement for consent election (Exhibit 5.6, NLRB-651). Through this form the regional director will make the final determination of any dispute regarding the conduct of the election. In Exhibit 5.7, NLRB-652, Stipulation for Certification upon Consent Election, a second form of consent agreement is outlined wherein the Board will be the final determinator of any dispute. Upon the setting of a date for the election, the Board will forward instructions to election observers (Exhibit 5.8, NLRB-722). This instruction sheet lists the duties of observers and guidelines regarding prohibited behavior. The Board will forward to the employer a notice of election (Exhibit 5.10, NLRB-707). This notice must be posted; it explains when and where the election is to be held and who is eligible to vote.

Exhibit 5.9, NLRB-4175, is a notice of election of representative along with the instructions to eligible employees voting by United States mail. This form is sent to effect absentee voting of eligible employees who cannot be present, either because of illness or other legitimate reasons. Upon conclusion of the election, the ballots are tallied by the Board representative and a tally of the ballots is prepared (Exhibit 5.11, NLRB-760). A certification is issued by the Board after the election is held, and this certification (Exhibit 5.12, NLRB-4279) reflects the majority choice of the employees who cast their ballots.

Exhibit 5.13, NLRB-4280, is a certification of the results of the election. The certification announces the results of the election when no union has been selected as the bargaining representative of the delineated unit. If an individual who presents himself as an eligible voter is challenged by either party, his ballot is placed in a challenge ballot secret envelope (Exhibit 5.14, NLRB-4646). The information necessary to identify the challenged individual is placed on the left of the envelope and includes the reason for the challenge. These envelopes are opened only after the challenge is adjudicated by the Board and only if the individual is deemed by the Board to be an eligible voter and such vote is or would be significant in the outcome of the election. Exhibit 5.15, NLRB-501, is a form for filing a charge against an employer, and Exhibit 5.16, NLRB-508, is a form for filing a charge against a labor organization or its agents.

A special form, Exhibit 5.17, NLRB-509, is provided for filing a charge alleging an unfair labor practice under Section 8(e) of the Act.

Exhibit 5.1. Challenge procedures as outlined in Section 102.69(a) of National Labor Relations Board Rules and Regulations

11338 Challenges: The challenge procedure provides a method whereby a voter's eligibility to vote may be called into question, the ruling on the question may be at least temporarily reserved, and the questioned voter may memorialize his desires in the event his desires should have relevance in the future--all without disrupting the regular flow of votes.

Any observer has the right to challenge a voter for cause. The Board agent must challenge anyone whose name is not on the eligibility list. Also, he must challenge a voter if he knows or has reason to believe that the voter is ineligible to vote, but, in this instance, he should not challenge until and unless none of the parties voice a challenge. The Board agent will not make challenges on behalf of the parties, whether or not such parties have observers present.

The reason for the challenge should be stated at the time the challenge is made.

11338.1 Challenge procedure: When a voter is challenged, a small "c" is placed beside his name by the checking observers. (If his name does not appear on the list, it should be added, in a supplemental list, and the "c" inserted.) The Board agent (at the checking table or, in a large election, at a challenge table) fills out the information called for on the stub of a challenged ballot envelope--the voter's name, clock number, job classification, employer, place and date of election, the reason given for the challenge, the identity of the challenger, and his (the agent's) initials. If time permits, he may elicit specific information surrounding the voter's status, for insertion on the reverse side of the stub, there to be initialed by the voter.

The voter is then given a ballot and instructed to enter the booth, mark the ballot, fold it so as to keep the mark secret and return to the voting table. Upon his return to the voting table, he is given a challenged ballot envelope. The voter places the marked ballot in the envelope, seals the envelope, and drops it in the box. Observers stationed at the voting booth area and/or the ballot box should make sure that the challenged voter, when he comes out of the booth, goes to the voting table and does not drop the ballot in the box before placing it in the envelope, and sealing the envelope.

11338.2 Notation of potential challenges: Observers may maintain lists of persons they intend to challenge, but the better practice is to permit the parties to note on the eligibility list, at the pre-election check, the persons they intend to challenge. Any such marks made prior to an election, however, must be easily distinguishable from the marks to be made by observers at the election.

11338.3 Proper time to challenge: Challenges should be handled as they come up. Challenged voters should not be told to return later, and they should not be allowed to congregate in the polling place awaiting a slack period.

In the oral instructions to observers, they should be urged to challenge as the voter comes up to the checking table. Normally, a challenge should be made before the questioned voter receives a ballot.

11338.4 Merit of challenge should not be argued: Arguments on the merits of a challenge should not be permitted. The challenge steps outlined above should be taken quietly and quickly, and the regular voting flow should be impeded as little as possible. The Board agent should be prepared to explain to the voter, quickly and lucidly, the measures which will be taken to protect the secrecy of the challenged ballot.

11338.5 Exclusions in decision: Persons in job classifications specifically excluded by the Decision and Direction of Election should be refused a ballot, even under challenge. The Board agent must exercise discretion in deciding whether to allow a vote (under challenge) when the person presents plausible reasons for being permitted to vote despite the exclusion, or if his actually being within the excluded group is not without question.

11338.6 Mail ballots challenged: Challenged mail ballots need not be placed in challenge envelopes. "Challenged" should be written across the face of the stub, and the information usually entered on a challenge envelope should be inserted on the reverse side of the mail-envelope stub.

Exhibit 5.2. Petition for Recognition: NLRB Form 502

Form NLRB-502
(11-64)

UNITED STATES OF AMERICA
NATIONAL LABOR RELATIONS BOARD

Form Approved
Budget Bureau No. 64 R002.14

PETITION

DO NOT WRITE IN THIS SPACE
CASE NO
DATE FILED

INSTRUCTIONS – Submit an original and four (4) copies of this Petition to the NLRB Regional Office in the Region in which the employer concerned is located.
If more space is required for any one item, attach additional sheets, numbering item accordingly.

The Petitioner alleges that the following circumstances exist and requests that the National Labor Relations Board proceed under its proper authority pursuant to Section 9 of the National Labor Relations Act.

1. Purpose of this Petition *(If box RC, RM, or RD is checked and a charge under Section 8(b)(7) of the Act has been filed involving the Employer named herein, the statement following the description of the type of petition shall not be deemed made.)*

(Check one)

☐ RC–CERTIFICATION OF REPRESENTATIVE – A substantial number of employees wish to be represented for purposes of collective bargaining by Petitioner and Petitioner desires to be certified as representative of the employees.

☐ RM–REPRESENTATION (EMPLOYER PETITION) – One or more individuals or labor organizations have presented a claim to Petitioner to be recognized as the representative of employees of Petitioner.

☐ RD–DECERTIFICATION – A substantial number of employees assert that the certified or currently recognized bargaining representative is no longer their representative.

☐ UD–WITHDRAWAL OF UNION SHOP AUTHORITY – Thirty percent (30%) or more of employees in a bargaining unit covered by an agreement between their employer and a labor organization desire that such authority be rescinded.

☐ UC–UNIT CLARIFICATION – A labor organization is currently recognized by employer, but petitioner seeks clarification of placement of certain employees *(Check one)* ☐ In unit not previously certified
☐ In unit previously certified in Case No. ______

☐ AC–AMENDMENT OF CERTIFICATION – Petitioner seeks amendment of certification issued in Case No. ______

Attach statement describing the specific amendment sought.

2. NAME OF EMPLOYER	EMPLOYER REPRESENTATIVE TO CONTACT	PHONE NO

3. ADDRESS(ES) OF ESTABLISHMENT(S) INVOLVED *(Street and number, city, State, and ZIP Code)*

4a. TYPE OF ESTABLISHMENT *(Factory, mine, wholesaler, etc.)*	4b. IDENTIFY PRINCIPAL PRODUCT OR SERVICE

5. Unit Involved *(In UC petition, describe PRESENT bargaining unit and attach description of proposed clarification.)*

Included

Excluded

(If you have checked box RC in 1 above, check and complete EITHER item 7a or 7b, whichever is applicable)

6a. NUMBER OF EMPLOYEES IN UNIT
PRESENT ______
PROPOSED (BY UC/AC) ______

6b. IS THIS PETITION SUPPORTED BY 30% OR MORE OF THE EMPLOYEES IN THE UNIT?*
☐ YES ☐ NO
*Not applicable in RM, UC, and AC

7a. ☐ Request for recognition as Bargaining Representative was made on .... *(Month, day, year)* and Employer declined recognition on or about .... *(Month, day, year)* *(If no reply received, so state)*

7b. ☐ Petitioner is currently recognized as Bargaining Representative and desires certification under the act.

8. Recognized or Certified Bargaining Agent *(If there is none, so state)*

NAME	AFFILIATION
ADDRESS	DATE OF RECOGNITION OR CERTIFICATION

9. DATE OF EXPIRATION OF CURRENT CONTRACT, IF ANY *(Show month, day, and year)*	10. IF YOU HAVE CHECKED BOX UD IN 1 ABOVE, SHOW HERE THE DATE OF EXECUTION OF AGREEMENT GRANTING UNION SHOP *(Month, day, and year)*
11a. IS THERE NOW A STRIKE OR PICKETING AT THE EMPLOYER'S ESTABLISHMENT(S) INVOLVED? YES ...... NO	11b. IF SO, APPROXIMATELY HOW MANY EMPLOYEES ARE PARTICIPATING?

11c. THE EMPLOYER HAS BEEN PICKETED BY OR ON BEHALF OF .... *(Insert name)* A LABOR ORGANIZATION, OF .... *(Insert address)* SINCE .... *(Month, day, year)*

12. ORGANIZATIONS OR INDIVIDUALS OTHER THAN PETITIONER (AND OTHER THAN THOSE NAMED IN ITEMS 8 AND 11c), WHICH HAVE CLAIMED RECOGNITION AS REPRESENTATIVES AND OTHER ORGANIZATIONS AND INDIVIDUALS KNOWN TO HAVE A REPRESENTATIVE INTEREST IN ANY EMPLOYEES IN THE UNIT DESCRIBED IN ITEM 5 ABOVE (IF NONE, SO STATE.)

NAME	AFFILIATION	ADDRESS	DATE OF CLAIM *(Required only if Petition is filed by Employer)*

I declare that I have read the above petition and that the statements therein are true to the best of my knowledge and belief.

.... *(Petitioner and affiliation, if any)*

By .... *(Signature of representative or person filing petition)* .... *(Title, if any)*

Address .... *(Street and number, city, State, and ZIP Code)* .... *(Telephone number)*

WILLFULLY FALSE STATEMENT ON THIS PETITION CAN BE PUNISHED BY FINE AND IMPRISONMENT (U.S. CODE, TITLE 18, SECTION 1001)

GPO 861-256

Exhibit 5.3. Letters to parties regarding petition for an election: Regional Office Form 29-R-70

29-R-70
(9/67)

NATIONAL LABOR RELATIONS BOARD

REGION 29

16 Court Street

Brooklyn, New York 11241 **Telephone 596-3535**

Re:

Case No.:

Gentlemen:

A petition under Section 9(c) of the National Labor Relations Act has been filed with this office, a copy of which is enclosed.

The investigation of this case has been assigned to (Telephone No. 596-).

Attention is called to your right, and the right of any party, to be represented by counsel or other representative in any proceeding before the National Labor Relations Board. In the event you choose to have a representative appear on your behalf, please have your representative complete "Notice of Appearance" Form NLRB-4701 and forward it promptly to this office.

The parties are requested to submit to this office as soon as possible the following information:

a) Correct name of your organization.

b) Copies of correspondence and existing or recently-expired collective bargaining contracts, if any, covering any of the employees in the unit alleged in the petition.

c) Name of any other labor organization claiming to represent any of the employees in the proposed unit.

d) Your position as to the appropriateness of the unit.

e) Whether you will agree to an election to be conducted by the Board to determine the question concerning representation.

In addition the Employer is requested to furnish the following:

f) The enclosed commerce questionnaire filled out in the appropriate sections.

g) An alphabetized list of employees described in the petition, together with their job classifications for the pay-roll period immediately preceding the date of this petition.

In the event an election is agreed to or directed in this case, the Board requires that a list of names and addresses of all the eligible voters be filed by the Employer with the undersigned, who will in turn make it available to all parties to the case. The list must be furnished to the undersigned within seven (7) days of the direction of or agreement to election. I am advising you now of this requirement so that you will have ample time to prepare for the eventuality that such a list may become necessary. (This list is in addition to the list of employees requested in the proposed unit by job classification in Item (g) above.)

At this point in the handling of this case, we of course do not know what disposition will be made of the petition, but experience tells us that an explanation of rights, responsibilities, and Board procedures can be helpful to your employees.

The Board believes that employees should have readily available information about their rights and the proper conduct of employee representation elections. At the same time employers and unions should be apprised of their responsibilities to refrain from conduct which could impede employees' freedom of choice.

Accordingly, the Employer is requested to post the enclosed Notice to Employees in conspicuous places in areas where employees in the requested unit work. Copies of this Notice are being made available to the labor organization(s) involved.

In the event an election is not conducted pursuant to this petition the Employer is requested to remove the posted Notice.

- 2 -

Additional copies of the Notice to Employees are available for posting if the Employer should need them. I would appreciate it if the Employer advise me, on the enclosed Certification of Posting form, the date when the Notice was posted.

If there are any questions about this matter and if we can be of any assistance do not hesitate to call the Board Agent assigned to this case.

Your cooperation with this office is invited so that all facts of the case may be considered.

Very truly yours,

Samuel M. Kaynard
Samuel M. Kaynard
Regional Director

Enclosures

CC:

Exhibit 5.4. Notice to employees regarding petition for an election: NLRB Form 666

Form NLRB 666
(7-72)

★NOTICE TO EMPLOYEES

FROM THE

National Labor Relations Board

A PETITION has been filed with this Federal agency seeking an election to determine whether certain employees want to be represented by a union.

The case is being investigated and NO DETERMINATION HAS BEEN MADE AT THIS TIME by the National Labor Relations Board. IF an election is held Notices of Election will be posted giving complete details for voting.

It was suggested that your employer post this notice so the National Labor Relations Board could inform you of your basic rights under the National Labor Relations Act.

YOU HAVE THE RIGHT under Federal Law

- To self-organization
- To form, join, or assist labor organizations
- To bargain collectively through representatives of your own choosing
- To act together for the purposes of collective bargaining or other mutual aid or protection
- To refuse to do any or all of these things unless the union and employer, in a state where such agreements are permitted, enter into a lawful union security clause requiring employees to join the union.

It is possible that some of you will be voting in an employee representation election as a result of the request for an election having been filed. While NO DETERMINATION HAS BEEN MADE AT THIS TIME, in the event an election is held, the NATIONAL LABOR RELATIONS BOARD wants all eligible voters to be familiar with their rights under the law IF it holds an election.

The Board applies rules which are intended to keep its elections fair and honest and which result in a free choice. If agents of either Unions or Employers act in such a way as to interfere with your right to a free election, the election can be set aside by the Board. Where appropriate the Board provides other remedies, such as reinstatement for employees fired for exercising their rights, including backpay from the party responsible for their discharge.

NOTE:

The following are examples of conduct which interfere with the rights of employees and may result in the setting aside of the election.

- Threatening loss of jobs or benefits by an Employer or a Union
- Misstating important facts by a Union or an Employer where the other party does not have a fair chance to reply
- Promising or granting promotions, pay raises, or other benefits, to influence an employee's vote by a party capable of carrying out such promises
- An Employer firing employees to discourage or encourage union activity or a Union causing them to be fired to encourage union activity
- Making campaign speeches to assembled groups of employees on company time within the 24-hour period before the election
- Incitement by either an Employer or a Union of racial or religious prejudice by inflammatory appeals
- Threatening physical force or violence to employees by a Union or an Employer to influence their votes

Please be assured that IF AN ELECTION IS HELD every effort will be made to protect your right to a free choice under the law. Improper conduct will not be permitted. All parties are expected to cooperate fully with this agency in maintaining basic principles of a fair election as required by law. The National Labor Relations Board as an agency of the United States Government does not endorse any choice in the election.

NATIONAL LABOR RELATIONS BOARD ★

NATIONAL LABOR RELATIONS BOARD
an agency of the
UNITED STATES GOVERNMENT

THIS IS AN OFFICIAL GOVERNMENT NOTICE AND MUST NOT BE DEFACED BY ANYONE

☆U.S. GOVERNMENT PRINTING OFFICE 1972 O—472-000

Exhibit 5.5. Commerce questionnaire: Regional Office Form 29-C-5A

29-C-5a
(1-65)

NATIONAL LABOR RELATIONS BOARD
REGION 29
16 Court Street
Brooklyn, New York **11241**

Telephone -- 596-3535

____
Case Name and Number

COMMERCE QUESTIONNAIRE

/Please return completed questionnaire promptly to the Twenty-Ninth Regional office of the National Labor Relations Board, at the address listed above. If you have any question concerning the information requested, please communicate with the staff member designated in the accompanying letter./

1. **The undersigned firm is a: (Check appropriate one) - a) Corporation___ b) Partnership___ c) Individual Enterprise___ which was incorporated, or registered in ______________________ during__________.**
(Year)

2. **FOR CORPORATIONS:**

Name as set forth on Certification of Incorporation:__________

____

Names and addresses of parent and subsidiary corporations, if any:

____

____

FOR PARTNERSHIPS:

Names and addresses of all partners:__________

____

____

FOR INDIVIDUAL ENTERPRISES:

Name as it appears on certificate of doing business:__________

____

____

29-C-5a
(1-65)

3. **Names of other corporations or enterprises, not previously listed above, which are operated in connection with the undersigned:**

____

____

____

4. **Name and address of any trade or employer-association with which the undersigned firm is affiliated:**

____

____

5. **General nature or type of business: (check which one)**

Manufacturer__________ **Wholesaler**__________ **Retailer**__________

Trucking__________ **Communications**__________ **Transit System**__________

Taxicab__________ **Service**__________ **Public Utility**__________

News Publisher__________ **Hotel-Motel**__________ **Office or Industrial Building**__________ **Building Construction**__________

Other (please specify)______________________________

6. **General Type of products handled or nature of services performed**

____

____

7. **Principal place of business located at:**______________________________

____

Branches located at:______________________________

____

____

____

8. **Approximate number of persons employed:**______________________________

29-C-5a
(1-65)

9. Check whether figures furnished below are for:

Calendar Year /__/ Fiscal Year /__/ Past 12 Months /__/

(Check appropriate boxes)

a. Gross annual revenue from sales: $500,000 or more /__/

Less than $500,000 /__/

If less than $500,000, please state amount $______________

b. Annual purchases of goods, supplies, commodities or services purchased directly from other firms located outside the State:

$50,000 or more /__/

Less than $50,000 /__/

If less than $50,000, please state amount $______________

c. Annual purchases of goods, supplies, commodities, or services purchased from firms located inside the State, but which originated outside the State:

$50,000 or more /__/

Less than $50,000 /__/

If less than $50,000, please state amount $______________

d. Annual revenue from sales of goods, products, or commodities delivered directly to points outside the State, or from services to firms located outside the State:

$50,000 or more /__/

Less than $50,000 /__/

If less than $50,000, please state amount $______________

e. Annual revenue from sales of goods, products, or commodities delivered to, or from services performed for, firms located within the State, which firms, in turn, made sales to customers located outside the State:

$50,000 or more /__/

Less than $50,000 /__/

If less than $50,000, please state amount $______________

29-C-5a
(1-65)

(Check appropriate boxes)

10. Engaged in performance of contracts to provide goods or services related to national defense:

Yes /__/

No /__/

During the past year the amount of such contracts totalled $________________________.

11. The name and title of the person who is best informed about the operation of the firm's business is:

____

12. The firm concedes that it is engaged in interstate commerce and subject to the jurisdiction of the National Labor Relations Board:

Yes /__/

No /__/

____
Firm Name

______________________ By____________________________
(Date) (Name and Title)

GPO 949-662

Exhibit 5.6. Agreement for consent election: NLRB Form 651

NLRB-651
(12-61)

UNITED STATES OF AMERICA
NATIONAL LABOR RELATIONS BOARD

AGREEMENT FOR CONSENT ELECTION

Pursuant to a Petition duly filed under Section 9 of the National Labor Relations Act as amended, and subject to the approval of the Regional Director for the National Labor Relations Board (herein called the Regional Director), the undersigned parties hereby waive a hearing and AGREE AS FOLLOWS:

1. SECRET BALLOT.—An election by secret ballot shall be held under the supervision of the said Regional Director, among the employees of the undersigned Employer in the unit defined below, at the indicated time and place, to determine whether or not such employees desire to be represented for the purpose of collective bargaining by (one of) the undersigned labor organization(s). Said election shall be held in accordance with the National Labor Relations Act, the Board's Rules and Regulations, and the applicable procedures and policies of the Board, provided that the determination of the Regional Director shall be final and binding upon any question, including questions as to the eligibility of voters, raised by any party hereto relating in any manner to the election, and provided further that rulings or determinations bv the Regional Director in respect of any amendment of any certification resulting therefrom shall also be final.

2. ELIGIBLE VOTERS.—The eligible voters shall be those employees included within the Unit described below, who were employed during the payroll period indicated below, including employees who did not work during said payroll period because they were ill or on vacation or temporarily laid off, employees in the military services of the United States who appear in person at the polls, employees engaged in an economic strike which commenced less than twelve (12) months before the election date and who retained their status as such during the eligibility period and their replacements, but excluding any employees who have since quit or been discharged for cause and employees engaged in a strike who have been discharged for cause since the commencement thereof, and who have not been rehired or reinstated prior to the date of the election, and employees engaged in an economic strike which commenced more than 12 months prior to the date of the election and who have been permanently replaced. At a date fixed by the Regional Director, the parties, as requested, will furnish to the Regional Director, an accurate list of all the eligible voters, together with a list of the employees, if any, specifically excluded from eligibility.

3. NOTICES OF ELECTION.—The Regional Director shall prepare a Notice of Election and supply copies to the parties describing the manner and conduct of the election to be held and incorporating therein a sample ballot. The parties, upon the request of and at a time designated by the Regional Director, will post such Notice of Election at conspicuous and usual posting places easily accessible to the eligible voters.

4. OBSERVERS.—Each party hereto will be allowed to station an equal number of authorized observers, selected from among the nonsupervisory employees of the Employer, at the polling places during the election to assist in its conduct, to challenge the eligibility of voters, and to verify the tally.

5. TALLY OF BALLOTS.—As soon after the election as feasible, the votes shall be counted and tabulated by the Regional Director, or his agent or agents. Upon the conclusion of the counting, the Regional Director shall furnish a Tally of Ballots to each of the parties. When appropriate, the Regional Director shall issue to the parties a certification of representatives or of results of election, as may be indicated.

6. OBJECTIONS, CHALLENGES, REPORTS THEREON.—Objections to the conduct of the election or conduct affecting the results of the election, or to a determination of representatives based on the results thereof, may be filed with the Regional Director within 5 days after issuance of the Tally of Ballots. Copies of such objections must be served upon the other parties at the time of filing with the Regional Director. The Regional Director shall investigate the matters contained in the objections and issue a report thereon. If objections are sustained, the Regional Director may in his report include an order voiding the results of the election and, in that event, shall be empowered to conduct a new election under the terms and provisions of this agreement at a date, time, and place to be determined by him. If the challenges are determinative of the results of the election, the Regional Director shall investigate the challenges and issue a report thereon. The method of investigation of objections and challenges, including the question whether a hearing should be held in connection therewith, shall be determined by the Regional Director, whose decision shall be final and binding.

7. RUN-OFF PROCEDURE.—In the event more than one labor organization is signatory to this agreement, and in the event that no choice on the ballot in the election receives a majority of the valid ballots cast, the Regional Director shall proceed in accordance with the Board's Rules and Regulations.

8. COMMERCE.—The Employer is engaged in commerce within the meaning of Section 2 (6) (7) of the National Labor Relations Act.

16—67080-7

9. WORDING ON THE BALLOT.—Where only one labor organization is signatory to this agreement, the name of the organization shall appear on the ballot and the choice shall be "Yes" or "No." In the event more than one labor organization is signatory to this agreement, the choices on the ballot will appear in the wording indicated below and in the order enumerated below, reading from left to right on the ballot, or if the occasion demands, from top to bottom. (If more than one union is to appear on the ballot, any union may have its name removed from the ballot by the approval of the Regional Director of a timely request, in writing, to that effect.)

First.

Second.

Third.

10. PAYROLL PERIOD FOR ELIGIBILITY.—

11. DATE, HOURS, AND PLACE OF ELECTION.—

12. THE APPROPRIATE COLLECTIVE BARGAINING UNIT.—

If Notice of Representation Hearing has been issued in this case, the approval of this agreement by the Regional Director shall constitute withdrawal of the Notice of Representation Hearing heretofore issued.

.... (Employer)	.... (Name of Organization)
By .... (Name and title) (Date)	By .... (Name and title) (Date)
Recommended:	
.... (Board Agent) (Date)	.... (Name of other Organization)
Date approved	By .... (Name and title) (Date)
.... Regional Director, National Labor Relations Board	
Case No.	

Exhibit 5.7. Stipulation for certification upon consent election: NLRB Form 652

NLRB-652
(1-63)

UNITED STATES OF AMERICA
NATIONAL LABOR RELATIONS BOARD

STIPULATION FOR CERTIFICATION UPON CONSENT ELECTION

Pursuant to a Petition duly filed under Section 9 of the National Labor Relations Act, as amended, and subjecf to the approval of the Regional Director for the National Labor Relations Board (herein called the Regional Director), the undersigned parties hereby AGREE AS FOLLOWS:

1. SECRET BALLOT.—An election by secret ballot shall be held under the supervision of the said Regional Director, among the employees of the undersigned Employer in the unit defined below, at the indicated time and place, to determine whether or not such employees desire to be represented for the purpose of collective bargaining by (one of) the undersigned labor organization(s). Said election shall be held in accordance with the National Labor Relations Act, the Board's Rules and Regulations, and the applicable procedures and policies of the Board.

2. ELIGIBLE VOTERS.—The eligible voters shall be those employees included within the Unit described below, who were employed during the payroll period indicated below, including employees who did not work during said payroll period because they were ill or on vacation or temporarily laid off, and employees in the military services of the United States who appear in person at the polls, also eligible are employees engaged in an economic strike which commenced less than twelve (12) months before the election date and who retained their status as such during the eligibility period and their replacements, but ***excluding*** any employees who have since quit or been discharged for cause and employees engaged in a strike who have been discharged for cause since the commencement thereof, and who have not been rehired or reinstated prior to the date of the election, and employees engaged in an economic strike which commenced more than twelve (12) months prior to the date of the election and who have been permanently replaced. At a date fixed by the Regional Director, the parties, as requested, will furnish to the Regional Director, an accurate list of all the eligible voters, together with a list of the employees, if any, specifically excluded from eligibility.

3. NOTICES OF ELECTION.—The Regional Director shall prepare a Notice of Election and supply copies to the parties describing the manner and conduct of the election to be held and incorporating therein a sample ballot The parties, upon the request of and at a time designated by the Regional Director, will post such Notice of Election at conspicuous and usual posting places easily accessible to the eligible voters

4. OBSERVERS.—Each party hereto will be allowed to station an equal number of authorized observers, selected from among the nonsupervisory employees of the Employer, at the polling places during the election to assist in its conduct, to challenge the eligibility of voters, and to verify the tally.

5. TALLY OF BALLOTS.—As soon after the election as feasible, the votes shall be counted and tabulated by the Regional Director, or his agent or agents. Upon the conclusion of the counting, the Regional Director shall furnish a Tally of Ballots to each of the parties.

6. POST-ELECTION AND RUN-OFF PROCEDURE.—All procedure subsequent to the conclusion of counting ballots shall be in conformity with the Board's Rules and Regulations.

7. RECORD.—The record in this case shall be governed by the appropriate provisions of the Board's Rules and Regulations and shall include this stipulation. Hearing and notice thereof, Direction of Election, and the making of Findings of Fact and Conclusions of Law by the Board prior to the election are hereby expressly waived.

8. COMMERCE.—The Employer is engaged in commerce within the meaning of Section 2(6) of the National Labor Relations Act, and a question affecting commerce has arisen concerning the representation of employees within the meaning of Section 9(c). ***(Insert commerce facts.)***

9. WORDING ON THE BALLOT.—Where only one labor organization is signatory to this agreement, the name of the organization shall appear on the ballot and the choice shall be "Yes" or "No." In the event more than one labor organization is signatory to this agreement, the choices on the ballot will appear in the wording indicated below and in the order enumerated below, reading from left to right on the ballot, or if the occasion demands, from top to bottom. ***(If more than one union is to appear on the ballot, any union may have its name removed from the ballot by the approval of the Regional Director of a timely request, in writing, to that effect.)***

First.

Second.

Third.

10. PAYROLL PERIOD FOR ELIGIBILITY.—

11. DATE, HOURS, AND PLACE OF ELECTION.—

12. THE APPROPRIATE COLLECTIVE BARGAINING UNIT.—

If Notice of Representation Hearing has been issued in this case, the approval of this stipulation by the Regional Director shall constitute withdrawal of the Notice of Representation Hearing heretofore issued.

....
(Employer)

....
(Address)

By ....
(Name and Title) (Date)

Recommended:

....
(Board Agent) (Date)

Date approved ....

....
Regional Director,
National Labor Relations Board.

Case No. ....

....
(Name of Organization)

....
(Address)

By ....
(Name and Title) (Date)

....
(Name of other Organization)

....
(Address)

By ....
(Name and Title) (Date)

GPO 878 416

Exhibit 5.8. Instructions to election observers: NLRB Form 722

FORM NLRB-722
(1-73)

UNITED STATES OF AMERICA
NATIONAL LABOR RELATIONS BOARD

INSTRUCTIONS TO ELECTION OBSERVERS

DUTIES *(General):*

1. Act as checkers and watchers.
2. Assist in identification of voters.
3. Challenge voters and ballots.
4. Otherwise assist agents of the Board.

THINGS TO DO *(Specific):*

1. Identify voter.
2. Check off the name of the person applying to vote. One check before the name by one organization. One check after the name by the other organization or the Company.
3. See that only one voter occupies a booth at any one time.
4. See that each voter deposits a ballot in the ballot box.
5. See that each voter leaves the voting room immediately after depositing his ballot.
6. Report any conflict as to the right to vote to the agent of the Board at your table.
7. Remain in the voting place until all ballots are counted in order to check on the fairness of the count, if ballots are counted at that time. If they are not counted immediately, you will be informed as to when and where ballots will be counted.
8. Report any irregularities to the Board agent as soon as noticed.
9. Challenge voters only for *good cause.*
10. Wear your observer badge at all times during the conduct of the election.
11. BE ON TIME. *(One-half hour before the time for the opening of the polls.)*

THINGS ***NOT*** **TO DO** *(Specific):*

1. Give any help to any voter. Only an agent of the Board can assist the voter.
2. Electioneer any place during the hours of the election.
3. Argue regarding the election.
4. Leave the polling place without the agent's consent.
5. Use intoxicating liquors.
6. Keep any list of those who have or have not voted.

As an official representative of your organization, you should enter upon this task with a fair and open mind. Conduct yourself so that no one can find fault with your actions during the election. You are here to see that the election is conducted in a fair and impartial manner, so that each eligible voter has a fair and equal chance to express himself freely and in secret.

NATIONAL LABOR RELATIONS BOARD

GPO 941-788

Exhibit 5.9. Notice of election of representative and instructions to eligible employees voting by United States mail: NLRB Form 4175

UNITED STATES OF AMERICA
NATIONAL LABOR RELATIONS BOARD

NOTICE OF ELECTION OF REPRESENTATIVE
and
INSTRUCTIONS TO ELIGIBLE EMPLOYEES VOTING BY UNITED STATES MAIL

NOTICE OF ELECTION

An election by secret ballot is being conducted under the supervision of the Regional Director of the National Labor Relations Board among the eligible voters to determine the representative, if any, desired by them for the purpose of collective bargaining with the employer named on the enclosed ballot. Your name appears on the list of those who are eligible to vote in this election.

PLEASE SEE THE OTHER SIDE OF THIS PAGE FOR AN IMPORTANT STATEMENT CONCERNING YOUR RIGHTS UNDER FEDERAL LAW AND HOW THE NLRB PROTECTS YOUR RIGHT TO A FREE CHOICE AND A FAIR ELECTION.

An OFFICIAL BALLOT and a RETURN-ADDRESSED SECRET ENVELOPE are enclosed. To vote by mail, carry out the following instructions:

INSTRUCTIONS TO ELIGIBLE EMPLOYEES VOTING BY UNITED STATES MAIL
(Read Carefully)

FROM THE TIME YOU OPEN THE ENVELOPE CONTAINING THE BALLOT, YOU SHOULD CONSIDER YOURSELF IN THE SAME POSITION AS THOUGH IN A VOTING BOOTH IN A MANUALLY CONDUCTED ELECTION. YOU SHOULD THEREFORE FOLLOW THE INSTRUCTIONS BELOW AND DROP YOUR BALLOT IN THE UNITED STATES MAIL BEFORE DISCUSSING IT WITH ANYONE. Read the official ballot carefully. *Ignore the instruction on the ballot to* "Fold and drop in ballot box," as this does not apply to persons who vote by mail. Mark an "X" in the square of your choice. Fold the ballot and put it in the envelope addressed to the National Labor Relations Board. Seal this envelope. *Sign your name (do not print it) on the outside of the envelope* in the space provided after the word "Signature." Deposit this envelope, which requires no postage, in the United States mail ***so that your ballot will be RECEIVED at the place shown on the return envelope not later than***

____
(Date)

This is a secret ballot election. YOUR BALLOT WILL BE VOID AND WILL NOT BE COUNTED *UNLESS* you:

1. Mark on the ballot only in the place provided for marking; *do not* identify yourself on the ballot.
2. Return the ballot in the same envelope which you received for that purpose.
3. Sign your name in your *own* handwriting on the outside of that envelope after the word "Signature," so that your name can be checked against the eligibility list.

After your name is checked against the eligibility list the detachable part of the envelope, the stub upon which your name appears, will be removed and destroyed. The remaining section of the envelope containing the ballot will be mixed with all other ballot sections before it is opened by agents of the Board and your ballot removed, thus insuring secrecy.

If you have any question about this election you can contact the Regional Director or his agent at the address below.

NATIONAL LABOR RELATIONS BOARD

Form NLRB—4175
(7–72)

Exhibit 5.10. Notice of election: NLRB Form 707

UNITED STATES OF AMERICA ★ NA

NOTICE OF

PURPOSE OF THIS ELECTION This election is to determine the representative, if any, desired by the eligible employees for purposes of collective bargaining with their employer. (See VOTING UNIT in this Notice of Election, for description of eligible employees.) A majority of the valid ballots cast will determine the results of the election.

SECRET BALLOT The election will be by SECRET ballot under the supervision of the Regional Director of the National Labor Relations Board. Voters will be allowed to vote without interference, restraint, or coercion. Electioneering will not be permitted at or near the polling place. Violations of these rules should be reported immediately to the Regional Director or his agent in charge of the election. Your attention is called to Section 12 of the National Labor Relations Act:

ANY PERSON WHO SHALL WILLFULLY RESIST, PREVENT, IMPEDE, OR INTERFERE WITH ANY MEMBER OF THE BOARD OR ANY OF ITS AGENTS OR AGENCIES IN THE PERFORMANCE OF DUTIES PURSUANT TO THIS ACT SHALL BE PUNISHED BY A FINE OF NOT MORE THAN $5,000 OR BY IMPRISONMENT FOR NOT MORE THAN ONE YEAR, OR BOTH.

An agent of the Board will hand a ballot to each eligible voter at the voting place. Mark your ballot in secret in the voting booth provided. DO NOT SIGN YOUR BALLOT. Fold the ballot before leaving the voting booth, then personally deposit it in a ballot box under the supervision of an agent of the Board.

A sample of the official ballot is shown at the center of this Notice.

ELIGIBILITY RULES Employees eligible to vote are those described under VOTING UNIT in this Notice of Election, including employees who did not work during the designated payroll period because they were ill or on vacation or temporarily laid off, and also including employees in the military service of the United States who appear in person at the polls. Employees who have quit or been discharged for cause since the designated payroll period and who have not been rehired or reinstated prior to the date of this election are not eligible to vote.

CHALLENGE OF VOTERS An agent of the Board or an authorized observer may question the eligibility of a voter. Such challenge MUST be made before the voter has deposited his ballot in the ballot box.

AUTHORIZED OBSERVERS Each of the interested parties may designate an equal number of observers, this number to be determined by the Regional Director or his agent in charge of the election. These observers (a) act as checkers at the voting place and at the counting of ballots, (b) assist in the identification of voters, (c) challenge voters and ballots, and (d) otherwise assist the Regional Director or his agent.

INFORMATION CONCERNING ELECTION The Act provides that only one valid representation election may be held in a 12-month period. Any employee who desires to obtain any further information concerning the terms and conditions under which this election is to be held or who desires to raise any question concerning the holding of an election, the voting unit, or eligibility rules may do so by communicating with the Regional Director or his agent in charge of the election.

SAM

WARNING: THIS IS THE ONLY OFFICIAL NOTICE OF THI

Form NLRB-707 (7-72)

LABOR RELATIONS BOARD

LECTION

RIGHTS OF EMPLOYEES

Under the National Labor Relations Act, employees have the right:

- To self-organization
- To form, join, or assist labor organizations
- To bargain collectively through representatives of their own choosing
- To act together for the purposes of collective bargaining or other mutual aid or protection
- To refuse to do any or all of these things unless the union and employer, in a State where such agreements are permitted, enter into a lawful union security clause requiring employees to join the union.

It is the responsibility of the National Labor Relations Board to protect employees in the exercise of these rights.

The Board wants all eligible voters to be fully informed about their rights under Federal law and wants both Employers and Unions to know what is expected of them when it holds an election.

If agents of either Unions or Employers interfere with your right to a free, fair, and honest election, the election can be set aside by the Board. Where appropriate the Board provides other remedies, such as reinstatement for employees fired for exercising their rights, including backpay from the party responsible for their discharge.

The following are examples of conduct which interfere with the rights of employees and may result in the setting aside of the election:

- Threatening loss of jobs or benefits by an Employer or a Union
- Misstating important facts by a Union or an Employer where the other party does not have a fair chance to reply
- Promising or granting promotions, pay raises, or other benefits, to influence an employee's vote by a party capable of carrying out such promises
- An Employer firing employees to discourage or encourage union activity or a Union causing them to be fired to encourage union activity
- Making campaign speeches to assembled groups of employees on company time within the 24-hour period before the election
- Incitement by either an Employer or a Union of racial or religious prejudice by inflammatory appeals
- Threatening physical force or violence to employees by a Union or an Employer to influence their votes

The National Labor Relations Board protects your right to a free choice

Improper conduct will not be permitted. All parties are expected to cooperate fully with this agency in maintaining basic principles of a fair election as required by law. The National Labor Relations Board as an agency of the United States Government does not endorse any choice in the election.

NATIONAL LABOR RELATIONS BOARD
an agency of the
UNITED STATES GOVERNMENT

ION AND MUST NOT BE DEFACED BY ANYONE

RIGHTS OF EMPLOYEES

Under the National Labor Relations Act, employees have the right:

- To self-organization
- To form, join, or assist labor organizations.
- To bargain collectively through representatives of their own choosing
- To act together for the purposes of collective bargaining or other mutual aid or protection
- To refuse to do any or all of these things unless the union and employer, in a state where such agreements are permitted, enter into a lawful union security clause requiring employees to join the union.

It is the responsibility of the National Labor Relations Board to protect employees in the exercise of these rights.

The Board wants all eligible voters to be fully informed about their rights under Federal law and wants both Employers and Unions to know what is expected of them when it holds an election.

If agents of either Unions or Employers interfere with your right to a free, fair, and honest election, the election can be set aside by the Board. Where appropriate the Board provides other remedies, such as reinstatement for employees fired for exercising their rights, including backpay from the party responsible for their discharge.

The following are examples of conduct which interfere with the rights of employees and may result in the setting aside of the election:

- Threatening loss of jobs or benefits by an Employer or Union
- Misstating important facts by a Union or an Employer where the other party does not have a fair chance to reply
- Promising or granting promotions, pay raises, or other benefits, to influence an employee's vote by a party capable of carrying out such promises
- An Employer firing employees to discourage or encourage union activity or a Union causing them to be fired to encourage union activity
- Making campaign speeches to assembled groups of employees on company time after ballots are scheduled to be dispatched by the regional office
- Incitement by either an Employer or a Union of racial or religious prejudice by inflammatory appeals
- Threatening physical force or violence to employees by a Union or an Employer to influence their votes

The National Labor Relations Board protects your right to a free choice

Improper conduct will not be permitted. All parties are expected to cooperate fully with this agency in maintaining basic principles of a fair election as required by law. The National Labor Relations Board as an agency of the United States Government does not endorse any choice in the election.

NATIONAL LABOR RELATIONS BOARD

an agency of the

UNITED STATES GOVERNMENT

GPO : 1972 O - 473-205

Exhibit 5.11. Tally of ballots: NLRB Form 760

FORM NLRB 760 (4-64)

UNITED STATES OF AMERICA
NATIONAL LABOR RELATIONS BOARD

Case No. ____________

Date issued ____________

Type of Election: (*Check one:*)
☐ Stipulation
☐ Board Direction
☐ Consent Agreement
☐ RD Direction

(*If applicable check either or both:*)
☐ 8(b) (7)
☐ Mail Ballot

TALLY OF BALLOTS

The undersigned agent of the Regional Director certifies that the results of the tabulation of ballots cast in the election held in the above case, and concluded on the date indicated above, were as follows:

1. Approximate number of eligible voters ____________ ____________
2. Void ballots ____________ ____________
3. Votes cast for ____________ ____________
4. Votes cast for ____________ ____________
5. Votes cast for ____________ ____________
6. Votes cast against participating labor organization(s) ____________ ____________
7. Valid votes counted (sum of 3, 4, 5, and 6) ____________ ____________
8. Challenged ballots ____________ ____________
9. Valid votes counted plus challenged ballots (sum of 7 and 8) ____________ ____________
10. Challenges are (not) sufficient to affect the results of the election.
11. A majority of the valid votes counted plus challenged ballots (item 9) has (not) been cast for:

____

For the Regional Director

____

The undersigned acted as authorized observers in the counting and tabulating of ballots indicated above. We hereby certify that the counting and tabulating were fairly and accurately done, that the secrecy of the ballots was maintained, and that the results were as indicated above. We also acknowledge service of this tally.

For ____________ For ____________

For ____________ For ____________

☆ U. S. GOVERNMENT PRINTING OFFICE: 1972—475-007

Exhibit 5.12. Certification of representative: NLRB Form 4279

FORM NLRB-4279

RC-RM-RD

UNITED STATES OF AMERICA
NATIONAL LABOR RELATIONS BOARD

TYPE OF ELECTION

(Check one)

☐ Consent Agreement
☐ Stipulation
☐ Board Direction
☐ RD Direction

(Also check box below where appropriate)

☐ 8(b)(7)

Case No.

CERTIFICATION OF REPRESENTATIVE

An election having been conducted in the above matter under the supervision of the Regional Director of the National Labor Relations Board in accordance with the Rules and Regulations of the Board; and it appearing from the Tally of Ballots that a collective bargaining representative has been selected; and no objections having been filed to the Tally of Ballots furnished to the parties, or to the conduct of the election, within the time provided therefor;

Pursuant to authority vested in the undersigned by the National Labor Relations Board, IT IS HEREBY CERTIFIED that a majority of the valid ballots have been cast for

and that, pursuant to Section 9(a) of the National Labor Relations Act, as amended, the said labor organization is the exclusive representative of all the employees in the unit set forth below, found to be appropriate for the purposes of collective bargaining in respect to rates of pay, wages, hours of employment, or other conditions of employment.

UNIT:

Signed at
On the day of 19

On behalf of

NATIONAL LABOR RELATIONS BOARD

Regional Director, Region
National Labor Relations Board

GPO 478-538

Exhibit 5.13. Certification of results of election: NLRB Form 4280

FORM NLRB-4280
(2-66)

RC-RM-RD

UNITED STATES OF AMERICA
NATIONAL LABOR RELATIONS BOARD

TYPE OF ELECTION

(Check one)

☐ Consent Agreement
☐ Stipulation
☐ Board Direction
☐ RD Direction

(Also check box below where appropriate)

☐ 8(b)(7)

Case No.

CERTIFICATION OF RESULTS OF ELECTION

An election having been conducted in the above matter under the supervision of the Regional Director of the National Labor Relations Board in accordance with the Rules and Regulations of the Board; and it appearing from the Tally of Ballots that no collective bargaining representative has been selected; and no objections having been filed to the Tally of Ballots furnished to the parties, or to the conduct of the election, within the time provided therefor;

Pursuant to authority vested in the undersigned by the National Labor Relations Board,

IT IS HEREBY CERTIFIED that a majority of the valid ballots has not been cast for any labor organization appearing on the ballot, and that no such organization is the exclusive representative of all the employees, in the unit herein involved, within the meaning of Section 9(a) of the National Labor Relations Act, as amended.

Signed at
On the day of 19

Regional Director, Region
National Labor Relations Board

GPO 903-732

Exhibit 5.14. Challenged ballot--secret envelope: NLRB Form 4646

CHALLENGED BALLOT

Secret ENVELOPE

FORM NLRB-4646
(2-65)

IDENTIFICATION STUB

NAME ____________________

CLOCK NO. ________ UNIT ________

JOB CLASS ____________________

COMPANY ____________________

POLLING PLACE ________ DATE ________

REASON FOR CHALLENGE ____________________

____

____

CHALLENGED BY ____________________

BOARD AGENT ____________________

PUT ADDITIONAL INFORMATION ON
THE BACK OF THIS STUB

Exhibit 5.15. Charge against employer: NLRB Form 501

FORM NLRB-501
(2-67)

Form Approved
Budget Bureau No. 64-R001.12

UNITED STATES OF AMERICA
NATIONAL LABOR RELATIONS BOARD

CHARGE AGAINST EMPLOYER

INSTRUCTIONS: File an original and 4 copies of this charge with NLRB regional director for the region in which the alleged unfair labor practice occurred or is occurring.

DO NOT WRITE IN THIS SPACE
Case No.
Date Filed

1. EMPLOYER AGAINST WHOM CHARGE IS BROUGHT

a. Name of Employer

b. Number of Workers Employed

c. Address of Establishment (Street and number, city, State, and ZIP code)

d. Employer Representative to Contact

e. Phone No.

f. Type of Establishment (Factory, mine, wholesaler, etc.)

g. Identify Principal Product or Service

h. The above-named employer has engaged in and is engaging in unfair labor practices within the meaning of section 8 (a), subsections (1) and ______ (List subsections) of the National Labor Relations Act, and these unfair labor practices are unfair labor practices affecting commerce within the meaning of the Act.

2. Basis of the Charge (Be specific as to facts, names, addresses, plants involved, dates, places, etc.)

By the above and other acts, the above-named employer has interfered with, restrained, and coerced employees in the exercise of the rights guaranteed in Section 7 of the Act.

3. Full Name of Party Filing Charge (If labor organization, give full name, including local name and number)

4a. Address (Street and number, city, State, and ZIP code)

4b. Telephone No.

5. Full Name of National or International Labor Organization of Which It Is an Affiliate or Constituent Unit (To be filled in when charge is filed by a labor organization)

6. DECLARATION

I declare that I have read the above charge and that the statements therein are true to the best of my knowledge and belief.

By ______ (Signature of representative or person filing charge) ______ (Title, if any)

Address ______ ______ (Telephone number) ______ (Date)

WILLFULLY FALSE STATEMENTS ON THIS CHARGE CAN BE PUNISHED BY FINE AND IMPRISONMENT (U.S. CODE, TITLE 18, SECTION 1001)

GPO 861-475

Exhibit 5.16. Charge against labor organization or its agents: NLRB Form 508

FORM NLRB-508
(4-73)

Form Approved
O.M.B. No. 64-R0003

UNITED STATES OF AMERICA
NATIONAL LABOR RELATIONS BOARD

CHARGE AGAINST LABOR ORGANIZATION OR ITS AGENTS

INSTRUCTIONS: File an original and 3 copies of this charge and an additional copy for each organization, each local and each individual named in item 1 with the NLRB regional director for the region in which the alleged unfair labor practice occurred or is occurring.

DO NOT WRITE IN THIS SPACE
Case No.
Date Filed

1. LABOR ORGANIZATION OR ITS AGENTS AGAINST WHICH CHARGE IS BROUGHT

a. Name
b. Union Representative to Contact
c. Phone No.

d. Address (Street, city, State and ZIP code)

e. The above-named organization(s) or its agents has (have) engaged in and is (are) engaging in unfair labor practices within the meaning of section 8(b), subsection(s) ________ (List Subsections) ________ of the National Labor Relations Act, and these unfair labor practices are unfair labor practices affecting commerce within the meaning of the Act.

2. Basis of the Charge (Be specific as to facts, names, addresses, plants involved, dates, places, etc.)

3. Name of Employer
4. Phone No.

5. Location of Plant Involved (Street, city, State and ZIP code)
6. Employer Representative to Contact

7. Type of Establishment (Factory, mine, wholesaler, etc.)
8. Identify Principal Product or Service
9. No. of Workers Employed

10. Full Name of Party Filing Charge

11. Address of Party Filing Charge (Street, city, State and ZIP code)
12. Telephone No.

13. DECLARATION

I declare that I have read the above charge and that the statements therein are true to the best of my knowledge and belief.

By ________________________ (Signature of representative or person making charge) ________________ (Title or office, if any)

Address ________________________ ________________ (Telephone number) ________________ (Date)

WILLFULLY FALSE STATEMENTS ON THIS CHARGE CAN BE PUNISHED BY FINE AND IMPRISONMENT (U.S. CODE, TITLE 18, SECTION 1001)

GPO 863-327

Exhibit 5.17. Charge alleging unfair labor practice under Section 8(e) of the Act: NLRB Form 509

FORM NLRB-509 (12-68)

Form Approved
Budget Bureau No. 64-R009.2

UNITED STATES OF AMERICA
NATIONAL LABOR RELATIONS BOARD

CHARGE ALLEGING UNFAIR LABOR PRACTICE UNDER SECTION 8(e) OF THE ACT

INSTRUCTIONS: File an original and 3 copies of this charge, and an additional copy for each organization, each local and each individual named in item 1 with the NLRB regional director for the region in which the alleged unfair labor practice occurred or is occurring.

Case No.

Date Filed

1. CHARGE FILED AGAINST: Employer and Labor Organization ☐ Employer ☐ Labor Organization ☐

a. Name of Labor Organization (Give full name, including local name and number)

b. Union Representative to Contact

c. Phone No.

d. Address (Street and number, city, State and ZIP code)

e. Name of Employer

f. Employer Representative to Contact

g. Phone No.

h. Location of Plant Involved (Street, city, State and ZIP code)

i. Type of Establishment (Factory, mine, wholesaler, etc.)

j. Identify Principal Product or Service

k. No. of Workers Employed

The above-named labor organization or its agents, and/or employer has (have) engaged in and is (are) engaging in unfair labor practices within the meaning of section 8(e) of the National Labor Relations Act, and these unfair labor practices are unfair labor practices affecting commerce within the meaning of the Act.

2. Basis of the Charge (Be specific as to facts, names, plants involved, dates, places, etc.)

3. Full Name of Party Filing Charge (If labor organization, give full name, including local name and number)

4a. Address (Street and number, city, State and ZIP code)

4b. Telephone No.

5. Full Name of National or International Labor Organization of Which It Is an Affiliate or Constituent Unit (To be filled in when charge is filed by a labor organization)

6. DECLARATION

I declare that I have read the above charge and that the statements therein are true to the best of my knowledge and belief.

By ______________________________ ______________________________
(Signature of representative or person filing charge) (Title, if any)

Address ______________________________ ______________ ______________
(Telephone number) (Date)

WILLFULLY FALSE STATEMENTS ON THIS CHARGE CAN BE PUNISHED BY FINE AND IMPRISONMENT (U.S. CODE, TITLE 18, SECTION 1001)

GPO 911-594

VI
Employer Unfair Labor Practices: Section 8(A) of the Law

UNFAIR LABOR PRACTICES: GENERAL

The original National Labor Relations (Wagner) Act passed in 1935 contained a section that delineated those practices which, when committed by managements or their agents, would be deemed to be unfair. The definition of these unfair labor practices was carried over unchanged in the 1947 amendments to the law (the Taft-Hartley Act) and now applies to health care facilities through the passage of P.L. 93-360. Sections concerning employee (or union) unfair labor practices were added to the law by the Taft-Hartley amendments in 1947--indeed, one of the primary reasons for passage of the amendments was the absence of a definition of employee unfair labor practices in the law as originally enacted. These now apply to unions or their agents with regard to their activities in seeking to gain recognition from and to bargain with a health care institution.

Section 8(a) of the Act delineates employer unfair labor practices--these practices are discussed in this chapter along with the practices listed in Section 8(e) which can only be committed by an employer and a union acting together. Section 8(b), which defines employee unfair labor practices, is discussed in Chapter VII. The substance and definition of unfair labor practices and the remedies for engaging in such activities are defined in the Act itself, in rulings of the National Labor Relations Board and in decisions of the federal court system (district, circuit and Supreme). This and the subsequent chapter will review each of these sources of interpretation when discussing unfair practices. However, due to the complexity of the issues involved, the discussion will not be exhaustive and will cover only the basic points. The objective of these two chapters is to provide the reader with a general and brief familiarization with both union and management unfair labor practices; specific interpretations regarding such actions should be obtained from labor relations and/or legal counsel.

PROHIBITED EMPLOYER PRACTICES

Section 8(a) of the National Labor Relations Act states that it is an unfair labor practice for management to

1. interfere with the rights guaranteed in Section 7 of the Act;
2. dominate or interfere with the formation or administration of a labor organization or contribute financial or other support to it;
3. discriminate with regard to hire or tenure of employment and to encourage or discourage membership in any union;
4. discharge or otherwise discriminate against an employee for filing charges or giving testimony under the Act; and
5. refuse to bargain in "good faith" with representatives designated or selected by the majority of the employees in a certified bargaining unit.

Each of these unfair labor practices will be discussed and analyzed in this chapter; examples of each type of unfair practice as they apply to health care facilities will be provided where meaningful.

SECTION 8(a)(1)--INTERFERENCE

Section 8(a)(1) provides that it is an employer unfair labor practice to "interfere with, restrain or coerce employees in the exercise of the rights guaranteed in Section 7." The rights guaranteed in Section 7 are as follows:

> Employees shall have the right to self-organization, to form, join or assist labor organizations, to bargain collectively through representatives of their own choosing, to engage in other concerted activities for the purpose of collective bargaining or other mutual aid or protection, and shall also have the right to refrain from any or all of such activities except to the extent that such right may be affected by an agreement requiring membership in a labor organization as a condition of employment as authorized in Section 8(a)(3).

This section is so worded that whatever unfair labor practice an employer commits, the action automatically implies a violation of 8(a)(1)--that is, employer action that interferes with the rights of employees to organize, form, join, bargain collectively or, on the other hand, to refrain from such activities is a violation of Section 8(a)(1). A violation of Sections 8(a)(2), (3), (4) or (5) is often referred to as a derivative violation of Section 8(a)(1).

Aside from derivative violations, Section 8(a)(1) can be violated directly. Violations of this section can generally be categorized as follows:

1. A health facility would violate the section by threatening, even by implication, the loss of jobs as the result of a union gaining collective bargaining status. This is true with regard to groups of employees as well as individual workers. For example, management could not imply that "if a union gained recognition and negotiated a contract the work force would have to be reduced because of the economic demands that would undoubtedly be made by the union." Similarly management of a health facility could not promise to "take care of" employees that promise not to vote for a union during a representational election. A company has been held in violation of Section 8(a)(1) because it threatened to go out of business entirely if a union won collective bargaining rights.

2. Health facility management would violate the interference prohibition if it attempted surveillance over employee union activity; even creating the impression of such action would be unlawful. Management is prohibited from questioning employees about their union activity if such questioning would lend the impression of being used for coercive purposes. Employers have been held in violation of the section for taking motion pictures of workers entering a union organizational meeting and for installing electronic listening devices to monitor union conversations.

3. Employers may implement rules limiting union activity on company working time if such regulations are uniformly applied; they cannot be established to give one union seeking recognition an unfair advantage over another union. Management may not prohibit or otherwise restrict union organizational activity during nonworking hours in locations separated from patient care areas (locker rooms, employee dining rooms, parking lots, etc.). Management may, in certain instances, place restriction on the size of union buttons, the wearing of union hats and the posting of notices and signs. Employers can call workers together during working hours to state management positions on union activity as long as statements made are not threatening or coercive (on their face or by implication)--management need not provide the union equal time.

It must be noted that an employer is responsible for interference actions prohibited under Section 8(a)(1) engaged in by agents of management. The employer can avoid responsibility for the unlawful acts of supervisors and other management personnel by instructing them to refrain, and making reasonable efforts to ensure that they do indeed refrain, from committing such acts.

SECTION 8(a)(2)--DOMINATION

Section 8(a)(2) of the Act provides that it is an unfair labor practice for an employer "to dominate or interfere with the formation or administration of any labor organization or contribute financial or other support to it..." It is not the intent of this section to prohibit an employee (accompanied by a union representative if desired) from conferring about grievances with an employer during working hours without loss of pay.

Employer-formed and -controlled unions are outlawed by this section of the Act. However, company unions not affiliated with an international organization are permissible as long as they deal "at arm's length" with management. Section 10(c) of the Act provides that the National Labor Relations Board in ruling on domination charges must treat independent (company) and affiliated (locals of an international union) unions alike. Domination is demonstrated where management actively participates in forming the union by establishing its organizational structure and/or actively solicits membership for it. Domination occurs when a union is established to meet management needs rather than to fulfill the wishes and represent the free choice of employees.

Employer involvement in union affairs may be less than domination and still be found to be an unfair labor practice under the section. For example, health facility management is prohibited from giving financial support to a union--an employer would violate the Act by allowing the union to make a profit by running concessions (vending machines, etc.) in the facility. Forwarding financial support to a union is further prohibited by the Labor-Management Reporting and Disclosure (Landrum-Griffin) Act of 1959 (this statute is discussed in Chapter X).

Analysis of past cases indicates that the NLRB constructs remedies for union domination and, somewhat differently, for assistance amounting to less than domination. Where the Board finds management domination of a labor organization it usually orders that union dissolved and prescribes that a new election be held. Management, when it is found to have assisted a union, is usually ordered to cease and desist from such activity.

SECTION 8(a)(3)--DISCRIMINATION FOR UNION ACTIVITY

Section 8(a)(3) denotes that it is illegal for an employer to discriminate with "...regard to hire or tenure of employment or any term or condition of employment to encourage or discourage membership in any labor organization." The section specifically provides that an employee may be discharged if he does not pay uniform and equitable union dues and fees where the union has obtained exclusive bargaining rights under a lawful union security agreement. (For example, a union shop contract provision provides that an employee must join the union after a specified period of employment.) However, the employer cannot be required to discharge the employee if membership in the union was not available to the worker under the same terms and conditions as available to other workers.

Through this section, health facility managements are forbidden from either discharging or discriminating against an employee with regard to terms and conditions of employment for engaging in labor organization activities. For example, managements under the Act cannot

1. fire an employee because he was instrumental in organizing labor union activity at the facility or because he urged fellow employees to instigate grievance procedures against the employer;
2. grant special privileges (e.g., pay increase, promotions, free medical care, time off, etc.) to employees not taking part in union activity;
3. refuse to hire a potential employee because he has been active in a union at his previous place of employment or because he belongs to a union--management cannot force applicants as a condition of employment to sign a contract stating they will not join a union;
4. grant superseniority to employees who refused to participate or were hired to replace workers engaged in a legal strike;
5. demote or otherwise discriminate (e.g., transfer of employee to a less desirable shift or job) against a worker for participation in a labor organization; or
6. refuse to reinstate an employee after he participated in a lawful strike if the position for which he is qualified is open.

The National Labor Relations Board, in determining employer discrimination, is interested in unlawful action as evidenced by actual behavior, intent and effect of the action. The Board in ruling upon discrimination under the section has given consideration to 1) forwarding inconsistent rationales for discharge or disciplinary actions; 2) neglect in employing customary discharge or disciplinary procedures (e.g., warnings, hearing procedures, conferences with employees, etc.); 3) the application of disproportionately severe punishment to those engaged in organized labor activities; 4) discharges because of past actions of the employee that were earlier condoned by the employer; 5) relationship between the point in time of the employer's alleged discriminatory action and the onset of the employee's engaging in union activity; 6) the degree to which the employee participated in labor organization activity; and 7) the effect of alleged employer discrimination upon the effectiveness of the union.

It must be emphasized that an employer may discharge an employee <u>for any reason</u> other than union activity (and discrimination with regard to race, creed, color, religion or national origin as provided for in Title VII of the 1964 Civil Rights Act). Employers, of course, must follow their own established administrative procedures in executing discharges or other disciplinary actions. The usual remedy employed by the Board when discrimination is demonstrated is to order reinstatement with back pay and benefits in the case of discharge, or reinstatement to the status prior to action in the case of discrimination. These actions by the Board are executed under the provision of Section 10(c) of the Act.

SECTION 8(a)(4)--DISCRIMINATION FOR ACTIVITY UNDER THE ACT

Under Section 8(a)(4) of the NLRA an employer cannot "discharge or otherwise discriminate against an employee because he has filed charges or given testimony under...[the] Act." This section was created to facilitate unimpaired administration and enforcement of the Act. Violations of this section are almost always also violations of 8(a)(3). As with the previous section, this unfair labor practice prohibits discharge, demotion, discrimination with regard to layoff and rehire, and discrimination in reinstatement after a lawfully conducted strike. In principle and application 8(a)(4) is a clarification and further specification of 8(a)(3).

SECTIONS 8(a)(3) AND 8(a)(4)--THE STATUS OF STRIKERS

The treatment of strikers by management deserves some elaboration. An economic striker is entitled to reemployment after the termination of a lawful job action if a vacancy exists for which the striker is qualified. The employer is, in every way, permitted to permanently replace economic strikers by hiring new regular employees. In such a case a vacancy may not exist for the economic striker to assume he will fill; the striker then would have no special right to reemployment and would be accorded the same status as any other applicant seeking work.

Strikers who are found to have violated employee unfair labor practices delineated in Section 8(b) of the Act (and discussed in Chapter VII) may be discharged from employment lawfully on a nondiscriminatory basis--the provisions of 8(a)(3) and 8(a)(4) cannot be violated in making such discharges. This also holds for employees who have violated a "no strike" provision of a legal collective bargaining contract or who have engaged in serious misconduct (e.g., violence in the conduct of a strike). Employees who engage in a strike because management has committed an unfair labor practice under Section 8(a) of the Act are protected with respect to their reemployment.

In the case where a "no strike" contract provision exists and that provision is violated by a job action resulting from a management unfair labor practice, job rights are protected, unless the "no strike" provision specifically prohibits employee action where the employer engages in unfair practices. Where employees violate a "no strike" contract clause as a response to a management unfair labor practice and they are then discharged, the Board will weigh the seriousness of the actions of both parties in determining a remedy under the language and intent of the Act.

SECTION 8(a)(5)--REFUSAL TO BARGAIN

Section 8(a)(5) of the NLRA states that it is an unfair labor practice for an employer "to refuse to bargain collectively with representatives of his employees, subject to the provisions of Section 9(a)." Section 9(a) specifies the rights of collective bargaining representatives as follows:

> Representatives designated or selected for the purposes of collective bargaining by the majority of the employees in a unit appropriate for such purposes shall be the exclusive representatives of all the employees in such unit for the purposes of collective bargaining in respect to rates of pay, wages, hours of employment, or other conditions of employment: Provided, that any individual employee or group of employees shall have the right at any time to present grievances to their employer and to have such grievances adjusted, without the intervention of the bargaining representatives, as long as the adjustment is not inconsistent with the terms of a collective bargaining contract or agreement then in effect: Provided further, that the bargaining representative has been given opportunity to be present at such adjustment.

Specifically, this section makes it unlawful for the employer to refuse to bargain in good faith regarding appropriate topics with a union that has been duly designated as a bargaining representative of a majority of the employees.

The subject matter of the bargaining process has been subdivided into mandatory, nonmandatory (discretionary) and prohibited topics. Mandatory subjects include matters dealing with but not necessarily limited to terms and conditions of employment, wages, work opportunity, fringe benefits, bonuses, grievance procedures, union security arrangements, safety practices, seniority, and procedures relating to discharge, layoff, recall and discipline. The NLRB has held that if an employer, in bargaining about wages, states that certain increases cannot be given because of internal economic conditions, sufficient data must be provided to the union so that it can evaluate this assertion. The employer must furnish individual employee wage data and information regarding work assignments and seniority. The law requires that management bargain with a union regarding such mandatory subjects, but it does not require that an agreement be reached. If an agreement is reached, Section 8(d) of the Act requires that a written contract be consummated at the request of either party to the negotiations. Nonmandatory items of negotiation are all issues that are not specifically prohibited by the Act: employers may bargain about such issues if they desire, but there is no requirement to do so. An example of a nonmandatory issue would be prices established by an independent contractor operating a company cafeteria. Once nonmandatory issues become the subject of bargaining, they might be viewed as mandatory issues during the next negotiating round. Through other sections (discussed in Chapter VII) the Act prohibits bargaining about payment for work not performed (featherbedding), closed shop and preferential hiring.

This section requires not only bargaining with regard to mandatory items but prescribes that such bargaining must be undertaken in good faith. Management is under no requirement to initiate the negotiation process; however, once bargaining has begun, there must be a demonstrated desire on the part of an employer to reach an agreement. The Board has found the following behavior to be evidence of non-good-faith collective bargaining: 1) insistence on dealing with individual employees rather than with the bargaining representative; 2) setting unreasonable times and/or locations for negotiating sessions; 3) refusing to send management representatives to bargaining sessions who have the authority to negotiate; 4) rejecting union bargaining proposals uniformly in the absence of forwarding counterproposals; and 5) repeatedly shifting positions or issues.

SECTION 8(e)--"HOT CARGO" AGREEMENTS

Section 8(e) was added to the Act in 1959 and prohibits an employer and a union from entering into what are commonly referred to as "hot cargo" agreements. The section states that

> It shall be deemed an unfair labor practice for any labor organization and any employer to enter into any contract or agreement, express or implied, whereby such employer ceases or refrains or agrees to cease or refrain from handling, using, selling, transporting or otherwise dealing in any products of any other employer, or to cease doing business with any other person, and any contract or agreement entered into heretofore or hereafter containing such an agreement shall be to such extent unenforceable and void...

Prior to 1959, such hot cargo agreements were common; they often provided that employees of an employer with whom a union had a contract would not be required to handle goods of a business that was labeled by the union as being unfair. Such contracts or agreements were often customary practice in the trucking industry: a trucking company would be forced by a union to deny service to businesses with whom the union (or an affiliated labor organization) had a representational dispute. This provision prohibits a union and an employer from entering into an agreement whereby the employer would not provide services (such as garbage removal) to health care facilities labeled by the union as being unfair. Similarly a union representing employees of a nursing home could not enter into an agreement with the home whereby it would admit patients only from hospitals whose employees were also represented by the union.

Section 8(e) contains specific exceptions that apply to the construction and textile industries. In the construction industry an employer and a union may make an agreement whereby the contracting and/or subcontracting of work on the construction site is limited. Usually the contract provides that if subcontracting is done, the subcontractor's employees must be members of the union. In the garment industry an agreement can be made that work to be done on the premises of a jobber or work that is part of an integrated process of production can be subcontracted only to an employer who has a contract with the union.

Agreeing to a hot cargo provision, even voluntarily, is a violation of the Act. Conversely, unions are prohibited from engaging in strikes, pickets or other job actions in order to force upon an employer a hot cargo agreement. Job actions designed to coerce employers into signing hot cargo provisions are specifically labeled as unfair labor practices under Section 8(b)(4) of the Act.

Evidence and Remedies

It is difficult if not impossible to determine purely on the basis of the actions themselves, whether many of the unfair labor practices discussed above (and those presented in the following chapter) have actually been committed. Additionally, the guilt or innocence involved in committing a prohibited practice often depends upon the intent of the person or persons engaging in the action. Because of these factors the NLRB often attempts to examine the total pattern of conduct of an employer or union accused of committing an unfair labor practice--that is, a series of acts, each of which taken alone would not be a violation, may be considered unfair when examined in total. Similarly, the Board looks to the effect of the alleged unfair practice and its timing. For example, an employer action such as a threat occurring immediately prior to an election might be considered unfair, whereas the same action committed months earlier could have been legal. Firing a union leader during an intense organizational drive without complete documentation as to cause might be questioned, whereas the same action taken against an ordinary union supporter might be overlooked. As will be discussed in Chapter XI, the National Labor Relations Board employs the same rules of evidence as the federal courts in conducting unfair labor practice hearings.

In remedying an unfair labor practice the NLRB has at its disposal a series of techniques provided for in Section 10 of the Act. The Board has the power to issue cease and desist orders and can make specific awards. For example, if a union is engaging in a strike that is deemed to be unfair, the Board can order the union to halt the job action so that the situation as it existed before the strike can be restored. Similarly, the Board can order an employer found guilty of discriminating against an employee for union activity to reinstate the employee with back pay and benefits. Furthermore, the Board can require an employer or union guilty of an unfair labor practice to make reports demonstrating the extent to which it has complied with the order.

Under the provisions of Section 10(e) the National Labor Relations Board is given the authority to petition federal (district or circuit) courts for injunctive relief regarding unfair labor practices. Two general types of relief provided by the courts are restraining orders and injunctions. Restraining orders are issued for a temporary period to prohibit a party from engaging in an anticipated action or to stop actions already in progress. An injunction restrains the commission of the enjoined action permanently. The issuance of injunctive relief is regulated by Section 2112, Title 28 of the United States Code.

VII

Union Unfair Labor Practices: Section 8(B) of the Act

PROHIBITED UNION PRACTICES

Until the 1947 (Taft-Hartley) amendments to the National Labor Relations Act, unions were regulated only through common law with respect to the types of labor practices they could engage in. The original National Labor Relations Act, passed in 1935, contained only prohibitions of certain management actions. Between 1935 and 1947 labor unions grew greatly in number, membership and power; certain abuses took place that the additions to the Act in 1947 were designed to rectify. Section 1 of the Act, as amended by the Taft-Hartley provisions, noted that experience under the law "...has further demonstrated that certain practices by some labor organizations...have the intent or the necessary effect of burdening or obstructing commerce by preventing the free flow of goods...through strikes and other forms of industrial unrest or through other concerted activities..." The Act as amended noted that "the elimination of such practices is a necessary condition to the assurances of the rights herein guaranteed."

Thus, the 1947 amendments to the law counterbalanced delineated employer unfair labor practices with the addition of a list of practices that, if committed by labor organizations, would be defined as illegal. Furthermore Section 7 of the Act was broadened to incorporate the right of employees not only to engage in union activities but also to refrain from engaging in such activities if they so desire. Section 8(b) of the Act specifies union unfair labor practices. The prohibition of such practices applies to labor organizations dealing with health care facilities. Section 8(b) provides that it is unlawful for a labor organization to

> (1): coerce or restrain employees in their right to engage in or to refrain from union activities, or to restrain employers in selecting their bargaining representative;
> (2): cause an employer to discriminate against an employee under a union security agreement, except where the employee fails to pay uniform and reasonable initiation fees and dues;
> (3): refuse to bargain in good faith;

(4): engage in conduct that influences the non-performance of work by employees for the purpose of forcing

(a) an employer or a person who is self-employed to join a labor or employer organization--or to force such person or organization to refuse to handle products of another company;
(b) another employer to recognize and bargain with an uncertified union;
(c) an employer to bargain with a union where another union has been previously certified; or
(d) the assignment of work to one group of employees rather than another unless ordered by the NLRB;

(5): assess excessive or otherwise discriminatory initiation fees and/or dues under a union security agreement;
(6): engage in the extraction of payment for work not actually performed; and
(7): engage in picketing to coerce unionization in the absence of seeking a certification election.

As is true with regard to management, the common law rules of agency apply to unions in determining if they are responsible for unfair labor practices. Unions are responsible for the acts of officials, business agents, consultants and union employees. A union has been held responsible for prohibited activities conducted during a picket or a strike by union members if union officials and/or agents participated in or directed such activities. Both the National Labor Relations Board and the courts have been extremely hesitant to hold the union liable for the individual actions of rank and file members--that is, members are not usually considered to be union agents because of their union membership per se.

The remainder of this chapter focuses upon providing a discussion of union unfair labor practices prohibited by Section 8(b) of the Act. As with the material presented in Chapter VI, this discussion is designed to be indicative rather than exhaustive. The application of these sections are governed by a host of National Labor Relations Board rulings and federal court decisions--the intent here is to familiarize the reader with the nature of union unfair labor practices in the most general sense. Managerial action in specific circumstances should be guided by competent labor relations and/or legal counsel.

SECTION 8(b)(1)--LABOR UNION COERCION

The first union unfair labor practices are grounded in Section 7 of the Act which holds that employees have the right to refrain from engaging in labor organization activity. Section 8(b)(1) states that it is an unfair labor practice for a labor organization

> ...to restrain or coerce (A) employees in the exercise of their rights guaranteed in Section 7: Provided, that this paragraph shall not impair the right of a labor organization to prescribe its own rules with respect to acquisition or retention of membership therein; or (B) an employer in the selection of his representatives for the purposes of collective bargaining or the adjustment of grievances. [emphasis in original]

Section 8(b)(1)(A) is a parallel to Section 8(a)(1). Neither unions nor managements have the right to coerce or restrain employees in their right to engage in or refrain from collective bargaining activity as guaranteed by Section 7 of the Act. The provision of Section 8(b)(1)(B) has no direct written parallel in Section 8(a). In the last chapter it was noted that violation of Section 8(a)(2) through (5) are also generally derivative violations of 8(a)(1). The NLRB has held, however, that the violation of other union unfair labor practices contained in Section 8(b) are not necessarily automatic derivative violations of 8(b)(1)(A). The one exception to this rule is that entering into illegal union security agreements (a violation of Section 8(b)(2)) is also unfair under 8(b)(1)(A)--such action has been held to compromise the rights guaranteed under Section 7.

Under this section both threats of violence and actual violence have been held illegal. For example, a union seeking representation at a health facility cannot threaten to physically harm employees who do not sign membership cards. They cannot suggest that if they win representation, employees who did not support the union will be treated unfavorably after a contract is negotiated. It is unlawful for unions to harass employees by such actions as constantly phoning workers at late hours in an abusive tone to force them to support a union recognitional drive and indicating that the pressure will subside only after they "join up." Similarly, a union cannot intimidate workers seeking to enter a struck plant; pushing, personal abuse (although not name calling), threats, destruction of workers' property and other such actions are illegal. The NLRB and the courts have ruled that large numbers of pickets outside a struck facility are not illegal. Such activity becomes a violation of the Act only when the picket line becomes a "picket fence"; that is, when the physical characteristics of the picket line prohibit entry to or exit from the facility.

Unions, like management, have the right of free speech in conducting their representational and collective bargaining activities. Abusive language and vague threats to nonpicketers or those not involved in strikes are not generally held as violations (unless they are embedded in a pattern of prohibited activity). As such, a proviso to Section 8(a)(1)(A) states that the unfair labor practice should not impede the union from implementing and enforcing its own rules. As such, a union does not violate the Act by fining a member who crosses a picket line or who works during a strike. The union's internal administration is its own business within certain limits. For example, a union cannot legally force the discharge of an employee for breaking output restrictions under a piecework system and a union security agreement (a fine would be legal, however). Under the Act a union is prohibited from fining a member for filing charges against it. Unions can press claims against members for fines in the courts.

Section 8(b)(1)(B) prohibits a union from restraining or coercing an employer in the selection of his bargaining representatives--such action might also be a violation of 8(b)(3), refusal to bargain in good faith. In other words, employers are protected in their right to representation and the manner of that representation. For example, a union could not strike one health facility to join a multiple-employer bargaining association. It would be unlawful for a union to strike in order to force members of a multiple-employer bargaining association to sign individual contracts with the union that are in conflict with a multiple-employer unit. A union could not strike or picket (or threaten such activity) in order to force the chief administrative officer of a health facility to be present at contract-negotiating sessions rather than a team or individuals selected by management.

SECTION 8(b)(2)--DISCRIMINATION

This unfair labor practice prohibits unions from forcing an employer to discriminate against an employee under Section 8(a)(3) of the Act. As noted in the preceding chapter, Section 8(a)(3) makes it an unfair labor practice for an employer to discriminate against an employee for labor organization activity. In this section, particular attention is paid to the illegality of discharging an employee where a union security agreement is in effect except for nonpayment of uniform and equitable dues and fees.

A union may violate this section by an act against an individual employee or a group of employees. As an example of the former, a union could not force an employer to demote a union member who has lost his good standing by breaking internally developed rules. Similarly a union would be held in violation of the section by forcing an employer to show preference with respect to wages or other conditions of employment to union members, thereby discriminating against employees who do not belong to the union.

Section 8(b)(2) has been held to prohibit preferential hiring practices. As will be noted in Chapter IX, a closed shop agreement--where potential employees are required to be union members prior to being hired--is prohibited under the Act. A closed shop arrangement is a violation of 8(b)(2) because nonunion members are discriminated against with regard to hire. Other preferential hiring practices are also barred by this section. It is unlawful for a union to require that all applicants for employment be cleared by it before being considered for employment. Requiring the possession of a work permit or a "good-standing card" as a condition of employment would also be illegal. For example, it would be an unfair labor practice violation under Section 8(b)(2) of the Act for a union to force a health facility to require, as a condition of employment, that a job applicant be a member of a specific professional association if such an organization is acting as a collective bargaining representative (irrespective of whether or not the association is a certified collective bargaining agent in the particular facility). Hiring halls--a mechanism where potential employees are referred to employers having job openings--are not in themselves prohibited by the Act, although referral preference must not be accorded union members.

This section of the Act also prohibits discrimination for "dual unionism"; this occurs where an employee is a member or works on behalf of more than one union. That is, an employee might be a member of one labor organization because of the requirements of a legal union security agreement but be actively engaged in assisting a rival organization; similarly a union cannot discriminate because of previous labor organization activity. A corollary exists to the above rule. With regard to its worker representation activities, a union is prohibited from discriminating against an employee who is not a member. A legally certified union that is the governmentally protected bargaining agent of a designated unit has the responsibility of representing all the employees in that unit irrespective of whether they belong to the union. That is, a certified union must represent members and nonmembers alike with regard to the negotiation of terms and conditions of employment and the resolution of grievances with the employer. This equal representation must take place even though the union cannot be required to admit all employees to membership. Racial discrimination in employment practices is prohibited by Title VII of the 1964 Civil Rights Act.

SECTION 8(b)(3)--REFUSAL TO BARGAIN

The Wagner Act passed in 1935 required that only employers engage in good-faith collective bargaining; unions were free to bargain or not to bargain with an employer as they saw fit. The 1947 amendments to the National Labor Relations Act through the provisions of Section 8(b)(3) now place similar requirements upon both managements and labor organizations. This section provides that it is an unfair labor practice for a union "to refuse to bargain collectively with an employer, provided it is a representative of his employees subject to the provision of Section 9(a)." The requirement for compliance under Section 8(b)(3) runs parallel to those placed upon management by Section 8(a)(5).

The union may engage in lawful nonviolent job actions and not be in violation of Section 8(b)(3). That is, unions can strike (providing that a no-strike agreement does not exist and other requirements of the Act, discussed later, have been met), and engage in other harassment techniques, such as slowdowns, walk-outs, sick-outs and admit-ins. However, the union cannot place unreasonable and/or unlawful demands upon the employer prior to or during negotiation. Examples of such actions would be demanding that the negotiations take place at unreasonable times or locations or forcing management to bargain about prohibited issues (hiring only employees referred by the union).

Section 8(d) of the Act requires that the party desiring a change in a negotiated collective bargaining agreement--usually the union--provide certain notices to the other party to the agreement and to the Federal Mediation and Conciliation Service. The requirements for health care facilities (which are different from those imposed upon unions dealing with other types of employers) are as follows:

1. They must serve written notice on the other party ninety days prior to the modification or termination of a collective bargaining agreement (Section 8(d)(1)).
2. They must notify the Federal Mediation and Conciliation Service sixty days prior to the termination or modification of a collective bargaining agreement (Section 8(d)(3)).
3. They must continue in full force, without resorting to strike or lockout, all the conditions of the existing contract during the notification period (Section 8(d)(4)).

Additionally, for health care institutions, the Act requires parties to engage in mandatory mediation with the assistance of the Federal Mediation and Conciliation Service (FMCS) during the period sixty days prior to the notice of termination. Health care facilities and labor organizations seeking representation therein also must file notice of attempts to reach agreement regarding an initial collective bargaining agreement with the FMCS (there is no corollary requirement for nonhealth facilities under the Act). Failure to meet the aforementioned requirements is a direct violation of Section 8(b)(3). For example, if a union struck a health care facility during the ninety-day notice period, such an action would be deemed an unfair labor practice and could be enjoined.

A more complete discussion of the notice and mediation requirements of the Act as they apply to health care facilities appears elsewhere in this book.

SECTION 8(b)(4)--PROHIBITED STRIKES

Section 8(b)(4) of the Act prohibits strikes, boycotts and other specified actions for the attainment of certain "objects" defined as illegal. The section contains two subparts: clauses (i) and (ii) delineate the prohibited actions, and subparagraphs (A) through (D) specify the illegal objects.

Section 8(b)(4)(i) prohibits a labor organization from engaging in a strike (or inducing or encouraging a strike) or other job actions by "...any individual employed by any person engaged in commerce or in an industry affecting commerce..." for the purpose of achieving an object listed in subparagraphs (A) through (D). The phrase "induce or encourage" has been interpreted very broadly; the courts have held that all forms of influence and persuasion are prohibited. Additionally, it is important to note that the prohibited activity need not actually happen for a labor union to be held in violation of the section. This provisions has been interpreted in such a way that it prohibits the inducement of organizational entities not covered by the Act for the purpose of achieving illegal objectives. For example, veterans hospitals and their employees are excluded from coverage of the Act. However, it would be illegal for a union to attempt to induce the employees of a veterans hospital to engage in a work stoppage or boycott for objects listed in subparagraphs (A) through (D). Section 8(b)(4)(ii) states that it is an unfair labor practice for a union to "...threaten, coerce, or restrain any person engaged in commerce or in an industry affecting commerce..." for the purpose of achieving the prohibited objects. This clause further defines the prohibition stated in (i).

The activities specified in 8(b)(4)(i) and (ii) cannot be employed where the object is to

> (A) force an employer to join an employer organization or to force an employer to enter into a hot cargo agreement;
> (B) for any person to cease dealing with another person or forcing or requiring any other employer to recognize or bargain with an uncertified union;
> (C) force an employer to recognize or bargain with a union in defiance of another labor organization's certification; and
> (D) force an employer to assign work to a group of employees rather than to another group unless specifically ordered by the National Labor Relations Board.

Section 8(b)(4)(A) makes it illegal for a union to engage in prohibited activities for the purpose of forcing an employer to join an employer organization. As already specified in Section 8(b)(1), employers are free to select their bargaining representatives as they see fit--engaging in activities to compromise this right is illegal. Employers are free to bargain with a union on an individual basis, or if a multiple-employer unit has been established, the employer can bargain through an association. Such multiple-employer bargaining units are becoming more common in the health industry. This section also prohibits coercive activities to force an employer to engage in a hot cargo agreement which is prohibited by Section 8(e) (this section of the Act was discussed in Chapter VI). For example, if a union is attempting to obtain recognition from a particular health facility, it would be illegal for the union to induce the employees of a food distributor not to make deliveries to the hospital until its management granted the union recognition. Similar action undertaken for the purpose of forcing the health facility to join a multiple-employer bargaining unit would also be illegal.

Section 8(b)(4)(B) is commonly known as the "secondary boycott" provision of the Act; it prohibits the forcing of one person to stop doing business with another. A secondary boycott would occur where a union has a dispute with an enterprise and the union forces another enterprise to stop handling the products of, or otherwise doing business with, the first. Here is an example. A union is seeking to negotiate a collective bargaining agreement with a particular nursing home; to apply pressure on the nursing home the union forces several hospitals, with which it has contracts, to stop transferring patients to the nursing home. In this instance the union's dispute is with the nursing home--the primary employer--although the action (prohibited in 8(b)(4) i or ii) is against a group of secondary employer hospitals; hence the designation "secondary boycott." In this case it would be illegal for the union to picket, strike or in any way force the hospitals to stop doing business with the nursing home.

The courts have ruled that in order for a secondary employer to be protected against union action prohibited by 8(b)(4)(B) the secondary employer must be a neutral in the dispute between the primary employer and the union. When a secondary employer is not neutral with respect to the primary dispute, he is considered an "ally" of the primary employer and may not be protected from certain union actions. Several criteria are employed by the National Labor Relations Board to determine if the secondary employer is an ally of the primary employer: 1) common ownership; 2) the existence of a closely integrated operation; and 3) behavior of the secondary employer. Where the primary and secondary employers are owned conjointly or where their operations are closely integrated they may be considered allies. Additionally, in situations where a secondary employer does not remain neutral to the dispute he may be considered an ally of the primary employer.

The House and Senate committee reports, expressing the intent of Congress in passing the 1974 amendments to the Act, elaborate on the "ally doctrine" with respect to health care facilities by stating:

> It has been held that where during the course of a labor dispute, a secondary employer performs work that, but for the existence of such labor dispute, would have been performed by the striking employees of the primary employer, the secondary employer loses his status as a neutral, and the labor organization is entitled to extend its economic activity to the secondary employer. It is the sense of the Committee that where such secondary institutions accept the patients of a primary employer or otherwise provide life-sustaining services to the primary employer, by providing the primary employer with an employee or employees who possess critical skills, such as an EKG technician, such conduct shall not be sufficient to cause the secondary employer to lose its neutral status. It should be clear, however, that where a secondary employer enmeshes itself into the primary dispute by providing supervisors, nurses or staff other than those described, it loses its status of neutrality.

Thus, a secondary employer can assist the primary employer in certain ways and still maintain its status as a neutral. The committee-report language clearly suggests that secondary actions against health care facilities should be viewed in a different manner by the National Labor Relations Board than similar disputes occurring in other sectors of the economy. The reports take into account that during a labor dispute at a health care facility, patients must be transferred to other facilities and those too ill to be transferred must be provided with life-sustaining services. It does not, however, allow the secondary facility a carte blanche with regard to the assistance it can provide to a primary employer.

Section 8(b)(4)(C) of the Act prohibits a union from engaging in activity to compel an employer to recognize and/or collectively bargain with any labor organization other than the one that has been certified as the representative of his employees. Prior to the enactment of this section, a rival union of one that currently had a contract with an employer was allowed to picket the employer for the purpose of forcing the employer to recognize it. This action, under the present Act, is illegal. If, however, a labor organization has not been certified as the bargaining representative of an employer's workers, a primary strike or picketing to seek recognition or other organizational purposes is not a violation of 8(b)(4)(C). It must be noted that picketing to force recognition of an uncertified union is subject to restrictions contained in Section 8(b)(7), which is discussed later in this chapter.

Section 8(b)(4)(D) of the Act prohibits a union from engaging in activities specified in clauses (i) and (ii) of Section 8(b)(4) for the purpose of: "...forcing or requiring any employer to assign particular work to employees in a particular labor organization or in a particular trade, craft or class rather than to employees in another labor organization or in another trade, craft or class..." unless the employer is failing to conform with an order issued by the National Labor Relations Board. For example, it would be a violation of this section for a union representing maintenance employees in a health facility to strike in order to force management to grant such employees the additional duties of operating the laundry. It is not a violation of this section, however, for a union to engage in activities not otherwise prohibited that are directed toward maintaining, within a unit, work already being done by employees in that unit. Work assignment disputes between groups of employees or unions do not violate the Act if they are not accompanied by actions prohibited in 8(b)(4)(i) and (ii); unions can request an employer to reassign work as long as there is no restraint or coercion involved.

Section 10(k) of the Act gives the National Labor Relations Board special powers with regard to disputes concerning the assignment of work. Where a dispute about work assignment is alleged to be an unfair labor practice (e.g., under 8(b)(4)(C)) the Board is required by the Act to decide the dispute by making an assignment of work unless the parties involved (within ten days of the date when the unfair labor practice charge was filed) show that 1) the dispute has been settled; or 2) a mechanism has been agreed upon to settle the dispute.

PROVISOS

This section contains several provisos clarifying the situation where employees refuse to cross a picket line and union informational activities.

The first proviso states that nothing contained in Sections 8(b)(1) through (7) of the Act

> ...shall be construed to make unlawful a refusal by any person to enter upon the premises of any employer...if the employees of such employer are engaged in a strike ratified or approved by a representative of such employees whom such employer is required to recognize under the Act...

Thus, it is not a violation of the Act, for example, for truck drivers to refuse to cross a picket line at a struck health facility if the strike is being conducted by a union that is a certified representative of that health facility's employees. In refusing to cross the picket line the truck driver must not violate the contract with his employer. The Board has ruled that an employer has the right to fire an employee who refuses to cross a picket line at another employer's premises.

The second proviso of this section states that nothing contained in 8(b)(4) shall be taken to prohibit publicity for the purpose of notifying the public that goods distributed by one employer are produced by a primary employer with whom the union has a dispute. Such publicity is prohibited if it has the effect of causing any persons other than the employees of the primary employer to stop handling goods or to stop performing services at the business where the publicity is taking place. For example, it is not a violation of the Act for employees of a hospital supply company to pass out handbills at a newly opened hospital stating that the facility bought equipment from a firm with whom the employees have a primary dispute. If, however, the action caused employees of the health facility to not enter the premises or to otherwise refrain from working, the action would be a violation of the Act.

SECTION 8(b)(5)--EXCESSIVE OR DISCRIMINATORY FEES

Section 8(b)(2), discussed earlier in this chapter, prohibits unions from causing an employer to discriminate against employees where a valid union security agreement exists for any reason other than for nonpayment of uniform union dues and fees. This section makes it an unfair labor practice for a union to extract excessive or discriminatory fees or dues when a union security agreement is in effect. In making the determination of whether dues and fees are excessive or discriminatory, the Act requires that the Board consider "...the practices and customs of labor organizations in the particular industry, and the wages currently paid to the employees affected." The Act, in no way, places ceilings on what unions can implement as their dues and fee structures.

This provision would prohibit a union from charging employees who did not join a union before it was recognized as a certified bargaining agent a $100 initiation fee when it charged employees who were original members of the union only $10. Similarly, charging employees with more than one year of service with a company a $50 initiation fee and new employees $10 would be illegal, since it penalizes employees for not joining the union when they were hired. A high dues rate might not be ruled excessive in one classification where wages are large, while similar dues in other classifications might be deemed an unfair labor practice.

SECTION 8(b)(6)--FEATHERBEDDING

This section prohibits a labor organization from causing "...or attempting to cause an employer to pay or deliver or agree to pay or deliver any money or other thing of value, in the nature of an exaction, for services which are not performed or not to be performed." Thus, this section makes it an unfair labor practice to engage in what is commonly referred to as featherbedding. In actuality, only a very restricted form of featherbedding is prohibited by the Act. This section does not forbid a labor organization from attempting to cause an employer to pay for unnecessary or useless work; rather, it addresses the payment for work not actually performed or work that will not be performed in the future.

A common form of a featherbed practice in industry is chaperoning. Here two men are assigned to a job that one man could reasonably do by himself; the extra worker is employed as a watcher and performs no useful service to the employer. Although the additional employee performs no service of value, he is fulfilling his job designation of watching. A union that seeks to have an employer hire chaperons in such instances would not be in violation of Section 8(b)(6). Another common practice (especially in the construction trades) involves certain services that may be required and are of value to an employer, but even though the employer pays for such services they are not executed. For example, a union steward who is being paid for ostensibly performing a task actually works full time at the job site handling union matters; if the agreement between the union and the employer calls for payment of the worker under such conditions, this would not be a prohibited practice. A final example of featherbedding is the situation where a union will negotiate with an employer to set up special job categories and make work assignments for disabled or old workers. As noted before, such assignments are not a violation of the section if the job designations were agreed to and some work (however meaningless) is performed.

SECTION 8(b)(7)--RECOGNITIONAL PICKETING BY NONCERTIFIED UNIONS

Section 8(b)(7) of the Act was added through a 1959 amendment and prohibits a union from picketing (or threatening to picket) an employer for the purposes of forcing him to recognize or bargain with a union where

> (A) the employer has lawfully recognized any other labor organization under the provisions of the Act;
> (B) a valid election has been conducted within the last twelve months; or
> (C) a representational petition has not been filed within a reasonable time period, not to exceed thirty days from the commencement of such picketing.

Thus Sections 8(b)(7)(A) and (B) of the Act hold that a union cannot, for example, picket a health facility for organizational or recognitional purposes when the employees are already represented by a union authorized under the Act or when a valid union election has been held within the last year (even though the union may have lost the election and the employees are unorganized).

Section 8(b)(7)(C) is of particular importance to health facilities. Prior to the 1947 amendments a union could picket an employer up to thirty days for recognition. That is, an unfair labor practice could be filed against a union if it failed to request a representational petition within a reasonable time period from the point at which the picketing started; the Act defines thirty days as a "reasonable time period." If an 8(b)(7)(C) charge is filed against a union and a representational petition has not been requested within a reasonable time period, subpart (C) of the section provides that the Board should direct that an election be held quickly. This election is called an "expedited election" and requires neither a "showing of interest" by the employees nor a hearing; the procedure can be executed much more quickly than under the regular election provisions of Section 9(c). If the union has filed a recognitional petition within a reasonable time, no expedited election will be directed.

Prior to the 1974 amendments to the Act, even if a union followed the provisions it could picket a health facility up to thirty days for organizational or recognitional purposes. The committee reports (expressing the intent of Congress in enacting the amendments), however, provide that

> In recognition picketing cases under Section 8(b)(7)(C), the National Labor Relations Board has ruled that a reasonable period of time is thirty days absent unusual circumstances such as violence or intimidation. <u>It is the sense of the committee that picketing of a health care institution would in itself constitute an unusual circumstance justifying the application of a period of time less than thirty days</u>. [emphasis added]

Thus, Congress believes that upon picketing a health facility, a union should petition for representation quickly or be held in violation of 8(b)(7)(C). The period of time within which a union must file a representational petition will be determined by the National Labor Relations Board. The intent is clear: representational picketing of health care facilities is to be given less latitude than in other sectors of the economy.

Section 8(b)(7)(C) is subject to several provisos. Picketing is permitted where the purpose is to truthfully advise the public (including consumers) that the employer either does not employ union members or does not have a contract with a labor organization. Such picketing is protected unless it has the effect of inducing any worker employed by another person not to pick up or deliver or to cease doing business. The National Labor Relations Board has ruled that the picket must be "sufficiently disruptive" to be declared a violation of the section. For example, if such a picket causes one of many deliveries not to be made it would probably not be held illegal.

VIII
Labor Management Disputes

TOWARD THE REDUCTION OF STRIKES

Uppermost in the minds of health administrators when a union begins its organizational drive at their institution is the possibility of strikes. Strikes, or the threat of strikes, are indeed an integral part of the total industrial collective bargaining experience. Many administrators believe that the recognition of a union is a direct invitation to strikes. Labor law where it is applicable usually requires that management and labor bargain "in good faith." It does not compel them to agree to terms of a contract. Therefore, unions go on strike in order to support the positions that they have taken across the bargaining table.

The concern over the possibility of strikes in health care facilities as a result of increased organizational activity upon removal of the industry's exemption from the Act was foremost in the minds of legislators when considering such removal. Several aspects of this enormously important problem require careful attention at this juncture. Section 8(d) of the Act has been amended to provide the following:

1. Parties to a collective bargaining agreement involving a health care facility must provide the other party ninety days' notice before terminating the agreement.
2. The Federal Mediation and Conciliation Service must be given a sixty-day notice of such collective bargaining agreement termination or expiration.
3. In initial contract negotiations, a thirty-day notice must be provided to the Federal Mediation and Conciliation Service.
4. The health care institution and labor organization will be required to participate in mediation at the direction of the Federal Mediation and Conciliation Service (FMCS).

In addition, subsection (g) of Section 8 provides that labor organizations must give a ten-day written notice to a health care institution and the FMCS of their intent to picket, strike or participate in other concerted refusal to work.

CONTRACT NOTICE REQUIREMENTS

Prior to the 1974 amendments, Section 8(d) required an employer and the representative of his employees to meet at reasonable times and confer in good faith about certain matters and to put into writing any agreement reached if requested by either party. The parties were required to confer in good faith with respect to wages, hours, other terms and conditions of employment, the negotiation of the agreement, or any question arising under the agreement. It further stated that where there where there was a collective bargaining agreement in effect, neither party could end or change that contract unless that party, wishing to make such a move, took the following steps:

1. The party was required to notify the other party to the contract, in writing, regarding intent to terminate or modify that contract sixty days before the date on which the contract was scheduled to expire. In cases where there was no specific date of expiration, such notice was required to be served sixty days before the time when it was proposed that the termination and modification take effect.
2. The party was required to offer to meet and confer with the other party with the intent to negotiate a new contract.
3. In addition, the party was required to notify the FMCS thirty days after the notice to the other party of the existence of a dispute if no agreement had been reached by that time. In addition, the party was required to notify any state mediation or conciliation service with jurisdiction in the area where the dispute occurred.
4. Finally, the party was required to continue, in full force and effect without resorting to strike or lockout, the terms of the current contract until sixty days after the notice to the other party was given or until the date the contract was scheduled to expire, whichever was later.

The Act, as amended for health care institutions, now extends the sixty-day notice period to ninety days and requires the FMCS to receive sixty days' notice instead of thirty days' notice in the case of health care institutions. Before amendment, the Act provided no obligation on either party's part to participate in mediation. As it is now constituted, it provides for mandatory mediation by the parties with the FMCS in the case of collective bargaining involving health care institutions.

TEN-DAY STRIKE NOTICE

Legislative committees considering the amendment of the Act to include health care facilities strongly urged that it was in the public interest to ensure the continuity of health service to the community and reduce the possibility of an interruption of care to patients of such facilities. This concern was translated into a required advance notice by a union of any anticipated strike or picketing. Section 8(g) prohibits a union from striking or picketing a health care institution without first giving ten days' notice. Violation of this provision constitutes an unfair labor practice and failure to give statutory notice will be subject to remedy under Section 10(j) of the Act. Section 10 is entitled the "Prevention of Unfair Labor Practices." Section 10(j) provides the Board with the power, upon issuance of a complaint charging a party with engaging in an unfair labor practice, to petition any district court of the United States where the unfair labor practice is alleged to have occurred for appropriate temporary relief or a restraining order. Although this section does not require that injunctive relief be sought, it does make it possible for the Board to do so in cases where it is considered appropriate. The ten-day-notice period provides the Board with the opportunity, where charges are filed, to make a determination as to the legality of any strike or picketing before it occurs.

Section 8 of the Act is amended by the addition of the following new subsection:

> (g) A labor organization before engaging in any strike, picketing or other concerted refusal to work at any health care institution shall, not less than ten days prior to such action, notify the institution in writing and the Federal Mediation and Conciliation Service of that intention, except that in the case of bargaining for an initial agreement following certification or recognition, the notice required by this subsection shall not be given until the expiration of the period specified in clause (B) of the last subsection of Section 8(b) of this Act. The notice shall state the date and time that such action will commence. The notice, once given, may be extended by the written agreement of both parties.

The intent of Congress in providing this ten-day notice was to give the health care institutions sufficient advance notice of a strike or picketing so as to allow them to plan and effect a program for continuity of patient care in face of such action. During the notice period, the health care institution remains free to take whatever action it deems necessary to ensure the maintenance of health care, but Congress warned in its report that such actions should not undermine the bargaining relationship that would otherwise exist. The institution is not free to bring in large numbers of supervisory help, nurses, staff and other personnel from other facilities for replacement purposes. It could receive supplies, but would not be free to take extraordinary steps to stock up on ordinary supplies for an unduly extended period. Although such actions are not a violation of the Act, the Board could construe them as a violation of principles enumerated in the Congressional report and could release the labor organization from its obligation not to engage in economic action during the course of the ten-day-notice period.

THIRTY-DAY COOLING-OFF PERIOD--EMERGENCY DISPUTES

The Act, as amended, provides procedures for handling "emergency" labor disputes in the health care industry. The mechanism to effect such conciliation is provided for under Section 2, Title II, by the addition, at the end of the section, of the following provision:

> Conciliation of Labor Disputes in the Health Care Industry
>
> Sec. 213(a) If, in the opinion of the Director of the Federal Mediation and Conciliation Service a threatened or actual strike or lockout affecting a health care institution will, if permitted to occur or continue, substantially interrupt the delivery of health care in the locality concerned, the Director may further assist in the resolution of the impasse by establishing within 30 days after the notice to the Federal Mediation and Conciliation Service under clause (A) of the last sentence of Section 8(d) (which is required by clause (3) of such Section 8(d)), or within 10 days after the notice under clause (B), an impartial Board of Inquiry to investigate the issues involved in the dispute and to make a written report thereon to the parties within fifteen (15) days after the establishment of such a Board. The written report shall contain the findings of fact together with the Board's recommendations for settling the dispute, with the objective of achieving a prompt, peaceful and just settlement of the dispute. Each such Board shall be composed of such number of individuals as the Director may deem desirable. No member appointed under this section shall have any interest or involvement in the health care institutions or the employee organizations involved in the dispute.
>
> (b)(1) Members of any board established under this section who are otherwise employed by the Federal Government shall serve without compensation but shall be reimbursed for travel, subsistence, and other necessary expenses incurred by them in carrying out its duties under this section.
>
> (2) Members of any board established under this section who are not subject to para-

> graph (1) shall receive compensation at a rate prescribed by the Director but not to exceed the daily rate prescribed for GS-18 of the General Schedule under section 5332 of title 5, United States Code, including travel for each day they are engaged in the performance of their duties under this section and shall be entitled to reimbursement for travel, subsistence, and other necessary expenses incurred by them in carrying out their duties under this section.
>
> (c) After the establishment of a board under subsection (a) of this section and for 15 days after any such board has issued its report, no change in the status quo in effect prior to the expiration of the contract in the case of negotiations for a contract renewal, or in effect prior to the time of the impasse in the case of an intial bargaining negotiation, except by agreement, shall be made by the parties to the controversy.
>
> (d) There are authorized to be appropriated such sums as may be necessary to carry out the provisions of this section.

Thus, this section provides that the emergency mechanism is to be implemented at the discretion of the director of the Federal Mediation and Conciliation Service when it is felt that a threatened strike has the potential to significantly affect the provision of health services in a specific locality. It is the intent of Congress that the mechanism not be indiscriminately applied. If an emergency is deemed to exist, the director of the Federal Mediation and Conciliation Service would establish a board of inquiry thirty days after it received notice of a contract termination under Section 8(d) of the Act. The board of inquiry would have fifteen days to report its findings and recommendations to the parties; the parties would then have fifteen days to engage in continued negotiations before a work stoppage or a lockout could take place. In the case of initial contract negotiations, Section 8(d) requires that after union certification the Federal Mediation and Conciliation Service must be provided with thirty days' prior notice of a dispute. Section 213 states that if an emergency is deemed to exist, the board of inquiry must be convened no less than ten days after receiving notice of the dispute. After the emergency procedure has been implemented, the process is the same as under agreement renegotiation.

The committee report in clarifying the intent of Congress in enacting the emergency disputes provision stated:

> The Conferees intend that the appointment of a Board of Inquiry shall not operate to interrupt medi-

> ation by the FMCS which is made mandatory under other provisions of this legislation, and that the service will pursue these parallel procedures to bring about a fair, prompt and just settlement of any dispute. The Conferees further intend that the Board of Inquiry, in formulating its recommendations for settlement of a dispute shall take into account all those factors normally considered by similar tribunals in formulating recommendations for the settlement of labor disputes.
>
> The Committee, in adding special mediation and conciliation procedures, including the Board of Inquiry, for the health care industry, recognizes the need for continuity of health services during labor-management disputes and that the labor organizations representing health care workers have publicly pledged their best efforts to persuade their affiliates voluntarily to avoid work stoppages through acceptance of arbitration in the event of an impasse in negotiations. Under these new procedures, it is anticipated that, in the event of such an impasse, the findings of fact and recommendations of the Board of Inquiry would provide the framework of the arbitrator's decision.

This provision of a cooling-off period during the final thirty days of the term of the collective bargaining agreement was strongly resisted by the American Hospital Association, which maintained that such a procedure should become effective after the contract terminated. It is unusual for a cooling-off period to be effected during the life of a contract, since, with rare exceptions, strikes or lockouts occur upon termination of a collective bargaining agreement. Still another controversial aspect of this amendment is the provision for an impartial board of inquiry to investigate the issues in the dispute and to issue a written report within fifteen days after entering the dispute. The fact-finding report would be made available to the parties to the controversy. Since there is no mandatory implementation of the recommendations contained in the report, such a report, if not accepted by both parties, might establish a situation in which the union may well wish to extract a further series of concessions from the health care facility.

JURISDICTIONAL DISPUTES

The term "jurisdictional disputes" is defined as a dispute between two or more unions over work assignments. The employer is the innocent bystander. Under Section 8(b)(4)(D), it is an unfair labor practice to force or require an employer to assign work to one group of employees rather than to another. The only exception to this rule is where an employer fails to adhere to a Board order or certification. This type of problem may appear at first impression to be of little or no pertinence to the health care facility. Such may not be the case with the growth of professional unions along with the usual service and maintenance unions which are present in such facilities. It may well become less unusual to find a jurisdictional dispute between a nursing union and a service union over specific elements of patient care delivery.

The Board provides special procedures to be used in jurisdictional dispute cases where a charge is filed with the Board alleging a violation of Section 8(b)(4)(D). The Board derives its powers through Section 10(k), which states that

> Whenever it is charged that any person has engaged in an unfair labor practice within the meaning of paragraph (4)(D) of Section 8(b), the Board is empowered and directed to hear and determine the dispute out of which such unfair labor practice shall have arisen unless within 10 days after notice that such charge has been filed, the parties to such dispute submit to the Board satisfactory evidence that they have adjusted or agreed upon methods for the voluntary adjustment of the dispute. Upon compliance by the parties to the dispute with the decisions of the Board or upon such voluntary adjustment of the dispute, such charges shall be dismissed.

The Board has been delegated the authority through the Act to obtain injunctive relief against violations of the jurisdictional dispute provisions of the Act. The Board may exercise this option while the case is pending before it.

UNFAIR LABOR PRACTICE AND ECONOMIC STRIKES

If an employer has committed an unfair labor practice and employees go out on strike in protest of such unfair labor practice, the employer is required under the law to reinstate these striking employees to their former jobs, upon completion of their job action, notwithstanding the fact that replacements have been hired for such employees. It is important to differentiate such strikers (whose activities are in protest against an unfair labor practice committed by the employer) from purely economic strikers (those involved in strikes usually associated with a union's attempt to win concessions from an employer during contract negotiation periods). Employees who are on strike maintain their status as employees during that period as provided in Section 2(3) of the Act:

> The term "employee" shall include any employee, and shall not be limited to the employees of a particular employer, unless the Act explicitly states otherwise, and shall include any individual whose work has ceased as a consequence of, or in connection with, any current labor dispute or because of any unfair labor practice, and who has not obtained any other regular and substantially equivalent employment...

Economic strikers are considered separately from those strikers involved in unfair labor practice strikes. The Court has ruled that the employer has "the right to protect and continue his business by permanently replacing economic strikers.... He is not bound to discharge those hired to fill the places of strikers." It follows that if an employee participates in an economic strike--a strike to obtain economic gains--the employer may replace such employees, and if the economic striker's job has been filled by a permanent replacement the employer is free from obligation to provide reemployment. The employer is only required to replace an economic striker if a vacancy exists at the time such an employee applies for reinstatement. It is well to note that an employer may not discharge an employee for engaging in an economic strike, but may, indeed, replace such employees. As long as such replacements are qualified and continue to work after the strike has been terminated, the employer need not offer the economic striker reinstatement. The employer does have an obligation to such strikers who have been replaced inasmuch as they are entitled to reinstatement if and when the replacement terminates. The employer's obligation to economic strikers is limited to disposing of the employee's application for reemployment on a nondiscriminatory basis. This does not include the termination of a replacement. Once an economic striker accepts regular employment with another employer in a position which is equivalent to the one he had left, his former employer (against whom he has struck) no longer has any obligation for reinstatement.

When strikers are guilty of misconduct on the basis of activities during the strike period, the employer is no longer obligated to reinstate them, whether or not they have been replaced during that period. If a striker is found guilty of violence on the picket line, or is involved in illegal actions on the employer's premises--such as a sit-down strike or destruction of the employer's property--the employer is no longer obligated to reinstate such employees under any circumstances. Under the rule established by the Supreme Court in NLRB v. Fansteel Metallurgical Corp. (306 U.S. 240), an employer may discharge or refuse to reinstate a striker who is guilty of unlawful conduct. Employees involved in economic strikes who are replaced and, therefore, lose their right to reinstatement still remain eligible to vote in representation elections which are held within a twelve-month period from the commencement of the strike. Generally, employees not currently employed are entitled to vote if there is reasonable expectation that they will be reemployed, on the basis that they may be affected by the presence or absence of a bargaining representative.

UNLAWFUL STRIKES

On the basis of the amendments to the Act covering health care facilities, unions that strike without first giving ten days' notice of their intent are involved in an unlawful strike. In addition, it is unlawful for a union to strike in a situation where the employer has lawfully recognized another union and where the striking union has not petitioned for a representation election. It is also unlawful for a union to strike to gain recognition where the Board has conducted an election within the preceding twelve months. Other strikes have been deemed unlawful--such as:

1. A sit-down strike where employees remain in the institution and prevent work from going on.
2. A strike which is violent in nature.
3. A wildcat strike--one which is not authorized by the union.
4. Strikes in defiance of existing certification.
5. Jurisdictional strikes.
6. Secondary strikes and boycotts.
7. A strike to induce the violation of a valid statute.
8. A strike to obtain a featherbedding arrangement.

A strike in violation of a no-strike agreement deserves further attention. Many contracts contain no-strike clauses where the union, in return for a commitment that their members will not be "locked out" by management, agrees not to strike during the life of the agreement. The Supreme Court had initially determined in Sinclair Refining Company v. Atkinson (370 U.S. 195) that a federal district court lacked jurisdiction to grant an injunction to enforce a no-strike clause of a collective bargaining agreement which also contained a grievance and arbitration provision covering the dispute involved. This decision was further reinforced in 1968, when the Supreme Court ruled that an action in a state court solely for injunctive relief enforcing a no-strike clause could be removed to the federal court, where, under the previous Sinclair decision, the injunction would not be granted. But two years after that decision the present rule on injunctive relief was enshrined by the Supreme Court in Boys Market, Inc. v. Retail Clerks (398 U.S. 235). In this decision the Supreme Court reversed the Sinclair decision. The union involved in the case conducted a strike during the life of a contract which contained a no-strike provision. In addition, the contract contained a grievance procedure which culminated in arbitration, and the employer had indicated readiness and willingness to exhaust the procedure through arbitration. The Court, therefore, ruled that the federal district court had jurisdiction to enjoin the strike. An important part of the Court's decision follows:

> A District Court entertaining an action under Section 301 may not grant injunctive relief against concerted activity unless and until it decides that the case is one in which an injunction would be appropriate despite the Norris-La Guardia Act. When a strike is sought to be enjoined because it is over a grievance which both parties are contractually bound to arbitrate, the District Court may issue no injunctive order until it first holds that the contract does have that effect; and the employer should be ordered to arbitrate, as a condition of his obtaining an injunction against the strike. Beyond this, the District Court must, of course, consider whether issuance of an injunction would be warranted under ordinary principles of equity--whether breaches are occurring and will continue, or have been threatened and will be committed; whether they have caused or will cause irreparable injury to the employer; and whether the employer will suffer more from the denial of the injunction than will the union from its issuance.

The Court in Boys Market, therefore, established that state courts could enjoin a strike in breach of a contract. Of course, the Supreme Court made it clear that in order to effect Boys Market, the collective bargaining agreement in effect must contain a grievance and arbitration procedure mandatory in nature and applicable to the dispute involved in the strike which the employer seeks to enjoin.

DAMAGES FOR UNLAWFUL STRIKES

An employer who is subjected to an unlawful strike may sue for damages. The Act provides for such suit as follows:

> Section 303(a). It shall be unlawful, for the purpose of this section only, in an industry or activity affecting commerce, for any labor organization to engage in any activity or conduct defined as an unfair labor practice in Section 8(d)(4) or 8(g) of

> the National Labor Relations Act as amended.
> (b) Whoever shall be injured in his business or property by reason of any violation of subsection (a) may sue therefore in any District Court of the United States subject to the limitations and provisions of Section 301 hereof without respect to the amount in controversy, or in any other court having jurisdiction of the parties, and shall recover the damages by him sustained and the cost of the suit.

The injured party may bring suit for damages which result from an unlawful strike and can recover actual dollar losses plus court costs. Such damage suits may be brought in state as well as federal courts or in any other court having jurisdiction of the parties. It is well to note that unions are bound by the acts of their agents whether or not the acts are specifically authorized or subsequently ratified.

IX
Union Security Arrangements

TYPES OF UNION SECURITY AGREEMENTS

Once a union has been certified as the collective bargaining agent for the employees in a health care facility, one of its primary aims is to obtain a contractual provision that gives it (the union) maximum protection as to its continued existence in that institution. It, therefore, attempts to bargain some form of compulsory union membership. These provisions are called union security arrangements. There are five major forms of union security:

1. closed shop;
2. union shop;
3. modified union shop;
4. maintenance of membership shop; and
5. agency shop.

Closed Shop

A closed shop requires applicants for employment to be members of the union before they can be hired. This form of union security was usually accompanied by a union hiring hall provision. The union is notified of the employment needs of the employer and forwards applicants to fill the jobs. A sample closed shop clause follows:

> The health care facility shall hire only applicants for employment who are members of the union. The union shall furnish such applicants for employment provided that, however, if the union is unable to fill such request, the health care facility may hire applicants who are not members of the union, but such applicants must become members of the union immediately upon being hired.

Under Section 8(a)(3), the closed shop is declared illegal.

Union Shop

The great majority of collective bargaining agreements contain a union shop clause. This type of union security provides that all employees in the bargaining unit must join the union within a specified period of time after hire, usually at the end of a probationary period. Under the Act, any union shop agreement must provide new employees with a minimum of thirty days in which to become members of the union. It is an unfair labor practice to allow nonmembers less than thirty days to join a union. It is also illegal to maintain a requirement that a nonmember must state his intent to join before thirty days of employment. A sample union shop provision follows:

> All employees on the active payroll at the time of the signing of the contract who are members of the union shall maintain their membership in the union in good standing as a condition of continued employment. All employees on the active payroll as of the time of the signing of the contract who are not members of the union shall become members of the union within thirty (30) days after the effective date of the contract. All employees hired after the effective date of the contract shall become members of the union no later than the 30th day following the beginning of such employment and shall thereafter maintain their membership in the union in good standing as a condition of continued employment.

Under the union shop arrangement, if an employee fails to join the union within the prescribed period of time (thirty days or longer), the union may request the discharge of such an employee.

Modified Union Shop

A modified union shop arrangement provides an option to employees currently on the payroll. Those who are members of the union must maintain their membership, but those who have not joined the union need not join. As to new employees, they must join the union within a specified period of time after hire--again, usually after the probationary period. This form of union security is a compromise which protects current employees who do not wish to join the union. The movement from a modified union shop to a union shop is sometimes effected by a clause which states that after a certain percentage of employees have joined the union, all those remaining out must join the union.

Maintenance of Membership

A more permissive union security arrangement is a maintenance-of-membership arrangement. In the maintenance-of-membership shop, members of the bargaining unit are not required to become members of the union to keep their jobs, but those employees who do decide to join the union must maintain their membership in the union for a specific length of time: either one year or for the duration of the contract. This is called an "escape" period. It clarifies the time when union members may drop out of the union without losing their jobs. The following is a typical maintenance-of-membership clause:

> Any employee who is a member in good standing of the union at the end of thirty (30) days from the date the provision becomes effective or who thereafter joins the union during the term of this agreement shall remain a member of the union in good standing as a condition of employment with the health care facility.

It is clear under this agreement that nonmembers have no duty to join the union.

Agency Shop

The agency shop was a comparatively rare form of union security which had a rebirth as a counterposition of unions to right-to-work laws. Section 14(b) gave state "right-to-work" laws precedence over union shop provisions of the Act. It stated:

> Nothing in this Act shall be construed as authorizing the execution or application of agreements requiring membership in a labor organization as a condition of employment in any State or Territory where such... is prohibited....

Right-to-work laws outlawed mandatory or compulsory union membership. Under an agency shop requirement, the employee can join or not join the union and can remain a member or drop out, but all employees in the bargaining unit represented by the union must pay a service fee to support the union as a condition of employment. This service fee is usually equal to the amount paid by union members for dues. The Supreme Court, in NLRB v. General Motors Corporation (373 U.S. 734, 53 LRRM 2313, 1963), upheld union security provisions calling for an agency shop. The Court stated in its decision that Congress, in passing the Taft-Hartley Act, did not intend to make the union shop the only valid union security device, but, rather, meant to limit the union's power to obtain discharge for any reason other than nonpayment of dues. The Court held that the agency shop is "the practical equivalent of union 'membership' as Congress used the term in the proviso to 8(a)(3)" and is therefore legal. Right-to-work laws have been enacted in twenty states. Fourteen states have provided for such arrangements by statute: Alabama, Georgia, Iowa, Louisiana, Nevada, North Carolina, North Dakota, South Carolina, South Dakota, Tennessee, Texas, Utah, Virginia and Wyoming. In the case of Louisiana, the statute applies only to agricultural workers. Six states provided constitutional amendments dealing with the right to work: Arizona, Arkansas, Florida, Kansas, Mississippi and Nebraska.

The absence of any form of union security is generally referred to as an open shop. Under the open shop, employees can join or not join the union as they see fit and can remain in or drop out of the union without losing their jobs.

ARGUMENTS ABOUT MANDATORY UNION MEMBERSHIP

Specific forms of union security are not mandated items which employers must incorporate in a collective bargaining agreement. The employer must bargain over the form and extent of a union security provision across the table. Labor leaders in presenting their arguments in favor of compulsory union membership base their position primarily on the so-called "free rider" inequity. The "free rider" employee, labor leaders argue, reaps all the advantages hard won by the union in their negotiations with the institution, yet is not required to support the union. Regardless of the type of union security agreement, all employees (even those that do not belong to the union) are covered by conditions of the contract if they are part of the bargaining unit. If the employees are given the option to remain out of the union, they are nonetheless covered by all provisions of the collective bargaining agreement including the grievance procedure; however, they may not attend meetings and may not vote on union issues. Union leaders maintain that the philosophy of compulsory union membership is rooted in a basic democratic principle: the rule of the majority. It is their position that given a free choice, employees will join the union but that usually they remain out because of fear of reprisal or promise of reward by the employer.

Management, in defending its position for optional membership across the table in collective bargaining, usually does so on the basis of the inherent right of the individual to make choices and therefore to withhold his membership from any organization. It is well to note that in actual practice, there are some advantages to management in agreeing to a compulsory union security provision. Too often when the employees are given an option to join or not join the union, only the most militant and outspoken critics of management join the union and their views are not modified by those of more conservative employees. Additionally, in a modified union security arrangement, the union continues its drive to enroll employees and often undertakes this activity during the normal workdays throughout the year.

In summary, the position of the union in support of its argument across the negotiating table for compulsory union membership is based on its need to continue its existence and to service the employees effectively; it maintains that in order to do this it must have financial support from all employees. Its argument is bolstered by its very presence at the negotiating table which was established by majority rule. Union leaders maintain that since a majority of the employees voted for the union, all employees in the bargaining unit should be required under the compulsory union security clause to join the union. This, they further state, will reduce strife and factionalism. On the other side of the table, employers, in negotiating union security agreements, state that compulsory union membership is an undemocratic mechanism. They wish to insure freedom of choice. Employers maintain that their position in support of a lesser form of union security is not part and parcel of an attempt to undermine the union. They further state that forcing employees to join the union when they do not wish to will not contribute to more harmonious or responsible labor relations. In fact, employees who are forced to join a union under a compulsory union security arrangement often are resentful and may indeed terminate their employment.

UNION SECURITY DISCHARGES

Section 8(a)(3) of the Act forbids the discharge or suspension of an employee under a union shop contract for loss of membership in good standing in the union except where such loss of membership is caused by the employee's failure to pay or tender payment of his union dues and initiation fee. It also forbids the discharge of an employee under a union shop contract if the employee was denied membership in the union on the same terms and conditions as all other employees who are members of the union. The Board has ruled that union membership must be available on a fair and nondiscriminatory basis. It has further stated that any requirement for membership in addition to dues and an initiation fee may not be used as a basis for the nonmember's discharge even if such requirement is fair and nondiscriminatory. Where an employee tendered the requisite money to the union but refused to attend meetings or take an oath of loyalty, the Board found both the institution and the union guilty of unfair labor practices for discharging the employee for nonmembership.

It is clear that after an employee joins a union, he can only be discharged for violation of a union shop agreement on the basis of his failure to tender his dues to the union.

CHECKOFF

The checkoff is an arrangement included in a collective bargaining agreement under which the dues and initiation fees of members of the bargaining unit are deducted from employee payroll checks by the employer and forwarded to the union. It is illegal to automatically checkoff union dues. In order to legally effect a checkoff arrangement under provisions of the Act, the employer must obtain written authorization cards from each employee. Section 302(c) of the Act authorizes an employer to deduct union dues from the employee's pay and forward such funds to the union only on the basis of an authorization card signed by the employee--such authorization cannot be irrevocable for more than one year or the duration of the existing collective bargaining agreement providing for the checkoff, whichever is the shorter period. The term "dues" has been interpreted to include initiation fees and general assessments uniformly leveled. A sample checkoff clause follows:

> 1. Upon receipt of a written authorization from an employee, the health care facility shall, pursuant to such authorization, deduct from the wages due said employee each month, starting not earlier than the first pay period following the completion of the employee's first thirty (30) days of employment, and remit to the union regular monthly dues and initiation fees, as fixed by the union. The initiation fee shall be paid in two (2) consecutive monthly installments beginning the month following the completion of the probationary period.
> 2. Employees who do not sign written authorizations for deductions must adhere to the same payment procedure by making payments directly to the union.
> 3. The health care facility shall be relieved from making such "check-off" deductions upon (a) termination of employment, or (b) transfer to a job other than one covered by the bargaining unit, or (c) lay-off from work, or (d) an agreed leave of absence, or (e) revocation of the check-off authorization in accordance with its terms or with applicable law. Notwithstanding the foregoing, upon the return of an employee to work from any of the foregoing enumerated absences, the health care facility will immediately resume the obligation of making said deductions, except that deductions for terminated employees shall be governed by paragraph 1 hereof. This provision, however, shall not relieve any employees of the obligation to make the required dues and initiation payment pursuant to the union constitution in order to remain in good

standing.
4. The health care facility shall not be obliged to make dues deductions of any kind from any employee who, during any dues month involved, shall have failed to receive sufficient wages to equal the dues deduction.
5. Each month, the health care facility shall remit to the union all deductions for dues and initiation fees made from the wages of employees for the preceding month, together with a list of all employees from whom dues and/or initiation fees have been deducted.
6. The health care facility agrees to furnish the union each month with the names of newly hired employees, their addresses, social security numbers, classifications of work, their dates of hire, and names of terminated employees, together with their dues of termination, and names of employees on leave of absence.
7. It is specifically agreed that the health care facility assumes no obligation, financial or otherwise, arising out of the provisions of this Article, and the union hereby agrees that it will indemnify and hold the health care facility harmless from any claims, actions or proceedings by any employee arising from deductions made by the health care facility hereunder. Once the funds are remitted to the union, their disposition thereafter shall be the sole and exclusive obligation and responsibility of the union.

Some institutions attempt to negotiate checkoff clauses in exchange for an arrangement which will reimburse the institution for the cost of operating such a program. In addition, a safeguard commonly found in checkoff provisions in collective bargaining agreements is a clause which clearly states that the union will assume responsibility for dues collection if the employee's earnings are curtailed. This is a guarantee that the union will relieve the institution of any legal liability growing out of improper deduction of union dues by the institution. No matter what shape or form the union's demand for a checkoff provision takes, the employer has a duty to bargain concerning the dues checkoff. This position was clearly stated by the Board (U.S. Gypsum Company, 94 NLRB 112, 28 LRRM 1015, 1951).

Although the checkoff is at times a controversial negotiating item and is often resisted by institutions, some employers feel that by agreeing to a checkoff provision they prevent the disruption and hostility which may develop from continuous activity on the part of union officers and delegates in their duties to collect dues.

RELIGIOUS OBJECTIONS AND UNION SECURITY

Section 19 was added to the Act by the 1974 amendments stating that

> Any employee of a health care institution who is a member of and adheres to established and traditional tenets or teachings of a bona fide religion, body, or sect which has historically held conscientious objections to joining or financially supporting labor organizations shall not be required to join or financially support any labor organization as a condition of employment; except that such employee may be required in lieu of periodic dues and initiation fees, to pay sums equal to such dues and initiation fees to a nonreligious charitable fund exempt from taxation under section 501 (c)(3) of the Internal Revenue Code, chosen by such employee from a list of at least three such funds, designated in a contract between such institution and a labor organization, or if the contract fails to designate such funds, then to any such fund chosen by the employee.

This section holds that employees of health care facilities who object on religious grounds to joining or financially supporting a labor organization shall not be required to do so as a condition of employment. It is important to note that this exclusion applies only to employees of health care facilities as defined in the Act. To be eligible for the exclusion the employee must be a member of a bona fide religion, body or sect that has historically held an objection to joining or financially supporting labor organizations. In lieu of union dues and fees the employee may be required to make payments to a nonreligious charitable fund. Designation of the funds can be made by the employer and union pursuant to the collective bargaining agreement.

X
The Labor Management Reporting and Disclosure (Landrum-Griffin) Act of 1959

BACKGROUND AND OBJECTIVES

The Labor-Management Reporting and Disclosure (Landrum-Griffin) Act was enacted into law in September 1959. The Act was a product of the McClellan committee which was chartered by the Senate to investigate alleged improper activities of managements and labor unions. Extensive investigations by the committee found "...that there [has] been a number of instances of breach of trust, corruption, disregard of the rights of individual employees, and other failures to observe high standards of responsibility and ethical conduct..." The objectives of the Act are stated in Section 2(a):

> The Congress, therefore, further finds and declares that the enactment of the Act is necessary to eliminate or prevent improper practices on the part of labor organizations, employers, labor relations consultants, and their officers and representatives which distort and defeat the policies of the Labor Management Relations Act of 1947, as amended...and have the tendency or necessary effect of burdening or disrupting commerce.

The Labor-Management Reporting and Disclosure Act (LMRDA) covers a broad range of topics; however, its major provisions can be grouped into the following additions to and alterations of the nation's labor law which

1. implement specific amendments to the National Labor Relations Act;
2. require the filing and reporting of certain acts committed by labor organizations and of information in their possession;
3. call for the disclosure of certain financial transactions by labor organization officers and employees;
4. require employers to report certain financial

dealings and agreements;
5. require the filing of reports by labor relations consultants engaged in certain activities;
6. specify the rights of union members;
7. delineate certain guidelines that must be followed with respect to union elections and the management of trust funds; and
8. bar members of the Communist Party and those convicted of certain crimes from holding office in a labor union or an employer association and prohibit such persons from acting as labor relations consultants.

The Taft-Hartley Act as enacted in 1947 contained provisions for filing certain reports and affidavits, but did not require unions to comply unless they wanted to use the services of the National Labor Relations Board. Since "local unions" were dealing with health care facilities not generally covered by the Act, and therefore not under NLRB jurisdiction, they had no reason or duty to file such material. As noted above, the LMRDA replaced the National Labor Relations Act's reporting requirements and established mandatory provisions. Although not covered by the Taft-Hartley Act, voluntary nonprofit health care facilities were nonetheless held to be included within the provisions of the LMRDA. In 1962 Arthur Goldberg, then Secretary of Labor, brought suit against the Public Building Service, Hospital and Industrial Employees' Union, Local 113. The union, which represented 2,500 nonprofessional employees in twenty voluntary hospitals and nursing homes in the Minneapolis area, was charged with failing to file copies of its constitution, bylaws and yearly financial statements with the Department of Labor. The union contended that it was involved in local activities only, and that as a result it should not be covered by the LMRDA. It also argued that reports were not filed because its members received no protection under federal labor law. The case was decided in favor of the Secretary's petition, thus confirming that labor unions who deal with enterprises then not covered by the NLRA were nonetheless susceptible to provisions of the LMRDA.

Although health care facilities are now covered by the NLRA as amended, their status under the LMRDA remains unchanged. Health facilities, unions dealing with them and labor relations consultants are subject to the requirements of the Act. The sections of this chapter that follow will examine selected provisions of the Labor-Management Reporting and Disclosure Act of 1959 as it applies to health care facilities.

TAFT-HARTLEY AMENDMENTS

The LMRDA made a series of amendments to the National Labor

Relations Act of 1947 in addition to enacting a series of new provisions. Some of the more important alterations in the NLRA are noted below.

1. Section 8(b)(7), which places restrictions on the picketing activities of noncertified unions, was added.

2. The "hot cargo" provisions of Section 8(e) were added. As noted in Chapter VI, such agreements between a labor organization and an employer are prohibited except in the garment and construction trades.

3. The construction industry was given broader latitude to negotiate union security agreements than other sectors of the economy under the jurisdiction of the Act.

4. Regional offices of the National Labor Relations Board were accorded expanded responsibilities to hear election cases.

5. Economic strikers were permitted to vote in representational elections up to twelve months following the initiation of a recognitional strike even though they might not be entitled to reinstatement.

When the LMRDA was enacted, twelve years had passed since the Taft-Hartley amendments to the NLRA had become law. As with the Taft-Hartley amending the Wagner Act of 1935, Congress realized that periodic adjustments were needed in the nation's labor laws. The amendments to the NLRA contained in the Labor-Management Reporting and Disclosure Act further refined the responsibilities of unions and managements with regard to their interrelationship in the process of collective bargaining.

LABOR ORGANIZATION REPORTING REQUIREMENTS

Title III, Section 201 (a), of the Labor-Management Reporting and Disclosure Act provides that every labor organization must adopt a constitution and bylaws and file a copy of each with the Secretary of Labor. In addition, in a report to the Secretary of Labor, a labor organization must file the following information:

1. the name of the labor organization, its mailing address, and any other addresses at which it maintains its principal office or at which it keeps records and papers referred to in the provisions of the Act;
2. the name and title of each union officer;
3. the initiation fees or other payments required of a new or transferred member and fees for work permits required by the reporting labor organization; and
4. the regular dues or fees or other such periodic payments required of a member to retain membership in the reporting labor organization.

In addition to the above reports, the labor organization must file detailed statements, or references to specific provisions of documents provided through the aforementioned requirements (e.g., constitution and bylaws), which demonstrate provisions made and procedures followed with respect to each of the following:

1. qualifications for and/or restrictions upon gaining membership to the labor organization;
2. levying of assessments;
3. participation in insurance and/or other benefit plans;
4. authorizations for disbursement of funds of the labor organization;
5. audit of financial transactions of the labor organization;
6. calling of regular and special meetings;
7. selection of officers and stewards and any representatives to other bodies composed of the labor organization's representatives, with a specific statement of the manner in which each officer was elected, appointed or otherwise selected;
8. discipline or removal of officers or agents for breach of trust;
9. imposition of fines, suspensions, and expulsions of members, including the grounds for such action and any provisions made for notice, hearings, judgment on the evidence and appeal procedures;
10. authorizations for bargaining demands;
11. ratification of contract terms;
12. authorizations for strikes or other job actions; and
13. issuance of work permits.

The aforementioned report must be filed by the union when it comes under the Act (i.e., in 1959, when the Act was passed) or when a new union gains a charter; special forms are available from the Department of Labor on which to report the requested information. Any changes in practices and procedures of the union must be transmitted to the Secretary of Labor at the end of the union's financial reporting period.

The Act specifies that unions must also report on certain financial transactions. The report must be filed no less than ninety days after the close of the union's accounting year. A special form (LM-3) has been designed for this purpose, although unions with less than $30,000 gross annual receipts are allowed to submit a simplified report. The Labor-Management Reporting and Disclosure Act provides that unions must provide a financial report detailing

1. assets and liabilities at the beginning and end of the fiscal year;
2. receipts of any kind and their source;
3. salary, allowances and other direct or indirect disbursements (including reimbursed expenses) to each officer and to each employee who during the reporting period received more than $10,000 from the labor organization or any labor organization affiliated with the union filing the report;
4. direct and indirect loans made to any officer, employee or member, which in the aggregate exceeded $250 during the fiscal year, together with a statement of the purpose of the loan, security for the loan (if any) and the method of repayment;
5. direct or indirect loans to any business enterprise, together with a statement of purpose of the loan, the security put forward (if any), and arrangements for repayment; and
6. other disbursements and their purposes.

Upon being filed with the Secretary of Labor the reports by labor organizations become public information. The Act, in Section 201 (c), specifies that information reported by the union be available for inspection by members. Union members also have the right to examine the union's financial reports, books, accounts and other such documents in order to verify the accuracy of the reports filed under the Act. Members can enforce these rights through the federal courts or in a state court. Copies of the reports filed by labor organizations can be obtained from the Department of Labor for the cost of their reproduction.

REPORTS OF LABOR-UNION OFFICERS AND EMPLOYEES

Title II, Section 202(a), of the Act specifies requirements regarding certain financial transactions of union officials and employees (with the exception of those workers hired to perform exclusively clerical or custodial tasks). As with other reports detailed in the previous section of this chapter, such information must be supplied to the Secretary of Labor no less than ninety days after the close of the individual's tax-reporting period. The requirements of this section stem from the McClellan committee findings that certain union officials had received both direct and indirect payments to negotiate "soft" or "sweetheart" contracts with managements (the reporting of payments by employers for these and other purposes are discussed later in this chapter). The Secretary has the authority to make reasonable investigations regarding the accuracy of information provided in the reports. As with reports filed by unions, the reports submitted by labor organization officials and employees are public information.

Specifically, officers and employees of labor organizations must file reports describing

> 1. any stock, bond, security or other interest, legal or equitable, which he directly or indirectly held in, and any income or any other benefit with monetary value (including reimbursed expenses) which he derived directly or indirectly from, an employer whose employees such labor organization represents or is actively seeking to represent, except payments and other benefits received as a bona fide employee of such employer;
> 2. any transaction in which he engaged, directly or indirectly, involving any stock, bond, security or loan to or from, or other legal or equitable interest in the business of, an employer whose employees such labor organization represents or is actively seeking to represent;
> 3. any stock, bond, security, or other interest, legal or equitable, which he directly or indirectly held in, and any income or any other benefit with monetary value (including reimbursed expenses) which he directly or indirectly derived from, any business of which a substantial part consisted of buying from, selling or leasing to, or otherwise dealing with, the business of an employer whose employees such labor organization represents or is actively seeking to represent;
> 4. any stock, bond, security or other interest, legal or equitable, which he directly or indirectly held in, and any income or any other benefit with monetary value (including reimbursed expenses) which he directly or indirectly derived from, a business of which any part consists of buying from, or selling or leasing directly or indirectly to, or otherwise dealing with, the labor organization;
> 5. any direct or indirect business transaction or arrangement between him and any employer whose employees his organization represents or is actively seeking to represent, except work performed and payments and benefits received as a bona fide employee of such employer and except purchases and sales of goods or services in the regular course of business at prices generally available to any employee of such employer; and

6. any payment of money or other thing of value (including reimbursed expenses) which he received directly or indirectly from any employer or any person who acts as a labor relations consultant to an employer, except payments of the kinds referred to in Section 302(c) of the Labor-Management Relations Act, 1947, as amended.

The term "he" has a wide definition in that it means the labor union official or employee, his wife and any minor unmarried children. These provisions should not be construed as a requirement of union officials or employees to report bona fide investments in stocks or bonds traded on a regular securities exchange. Such individuals are not required to file reports unless they engage in one or more of the actions listed in the section.

REPORTS BY EMPLOYERS AND LABOR RELATIONS CONSULTANTS

In addition to requiring labor unions and labor union officials and employees to provide certain information to the Secretary of Labor, the Labor-Management Reporting and Disclosure Act also places a series of requirements upon managements and labor relations consultants (when acting in certain capacities). These reports, like the ones provided by unions, become public information and can be obtained from the Department of Labor for the cost of reproduction. Managements and labor consultants must maintain for five years the records substantiating the reports filed under the Act. The Secretary is supplied with the authority and power to audit the accuracy and completeness of the information supplied.

A report detailing the nature of the following financial transactions and/or arrangements must be filed:

1. any payment or loan, direct or indirect, of money or other thing of value (including reimbursed expenses), or any promise or agreement therefor, to any labor organization of officer, agent, shop steward or other representative of a labor organization, or employee of any labor organization, except (a) payments or loans made by any national or state bank, credit union, insurance company, savings and loan association or other credit institution, and (b) payments permitted under the Labor-Management Relations Act, 1947, as amended;
2. any payment (including reimbursed expenses) to any employees, or any group or committee of such employees, for the purpose of causing such employee or group or committee of employees to

persuade other employees to exercise or not to exercise, or as to the manner of exercising, the right to organize and bargain collectively through representatives of their own choosing unless such payments were contemporaneously or previously disclosed to such other employees;

3. any expenditure, during the fiscal year, where an object, directly or indirectly, is to interfere with, restrain or coerce employees in the exercise of the right to organize and bargain collectively through representatives of their own choosing, or is to obtain information concerning the activities of employees of a labor organization in connection with a labor dispute involving such employer, except for use solely in conjunction with an administrative or arbitral proceeding or a criminal or civil judicial proceeding;

4. any agreement or arrangement with a labor relations consultant or other independent contractor or organization pursuant to which such person undertakes activities where an object thereof, directly or indirectly, is to persuade employees to exercise or not to exercise, or persuade employees as to the manner of exercising the right to organize and bargain collectively through representatives of their own choosing, or undertakes to supply such employer with information concerning the activities of employees or a labor organization in connection with a labor dispute involving such employer, except information for use solely in conjunction with an administrative or arbitral proceeding or a criminal or civil judicial proceeding; and/or

5. any payment (including reimbursed expenses) pursuant to an agreement or arrangement described in (4) above.

The reports submitted must detail the date and amount of each payment or arrangement; the name, address and position of the person and firm to which the payment was made and/or the arrangement concluded; and a full explanation of the circumstances and terms of all such payments and arrangements. Employers are not required to file reports unless payments or arrangements of the kind noted above were made.

Reports also must be filed by persons, who, pursuant to any agreement or arrangement with an employer, undertakes activities where the object (directly or indirectly) is to (1) persuade employees to exercise or not to exercise, or persuade employees as to the manner of exercising, the right to organize and bargain collectively through representatives of their own choosing; or (2) to supply an employer with information concerning the activities of employees or a labor organization in connection with a labor dispute involving such employer, except information for use solely in conjunction with an administrative or arbitral proceeding or a criminal or civil judicial proceeding. Such reports must be filed with the Secretary of Labor no later than thirty days after the person has entered into such an agreement with an employer.

Labor relations consultants need not file reports regarding the forwarding of advice to an employer or representing an employer before a court, administrative agency or tribunal, or engaging in collective bargaining on behalf of the employer. Attorneys are not required (under Section 204 of the Act) to file information which was lawfully communicated in the course of a legitimate attorney-client relationship.

UNION MEMBER'S BILL OF RIGHTS

Title I, Section 101(a), of the Labor-Management Reporting and Disclosure Act specifies a bill of rights for the members of labor organizations. In including these provisions in the Act it was the intent of Congress to facilitate the insurance of union democracy. The section states that the provisions of any union's constitution inconsistent with the bill of rights shall have no force or effect. The rights guaranteed union membership are as follows:

Equal Rights

Every member of a labor organization shall have equal rights and privileges within such organization to nominate candidates, to vote in elections or referendums of the labor organization, to attend membership meetings, and to participate in the deliberations and voting upon the business of such meetings, subject to reasonable rules and regulations in such organization's constitution and bylaws.

Freedom of Speech and Assembly

Every member of any labor organization shall have the right to meet and assemble freely with other members; and to express any views, arguments or opinions, and to express at meetings of the labor organization his views, regarding candidates in an election of the labor organization or upon any business properly before the meeting, subject to the organization's established and reasonable rules pertaining to the conduct of meetings. Provided, that nothing required shall be construed to impair the right of a labor organization to adopt and enforce reasonable rules as to the responsibility of every member toward the organization as an institution and to his refraining from conduct that would interfere with its performance of its legal or contractual obligations.

Dues, Initiation Fees and Assessments

Except in the case of a federation of national or international labor organizations, the rates of dues and initiation fees payable by members of any labor organization in effect on the date of enactment of the Act shall not be increased, and no general or special assessment shall be levied upon such members, except by voting procedures as prescribed in the Act.

Protection of the Right to Sue

No labor organization shall limit the right of any member to institute an action in any court, or in a proceeding before any administrative agency, irrespective of whether or not the labor organization or its officers are named as defendants or respondents in such action or proceeding; or the right of any member of a labor organization to appear as a witness in any judicial, administrative, or legislative proceeding, or to petition any legislature or to communicate with any legislator. Members may be required to exhaust reasonable hearing procedures (but not to exceed a four-month lapse of time) within such organization before instituting legal or administrative proceedings against such organization of any officer thereof. No interested employer or employer association shall directly or indirectly finance, encourage or participate in, except as a party, any such action, proceeding, appearance or petition.

Safeguards against Improper Disciplinary Action

No member of any labor organization may be fined, suspended, expelled or otherwise disciplined except for nonpayment of dues by such organization or by any officer thereof unless such member has been (1) served with written specific charges; (2) given a reasonable time to prepare his defense; and (3) afforded a full and fair hearing.

OTHER PROVISIONS OF THE ACT

In addition to the provisions noted above, the Labor-Management Reporting and Disclosure Act details requirements regarding the administration of trusteeships, the conduct of union elections and safeguards for labor organization.

Trusteeships

Section 301(a), Title III, of the LMRDA delineates procedures that must be followed by labor unions in the creation and administration of trusteeships. A parent labor union can put a subordinate organization (e.g., a local affiliate of the union) under trusteeship for "legitimate purposes," and then only in accordance with the parent union's constitution and bylaws. Within thirty days of the imposition of the trusteeship (and semiannually thereafter) the following information must be filed with the Secretary of Labor by the officers of both the parent and subordinate labor organization:

1. name and address of the subordinate organization;
2. the date of the trusteeship's establishment;
3. a detailed statement of the reasons for establishing or continuing the trusteeship; and
4. the nature and extent of participation by the membership of the subordinate organization in the selection of delegates to represent such organizations in regular or special conventions or other policy-determining bodies and in the election of officers at the labor organization which has assumed trusteeship over the subordinate.

The report must also include a complete account of the financial condition of the subordinate at the time trusteeship is assumed by the parent labor organization. During the period of the trusteeship the parent labor union is required to file financial reports for the subordinate organization which are required by the Act (i.e., labor union financial reports specified at Section 201(b) of the LMRDA).

The law specifies several reasons for which a trusteeship may be executed; some examples are (1) correcting corruption of financial malpractices on the part of the officers or executives of the subordinate organizations; (2) assuring the effective performance of collective bargaining agreements or other duties of a bargaining representative; (3) restoring democratic procedures in the subordinate organization; or (4) otherwise carrying out the legitimate objectives of such labor organization. After a period of eighteen months, the trusteeship of a subordinate organization is presumed to be invalid unless the parent union can demonstrate why it should be continued. If a member of the subordinate organization believes the trusteeship is illegal, he can file a complaint with the Secretary of Labor, who has authority to investigate the situation. If the Secretary of Labor finds cause to believe that the requirements of the Act have probably been violated, he may file a petition with the court to have the trusteeship dissolved or may seek to reinstate the status quo.

In the administration of a trusteeship, it is unlawful to count the vote of delegates from such body in any convention or election of officers of the labor organization unless the delegates have been chosen by secret ballot in which all the members in good standing of the subordinate body were eligible to vote. Second, the parent organization is restrained from transferring any funds from the subordinate group other than normal per capita taxes and assessments payable by subordinate bodies not in trusteeship.

Union Elections

Through Section 401, Title IV, the Labor-Management Reporting and Disclosure Act specifies in detail requirements and procedures that must be followed by labor organizations regarding terms of office and the conduct of elections.

Timing

Every national or international union organization must elect its officers not less than once every five years; each local union must elect officers at least once every three years. Such elections must be conducted by secret ballot among the members in good standing or at a convention of delegates chosen through a secret ballot.

Campaign Literature

Labor organizations must comply with all reasonable requests of any candidate for a union office to distribute, at the candidate's expense, literature supporting such person's election to all members in good standing. Unions are forbidden from discriminating in favor of or against candidates with regard to the disclosure of membership lists or other such records. Every bona fide candidate has the right to inspect the membership roster of the union within thirty days of the date established for the election.

Observers

The union is required to take all necessary steps to ensure that elections are conducted fairly. Every bona fide candidate is allowed to have one observer at each polling place and may have a representative present when the ballots are counted.

Committees and Boards

Officers of intermediate bodies of the labor organization such as general committees, joint councils, systems boards, etc., must be elected not less than once every four years through a secret ballot among members in good standing or by labor organization officers representative of such members who have been selected by secret ballot.

Nomination and Voting

Reasonable opportunity shall be accorded members of the union in good standing to either run for office or nominate candidates. Such members have the right to vote or otherwise support the candidates of his choice without being subject to penalty, discipline or improper interference or reprisal of any kind. Notice of the above rights must be mailed to each union member at his last known address not less than fifteen days prior to a scheduled election. No member whose dues have been withheld from his paycheck through a valid "checkoff" authorization can be declared ineligible to vote in an election by reason of alleged delay or default in the payment of dues.

Counting and Records

The votes cast by members of each local labor organization in a national or international union election must be counted and the results published separately. Ballots and all other records pertaining to the election of officers at that convention must also be retained for one year.

Campaign Financing

No funds received by a labor organization through dues, assessments or other levies can be employed to finance the candidacy of any person seeking office in an election subject to control of the Act. Employers are prohibited from making contributions to union campaigns. Unions are allowed to make expenditures for the distribution of factual notices, and a statement of issues not involving candidates and for other purposes necessary for the conduct of an election.

Members in good standing with the union may file a complaint with the Secretary of Labor regarding the abridgment of rights guaranteed by this section. Before filing a complaint the union member is required to have exhausted remedies available under the constitution and bylaws of the union. After a finding that probable cause exists for a violation of the Act, the Secretary may seek redress in the federal courts.

Safeguards for Labor Organizations

Title IV of the Labor Management Reporting and Disclosure Act seeks to provide certain safeguards for labor organizations regarding fiduciary responsibilities of officers (Section 501), bonding of union offices and agents (Section 502), the making of loans and the payment of fines (Section 503), and prohibitions against certain persons holding office in labor organizations.

Section 501 of the Act notes that the officers, agents, shop stewards and other representatives of labor organizations hold positions of trust with relationship to the organization and its members. The Act states that:

> It is, therefore, the duty of each such person, taking into account the special problems and functions of a labor organization, to hold its money and property solely for the benefit of the organization and its members and to manage, invest, and expend the same in accordance with its constitution and bylaws and any resolutions of the governing bodies adopted thereunder, to refrain from dealing with such organization as an adverse party or in behalf of an adverse party in any matter connected with his duties and from holding or acquiring any pecuniary or personal interest which conflicts with the interests of such organization, and to account to the organization for any profit received by him in whatever capacity in connection with transactions conducted by him or under his direction on behalf of the organization.

The Act holds that when an officer or agent is alleged to have violated the duties prescribed in the provision, any member of the labor organization may sue in a state or federal court to recover damages or to secure other appropriate relief. Embezzlement, theft or misappropriation of labor organization assets is punishable by a fine of not more than $10,000, imprisonment up to five years, or both.

Section 502 provides that labor organization officers, agents, shop stewards or other representatives who handle funds must be bonded for the faithful discharge of their duties. The bond of each person is required to be set at 10 percent of the funds handled by him (or his predecessor in that position) during the preceding accounting year, although the amount bonded need not exceed $500,000. Any person not bonded as required by the Act is prohibited from handling union funds.

Section 503 states that a labor organization cannot make a loan to officers and employees which results in a total indebtedness exceeding $2,000 on the part of such individuals to the union. The provision also prohibits the union from directly or indirectly paying the fine of any officer or employee convicted of a willful violation of the Act.

Prohibitions against certain persons holding office in a labor organization are specified in Section 504. Persons who have been members of the Communist Party or who have been convicted of certain crimes cannot serve

> 1. as an officer, director, trustee, member of any executive board or similar governing body, business agent, manager, organizer, or other employee (other than as an employee performing exclusively clerical or custodial duties) of any labor organization; or
> 2. as a labor relations consultant to a person engaged in an industry or activity affecting commerce, or as an officer, director, agent, or employee (other than as an employee performing exclusively clerical or custodial duties) of any group or association of employers dealing with any labor organization.

The prohibition has effect for a period of five years after termination of Communist Party membership or for five years subsequent to being convicted of specified crimes.

XI

Administration of the Act: Organization and Function of the National Labor Relations Board

THE NATIONAL LABOR RELATIONS BOARD

The National Labor Relations Act created the National Labor Relations Board. The Taft-Hartley amendments of 1947 modified the functions of the Board; the 1974 amendments broadened the jurisdiction of the Board to health care facilities. The National Labor Relations Board is comprised of five individuals (the Board had three members under the original Wagner Act). All appointments to the Board are made by the President of the United States with the advice and consent of the Senate; members of the Board are appointed for terms of five years each, except in the case of an individual chosen to fill a vacancy who is appointed only for the unexpired term of the member whom he succeeds.

The President also appoints the General Counsel of the Board who serves for a four-year term. The Board, General Counsel and his staff are located in Washington, D.C. To facilitate the work of the Board, thirty-one regional offices have been established (for a listing of regional offices and their directors see Exhibit 11.1). The Board is duly authorized under the Act to delegate to its regional directors any of its powers under Section 9, such as the determination of appropriate units, investigation of claims of representation including hearings, and the determination of whether a question of representation exists. The Board delegates to the regional directors the authority to conduct elections.

DUTIES OF THE BOARD

The principal functions of the Board are quasi-judicial in nature. The duties of the Board are to

1. conduct secret ballot elections among employees in appropriate units to determine whether or not the employees wish to be represented by a labor organization;
2. prevent and remedy unfair labor practices committed by either party (employers or unions);
3. poll employees on their employer's last offer

in national emergency situations;
4. determine the authority of representatives to have union shop provisions in their collective bargaining agreements; and to
5. determine jurisdictional disputes which have led to the filing of unfair labor practice charges.

Each of the five members of the Board (whose terms are staggered) have a Chief Counsel and an Assistant Chief Counsel plus a staff of approximately twenty-five attorneys. The Board also has an Executive Secretary who is responsible for administrative services and who functions much like the clerk of a court.

GENERAL COUNSEL

The Act provides that there shall be a General Counsel of the Board who is appointed by the President with the advice and consent of the Senate. The General Counsel serves for a term of four years; his functions and jurisdiction are outlined under Section 3(d) of the Act. They are as follows:

1. The General Counsel has final authority on behalf of the Board in respect to the investigation of charges and issuance of complaints under Section 10 and in respect to the prosecution of such complaints before the Board.
2. The General Counsel exercises general supervision over all attorneys employed by the Board except those serving as trial examiners or legal assistants to Board members. The Board has delegated to the General Counsel supervision of all non-attorney employees in its Washington offices.
3. The General Counsel is delegated authority to apply to the courts for injunctions.
4. The General Counsel is responsible for securing compliance with the Board's orders.
5. The General Counsel exercises supervision over the officers and employees of the Regional Offices.

TRIAL EXAMINERS' DIVISION

The Trial Examiners' Division conducts formal hearings on unfair labor practice complaints. The trial examiners are independent both of the Board and the General Counsel, although they are bound by Board precedent. Their independence is clearly established by Section 4(a) of the Act which stipulates that

> No Trial Examiner's report shall be reviewed either before or after its publication by any person other than a member of the Board or his legal assistant and no Trial Examiner shall advise or consult with the Board with respect to exceptions taken to his findings, rulings or recommendations.

The functions of the trial examiners can be compared to those of judges. They are appointed for life; they hear witnesses; they rule on the admissibility of evidence; they render initial decisions and findings of fact in unfair labor practice cases; they are not involved with the decision or consideration by the appellate body, which is the Board.

Two major functions of the Board are determining a bargaining representative and investigating and preventing unfair labor practices. The procedure for selecting or rejecting a bargaining representative by secret ballot is contained in Section 9(c) of the Act. The procedure for investigating and preventing unfair labor practices is listed in Section 8 of the Act.

SELECTING A BARGAINING AGENT

Section 9(c) sets forth the procedures under which employees may express their preference regarding union representation. The procedure is set in motion by the filing of a petition with the regional director for the region where the employee bargaining unit is located. The Act stipulates that a petition may be filed by

> 1. an individual or labor organization acting on behalf of a substantial number of employees;
> 2. an employer from whom one or more individuals or labor organizations claim recognition as exclusive bargaining representative of the employer's employees; or
> 3. an employee or group of employees claiming that a certified or properly recognized bargaining unit no longer represents a majority of the employees in an appropriate bargaining unit.

The Board has established rules and regulations which cover the procedure for the determination of questions concerning representation of employees (such procedures have been discussed in Chapter V). A brief review of the rules and regulations established by the Board for this process is warranted. The process is initiated through the filing of a petition for certification. It may be filed by any employee or group of employees or any individual or labor organization acting in their behalf. These petitions are filed in writing and submitted in the original plus four copies to the appropriate regional office. The Board will send both parties a copy of the petition and will forward a poster, which it suggests that the employer post, containing the rights of employees in representation cases. The employer need not post this notice. A Commerce Questionnaire to establish whether or not the Board can assert jurisdiction is forwarded at the same time. Soon thereafter, the employer receives an informal telephone call from the regional office to ascertain what his posture will be when the union requests recognition. The Board will request an Excelsior list, so named for a previous case which established the validity of such a request.[1] This list, containing the names and addresses of all unit employees, will be turned over to the union. The union must establish its showing of interest by demonstrating that at least 30 percent of the unit's employees have signed authorization cards. The Board will then schedule a representation hearing, usually thirty days after receipt of the petition. The hearing is usually conducted by a staff attorney and is nonadversary in nature. The regional office will then issue a decision and schedule an election for an appropriate unit or it may dismiss the petition. The mechanics of the election procedure have been discussed earlier.

INVESTIGATION AND PREVENTION OF UNFAIR LABOR PRACTICES

Another major responsibility of the Board is the investigation and prevention of unfair labor practices. The Board can only act upon the forwarding of a charge, which any individual or organization may file. The charge must be in writing and signed; the Board requires that it be either notarized or contain a declaration by the person signing it that its contents are true and correct. Such charges must contain the name and address of the person against whom the charge is made and a statement of the facts constituting the alleged unfair labor practice. The form upon which a charge is filed is made available at regional offices. It must be signed and sworn to or affirmed under oath. Under Section 10 of the Act, it is necessary for the Board to issue a complaint stating the charges and notifying the charged party of the hearing held concerning the charges. The regional office issues a complaint after investigation of the charges and then only if there is reasonable evidence supporting the fact that an unfair labor practice may have been committed. The regional director will request the person filing the charge to submit a statement of his position. A Board agent, generally a member of the field staff from a regional office, investigates the facts of the case. Section 10(l) provides that whenever a charge is filed alleging a violation of certain sections of the Act relating to boycotts, picketing and work stoppages, the preliminary investigation of the charge must be given priority over all other types of cases in the regional office where it is filed. The unfair labor practices subject to this priority concerning the investigation are those defined in Section 8(b)(4)(A), (B), or (C), all three paragraphs of Section 8(b)(7), and Section 8(e). Section 10(m) requires that second priority be given to charges alleging violations of Section 8(a)(3), the prohibition against employer discrimination to encourage or discourage membership in a union, and Section 8(b)(2), which forbids unions to cause or attempt to cause discrimination.

The regional director may dispense with any portion of the investigation if he deems it necessary. In making such a decision he considers the amount of time necessary to complete a full investigation and the nature of the proceeding and, most important, the public interest. The Board agent interviews the parties and may request written statements from all potential witnesses. If the Board agent, on the basis of his investigation, finds that the charge has no merit, the case will be withdrawn or dismissed. The complainant may request such withdrawal on his own. If it is the regional director's determination to recommend withdrawal of the charge, the complainant may accept the recommendation or request withdrawal on his own initiative. In that case the respondent will be notified of such withdrawal. If the complainant refuses to withdraw the charge as recommended by the regional director, the director may dismiss the charge. If the General Counsel upholds the regional director's action, there is no right to Board or court review. The charging party has ten days from the receipt of the regional director's letter notifying him of his action to appeal such action. If the investigation by the Board agent reflects merit in the charge, an attempt will be made to secure a settlement. There are two types of settlements: the informal and the formal. The regional director must approve all informal settlements. This type of settlement is commonly found where the Board determines that there is not a likelihood of a repetition of such action which caused the charge. It is often accompanied by a "nonadmission" clause, which in effect is a statement by the charged party that it will undertake to remedy the unfair labor practice without admitting guilt. Formal settlement is almost always included in a stipulation.

The regional office will provide forms for such settlement agreements. It is also possible to obtain a settlement after the issuance of a complaint even though the formal proceedings have started. The Board attempts at all points to arrive at an amicable adjustment which is in compliance with the law. In cases where the Board determines that the complaint has merit and a settlement is not obtained, the formal complaint will be issued and a hearing will be held before a trial examiner.

The government's case is handled by an attorney attached to the Board's regional office. The case is heard before an administrative-law judge, also known as a trial examiner. It is conducted in accordance with the provisions of the National Labor Relations Act, the Administrative Procedure Act and the Board's rules and regulations. The rules of evidence applicable in the district courts of the United States are in effect. The parties are given ample opportunity to present evidence and may be represented by an attorney or any other representative who, like the administrative-law judge, has the power to call, examine and cross-examine witnesses. An official reporter is present, and all matters presented in the hearing room are recorded except those that the trial examiner specifically notes as off-the-record discussions. Exhibits are permissible and the administrative-law judge (trial examiner) is called upon to rule on admissibility of exhibits and evidence. Both parties are entitled to make closing oral arguments, and before the close of the hearing, are entitled to file a brief.

At the end of the hearing, the trial examiner prepares and files with the Board a decision in which he states his findings of fact, his conclusions and the reasons for his determination. He has the option to recommend dismissal or to sustain the complaint in whole or in part and recommend that the respondent cease and desist from the unlawful act. When the trial examiner files his decision with the Board, his official connection with the case ceases and the Board transfers the case to itself. At this point the parties may accept the recommendations of the trial examiner, thereby ending the process. On the other hand, the parties or the counsel for the Board may file exceptions to the trial examiner's decision with the Board. The parties may, in support of their exception, request permission to appear and argue orally before the Board in Washington, D.C.

Section 10(b) provides that "no complaint shall issue based upon any unfair labor practice occurring more than six months prior to the filing of the charge with the Board and the service of a copy thereof upon the person against whom such charge is made." An exception is made if the charging party was prevented from filing such charge by reason of service in the Armed Forces, in which event the six-month period shall be computed from the day of his discharge. The Board is authorized by Section 10(c) not only to issue a cease and desist order, but to take such affirmative action, including reinstatement of employees with or without back pay, as will effectuate the policies of this Act.

Some typical affirmative actions of the Board in unfair labor practice cases are to order an employer to

1. disestablish an employer-dominated union;
2. offer certain named individuals immediate and full reinstatement to their former positions or, if those positions no longer exist, to substantially equivalent positions without prejudice to their seniority and other rights and privileges and with back pay including interest; or

3. upon request bargain collectively with a certain union as the exclusive representative of the employees in a certain described unit and sign a written agreement if an understanding is reached.

The Board may also require a union which it has found to have engaged in an unfair labor practice to

1. notify the employer and the employee that it has no objection to reinstatement of certain employees or employment of certain applicants whose discriminatory discharge or denial of employment was caused by the union;
2. refund dues or fees illegally collected plus interest; or
3. upon request bargain collectively with a certain employer and sign a written agreement if one is reached.

If a party found guilty of an unfair labor practice fails to comply with a Board order, the Board is empowered to either close the case or petition a U.S. court of appeals for a court decree enforcing its order. Section 10(j) gives the Board discretion and does not require that injunctive relief be sought. On petition of the Board for court enforcement made to a U.S. court of appeals, the court can enforce, modify or set aside in whole or in part the order. Further appeal of the court's order may be made to the Supreme Court. The Supreme Court in such cases can affirm, reverse or modify a circuit court of appeals order or, as it has done in many cases, remit the case back for further action. Section 10(f) provides that an aggrieved person--so aggrieved by an order of the Board which grants or denies in whole or in part the relief sought--may obtain a review of such order in any appropriate circuit court of appeals. Here again the court may enforce the order or remand it to the Board for reconsideration. It may also change the order or set it aside entirely. If the court of appeals issues a decree enforcing the Board order, failure to comply may be punishable by fine or imprisonment for contempt of court.

Footnotes

1. Excelsior Underwear, Inc., 156 NLRB 1236, 61 LRRM 1217 (1961). This decision provided for a requirement applicable to all election cases; within seven (7) days after the regional director has approved a consent-election agree-

ment entered into by the parties or after the regional director or the Board has directed an election, the employer must file with the regional director an election eligibility list, containing the names and addresses of all the eligible voters. The regional director, in turn, shall make this information available to all parties in the case. Failure to comply with this requirement shall be grounds for setting aside the election whenever proper objections are filed.

Exhibit 11.1. Directory of National Labor Relations Board: Regional Offices, Director and Attorneys

BOSTON, MASS. 02114, 7th floor, Bulfinch Bldg., 15 New Chardon St.; Telephone: (617) 223-3330
Director: Robert S. Fuchs; Regional Attorney: Harold M. Kowal

NEW YORK, N.Y. 10007, 36th floor, Federal Bldg., 26 Federal Plaza; Telephone: (212) 264-0300
Director: Sidney Danielson; Regional Attorney: Winifred Morio

BUFFALO, N.Y. 14202, 9th floor, Federal Bldg., 111 W. Huron St.; Telephone: (716) 842-3100
Director: Thomas W. Seeler; Regional Attorney: Thomas Ramsey

PHILADELPHIA, PA. 19107, 1700 Bankers Security Bldg., Walnut & Juniper Sts.; Telephone: (215) 597-7601
Director: Bernard L. Samoff; Regional Attorney: Leonard Leventhal

BALTIMORE, MD. 21201, Room 1019, Federal Bldg., Charles Center; Telephone: (301) 962-2822
Director: John A. Penello; Regional Attorney: David C. Sachs

PITTSBURGH, PA. 15222, 1536 Federal Bldg., 1000 Liberty Ave.; Telephone: (412) 644-2977
Director: Henry Shore; Regional Attorney: Edward A. Grupp

DETROIT, MICH. 48226, 500 Book Bldg., 1249 Washington Blvd.; Telephone: (313) 226-3200
Director: Jerome H. Brooks; Regional Attorney: Bernard Gottfried

CLEVELAND, OHIO 44199, Room 1695, Federal Office Bldg., 1240 E. 9th St.; Telephone: (216) 522-3715
Director: Philip Fusco; Regional Attorney: Carroll L. Martin

CINCINNATI, OHIO 45202, Room 2407, Federal Office Bldg., 550 Main St.; Telephone: (513) 684-3686
Director: John C. Getreu; Regional Attorney: C. Emil Farkas

ATLANTA, GA. 30308, Room 701, 730 Peachtree St. NE;
Telephone: (404) 526-5760
Director: Walter G. Phillips; Regional Attorney:
William J. Rains

WINSTON-SALEM, N.C. 27101, 16th floor,
Wachovia Bldg., 301 N. Main St.; Telephone:
(919) 723-9211, Ext. 360
Director: Reed Johnston; Regional Attorney:
Hugh F. Malone

TAMPA, FLA. 33602, Room 706, Federal Office Bldg.,
500 Zack St.; Telephone: (812) 228-7711, Ext. 227
Director: Harold A. Boire; Regional Attorney:
Joseph Moran

CHICAGO, ILL. 60604, Room 881, Everett McKinley
Dirksen Bldg., 219 S. Dearborn St.; Telephone:
(312) 353-7572
Director: Ross M. Madden; Regional Attorney:
William J. Cavers

PEORIA, ILL. 61602, 10th floor, Savings Center Tower,
411 Hamilton Blvd.; Telephone: (309) 673-9061,
Ext. 282
Officer-in-Charge: Raymond A. Jacobson

ST. LOUIS, MO. 63101, Room 448, 210 N. 12th Blvd.;
Telephone: (314) 622-4167
Director: Joseph H. Solien; Regional Attorney:
Gerald Fleischut

NEW ORLEANS, LA. 70113, T6024 Federal Bldg.
(Loyola), 701 Loyola Ave.; Telephone: (504) 527-6361
Director: Charles M. Paschal, Jr.; Regional
Attorney: Louis V. Balovin, Jr.

FORT WORTH, TEX. 76102, Room 8A24, Federal
Office Bldg., 819 Taylor St.; Telephone:
(317) 334-2921
Director: Elmer P. Davis; Regional Attorney:
William E. Youngblood

KANSAS CITY, MO. 64106, 610 Federal Bldg.,
601 E. 12th St.; Telephone: (816) 374-5181
Director: Thomas C. Hendrix; Regional Attorney:
Harry Irwig

MINNEAPOLIS, MINN. 55401, 316 Federal Bldg.,

110 S. 4th St.; Telephone: (612) 725-2611
Director: Clarence A. Meter; Regional Attorney:
Max Rotenburg

SEATTLE, WASH. 98101, 10th floor, Republic Bldg.,
1511 3d Ave.; Telephone: (206) 583-4532
Director: Charles M. Henderson; Regional Attorney:
Patrick H. Walker

PORTLAND, OREG. 97205, 310 Six Ten Broadway Bldg.,
610 SW Broadway; Telephone: (503) 226-3361, Ext. 1431
Officer-in-Charge: Robert J. Wiener

SAN FRANCISCO, CALIF. 94102, 13050 Federal Bldg.
450 Golden Gate Ave., Box 36047; Telephone:
(415) 556-3197
Director: Roy O. Hoffman; Regional Attorney:
Harvey Letter

HONOLULU, HAWAII 96814, Suite 308, 1311 Kapiolani
Blvd.; Telephone: (308) 546-5797
Officer-in-Charge: Dennis R. MacCarthy

LOS ANGELES, CALIF. 90014, Room 600, Eastern
Columbia Bldg., 849 Broadway; Telephone:
(213) 688-5254
Director: Wilford W. Johansen; Regional Attorney:
Daniel J. Harrington

NEWARK, N.J. 07102, 16th floor, Federal Bldg.,
970 Broad St.; Telephone: (201) 645-2100
Director: John J. Cuneo; Regional Attorney:
Bernard L. Balicer

HOUSTON, TEX. 77002, 4th floor, Dallas-Brazos Bldg.,
1125 Brazos St.; Telephone: (713) 226-4296
Director: Clifford Potter; Regional Attorney:
Arthur Safos

HATO REY, P.R. 00919, 7th floor, Pan Am Bldg.,
255 Ponce de Leon Ave.; Telephone: (809) 765-0404
Director: Raymond J. Compton; Regional Attorney:
Vincent Rotolo

INDIANAPOLIS, IND. 46204, 614 ISTA Center,
150 W. Market St.; Telephone: (317) 633-8921
Director: William T. Little; Regional Attorney:
George M. Dick

MEMPHIS, TENN. 38103, 746 Federal Office Bldg., 167 N. Main St.; Telephone: (901) 534-3161
Director: John J.A. Reynolds, Jr.; Regional Attorney: John F. Harrington

DENVER, COLO. 80202, Room 260, Federal Bldg., U.S. Customs House, 721 19th St.; Telephone: (303) 297-3551
Director: Francis Sperandeo; Regional Attorney: W. Bruce Gillis

ALBUQUERQUE, N. MEX. 87101, 7011 Federal Bldg. & U.S. Courthouse, 500 Gold Ave. SW, P.O. Box 2146; Telephone: (505) 843-2508
Director: C. Woodrow Greene; Regional Attorney: James W. Mast

BROOKLYN, N.Y. 11201, 4th floor, 16 Court St.; Telephone: (212) 596-3535
Director: Samuel Kaynard; Regional Attorney: Harold L. Richman

MILWAUKEE, WIS. 53202, 2d floor, Commerce Bldg., 744 N. 4th St.; Telephone: (414) 272-3600, Ext. 3861
Director: George F. Squillacote; Regional Attorney: William C. Humphrey

LOS ANGELES, CALIF. 90024, Room 12100, Federal Bldg., 11000 Wilshire Blvd.; Telephone: (212) 824-7351
Director: Abraham Siegel; Regional Attorney: Jerrold H. Shapiro

Resident Offices

LITTLE ROCK, ARK. 72201
3507 Federal Bldg., 700 W. Capitol Ave.; Telephone: (501) 372-4361, Ext. 5512
Resident Officer: William K. Harvey

BIRMINGHAM, ALA. 35203
1417 City Federal Bldg., 2026 2d Ave. North; Telephone: (205) 325-3877
Resident Officer: H. Carlton Bryan, Jr.

EL PASO, TEX. 79901
Room 1025, The Mills Bldg., 303 N. Oregon;

Telephone: (915) 533-9351, Ext. 5331
Resident Officer: Lloyd Porterfield

MIAMI, FLA. 33130
Room 826, Federal Office Bldg., 51 SW 1st Ave.;
Telephone: (305) 350-5391
Resident Officer: James L. Jeffers

PHOENIX, ARIZ. 85013
Room 207, Camelback Bldg., 110 W. Camelback Rd.;
Telephone: (602) 201-3717
Resident Officer: James W. Cherry

ALBANY, N.Y. 12207
7th Floor, Drislane Bldg., 60 Chapel St.;
Telephone: (518) 472-2215
Resident Officer: John M. Shea

NASHVILLE, TENN. 37203
403 West End Bldg., 1720 West End Ave.;
Telephone: (615) 242-8321, Ext. 5922
Resident Officer: Hutton Brandon

JACKSONVILLE, FLA. 32202
2d Floor, Federal Bldg., 400 W. Bay St.;
Telephone: (904) 791-2168
Resident Officer: Peter E. Donnelly, Jr.

XII
Labor Relations

PRACTICAL APPLICATION OF LABOR LAW

To the practitioner in the field, labor law is the frame of the picture; it is essential because it establishes the boundaries for behavior (both actions and reactions). However, the picture itself--the colors, the shapes--is, of course, equally important: this is the subject matter of labor relations where labor law meets the test of practical application. Specific health care facilities will not immediately and automatically be organized as a result of their inclusion under the Act. The life-style of an organization--the way it treats its employees--has a far more important impact in the determination of whether or not it will be organized by a union than the requirements of federal legislation.

Further down the road, negotiating a contract with a labor organization flows from the requirements under the law to bargain in good faith, but much of the outcome of such bargaining is determined by the structure of the union-management relationship and the personalities involved in collective bargaining. The mere fact that there are provisions of the law will not organize employees, nor will such provisions guarantee the negotiation of a sound collective bargaining agreement.

THE VULNERABILITY OF HEALTH CARE FACILITIES TO UNION ORGANIZATION

The choice of one health care facility rather than another as a target for organization is not a happenstance decision. Unions will select the health care facilities that are the most vulnerable: those who do not pay competitive wages, in comparison with other institutions in the field as well as with industries employing similar types of employees; those who do not have a wage and salary program which has established job descriptions and wage patterns providing for fair differentials between jobs based upon a careful analysis of responsibilities; those who have inconsistent shift rotation and who effect changes of shifts and/or hours without proper notice; those who do not have a formal and accessible grievance procedure which provides for third-party arbitration of disputes not settled within the institution; and those who do not have written and well-publicized personnel policy manuals and fail to recognize the contributions of employees in a meaningful and consistent manner. Among the list of irritants that drive employees into unions--for indeed institutions force employees into unions more often than unions organize employees--are the following:

1. poor working conditions
2. dissatisfaction with supervisors
3. poor morale
4. ineffectual channels of communication
5. inequality in wage structures
6. generally poor levels of wages

Goodfellow has provided a checklist on how union organizers rate a health care institution:[1]

1. Number of shifts: The first shift is most "loyal" to the hospital, while the second and third are less loyal. This develops because of generally poorer supervision on the second and third shifts.

2. Female/male ratio: Females are less interested in unions than males.

3. Housekeeping: A dirty, poorly maintained hospital stimulates employees to feel that the hospital cares little about hourly employees and even denigrates them.

4. Wage rates: Many hospital employees believe their supervisor is arbitrary and plays favorites in giving wage increases. Many employees are at the bottom of a job classification or near the bottom. Employees believe this is based upon unfair management; the absence of fair wage differentials are more important to employees than the dollar level of wages.

5. Overtime practices: Managements ask for trouble when they schedule overtime without asking the employee. A facet of poor overtime practices is the selection of only a few employees to share in the overtime available.

6. Seniority: Bypassing seniority or minimizing it is a self-defeating policy. If a new job opens up and employees are not given an opportunity to try for that job, they will resent it.

7. Job transfer: Too often the supervisors have sabotaged promotion from within or any job transfer plan because both create problems for the supervisor.

8. Fringe benefits: Most managements underrate their importance. Employees prefer better protection, even if they have to pay part of the cost themselves.

9. Discipline and grievance procedure: If there are no printed rules about what is punishable and what is not and to what degree, you may be certain that many supervisors will abuse their authority.

10. Treatment: Employees want clean and decent working and eating environments, sanitary toilets, fair hearings on objections to wage rates, respect and recognition for service and loyalty to the hospital, fair opportunity to improve themselves through available training and better job opportunities.

SUPERVISORS: THE VITAL LINK

The success or failure of a union in organizing employees in a health care institution is deeply rooted in supervisory actions. More people vote for or against their immediate supervisor than vote for or against an institution. The supervisor is the key to management's response to a union organization drive. Communicating with supervisors and prescribing "do's and don't's" during union organizing campaigns are steps most usually neglected by those responsible for health facility administration. Supervisors must be carefully prepared for their roles in the management campaign to thwart the union during an organizing drive. Getting across the administration story is essential in dealing with such organization. Jackson and Lewis provide a checklist on what supervisors may say and do during the management counter-attack:[2]

1. Supervisors may tell employees that the employer neither wants nor needs a union.

2. They may tell employees that the law gives them the right to refrain from joining the union and that employees may not be threatened or coerced into joining.

3. They may tell employees of the benefits they enjoy and may compare these benefits with those in unionized companies.

4. They may tell employees that if they are unionized, they may have to bring their problems to a shop steward instead of dealing with their supervisor.

5. They may tell employees of the disadvantages of belonging to a union--such as the payment of dues and initiation fees, the loss of income due to strikes, and the possibility of picket-line duty, fines and assessments. They may tell employees that if they engage in an economic strike, they may be permanently replaced and need be reinstated only if an opening occurs.

6. They may tell employees that a union will always out-promise an employer, but can guarantee nothing. They may point out the untruth of statements being made by the union. They may recall events from personal knowledge of unhappy union experiences.

7. Supervisors may tell employees that they do not have to sign authorization cards. They may tell employees that signing a union card is like signing a bank check. They may tell employees they do not have to speak to union organizers at their homes if they do not desire to do so.

8. Supervisors may campaign vigorously against the union.

They may distribute literature and speak to employees individually or in groups at the employees' work station, in the employee cafeteria or in other areas where employees are accustomed to being. They may request employees to vote against the union and ask them to tell others to do the same.

9. Supervisors may continue to operate normally. They need not tolerate insubordination or soldiering on the job. They may continue to discipline and discharge as warranted by the circumstances.

10. Supervisors may advise employees that the employer's policies with respect to merit pay adjustments, promotions and transfers will be continued as before.

Jackson and Lewis then list what supervisors may not say or do:

1. They may not promise employees pay increases, promotions, improved working conditions and additional benefits or special favors on condition that the employees refuse to join the union or vote against it.

2. They may not threaten employees with loss of job or reduction in wages or use threatening or intimidating language calculated to influence an employee in the exercise of his right to support a union.

3. They must not discriminate against an employee who is taking part in union activities by separating him from other employees, nor may they intentionally assign or transfer employees to undesirable tasks because of their union activities.

4. They may not threaten, actually discipline or discharge an employee for soliciting other employees to sign authorization cards or for engaging in other union activity during his nonworking time. Lunch periods and coffee breaks are considered nonworking time, even though the employee may be paid during these periods. Similarly, an employee standing in line waiting to punch out is on nonworking time. However, even though an employee is on nonworking time himself, he may be warned and disciplined if he is interfering with another employee who is at work.

5. Supervisors may not engage in surveillance of employees attending union meetings or receiving union handbills or give the impression that employee activities are being watched.

6. They may not question employees about their prior or present union affiliations, internal union affairs or union meetings, nor may they ask an employee whether he has signed a union card. It is not improper, however, for a supervisor to receive such information if an employee volunteers it.

7. Supervisors may not call employees away from their places of work to their office or any similar place on the premises where employees are unaccustomed to being in order to urge them to vote against the union.

8. They may not ask employees their personal opinions about the union or the feelings of other employees.

9. Supervisors may not systematically visit the homes of employees to urge them to vote against the union.

10. They may not solicit or encourage employees to request the return of their authorization cards or assist them by writing letters to the union or the NLRB. However, they may respond affirmatively to employees' questions as to whether they can get their cards back, and if this is their desire, advise them to contact the person who solicited their signature.

"PREVENTIVE MEDICINE"

Many employers arrange for a series of meetings with their supervisors to communicate their position on union organization. In addition, meetings are conducted with employees to discuss the benefits enjoyed by the institution's employees, the disadvantages of joining a union, and the personnel policies and practices of the institution which ensure due process and appropriate recognition. Getting across the administration's story is essential in dealing with union organization. The actions of the administration during the organization campaign are, more often than not, secondary to the overall record of the administration during prior years. The management campaign, of course, is important in the outcome of a certification election, but "the poor personnel practices" that may have been part of the record of employee-management relations over the years--low wages, substandard fringe benefits, lack of communication, unfavorable working conditions, favoritism, poor supervision--are likely to override any other consideration.

"Preventive medicine" is the key to maintaining a union-free management. Such a program includes the following:

1. Selecting new employees and rewarding present employees on the basis of qualifications and merit. Favoritism has no place in the proper administration of an employee-relations program.

2. Maintaining a fair level of wages and salaries by attempting to establish the institution's rates at a level which is at least equal to the prevailing rates for comparable positions in the community and by rewarding outstanding work performance through periodic merit increases.

3. Maintaining reasonable hours of work and informing employees as far as possible in advance of changes in their work schedules.

4. Maintaining good working conditions. An employee's second home is in the institution.

5. Providing steady employment and a fair seniority policy.

6. Placing employees in the kind of work best suited to their ability, providing for upward mobility and lateral transfer.

7. Providing opportunities for employees to obtain added knowledge through training programs, both on and off institution

premises during and after working hours.

8. Discharing employees only for cause, providing due process for all aggrieved employees.

9. Giving each employee the right to discuss any matter of concern.

THE "FREE SPEECH" DOCTRINE

Section 8(c) of the Act states:

> The expressing of any views, argument or opinion, or the dissemination thereof, whether in written, printed, graphic or visual form shall not constitute or be evidence of an unfair labor practice under any of the provisions of this Act if such expression contains no threat of reprisal or force or promise of benefit.

The right to speak is not an unlimited one. It is not only important what is said, but how it is said. The surrounding circumstances in each case are weighed when charges of unfair labor practices are levied by either side. The Board looks at the "total context" to determine whether the expression of opinions were coercive or threatening. The actions as well as speeches by either party may subject it to charges of unfair labor practices. The administration is not required to be neutral in representation elections. An employer who prefers not to recognize a union may speak to his employees and tell them just that. He can go into all the details he deems necessary in explaining why he wishes to maintain a union-free institution. The Board looks to the atmosphere of the election and the effect that the employer's speech has upon that atmosphere. The Board will not tolerate threats of loss of employment, threats of closing of institutions, threats of moving the institution to a new location, threats of the loss or reduction in pay or overtime, threats of loss of promotion and threats of violence. The Board has ruled that a "prophecy that unionization might ultimately lead to loss of employment is not coercive where there is no threat that the employer will use his economic power to make its prophecy come true."[3]

BUTTONS AND INSIGNIAS

One of the more emotional aspects involved in the union-organizing drive occurs when employees first sprout union insignia or buttons. Section 7 of the National Labor Relations Act has been interpreted to permit employees to wear buttons or other insignia at their place of work. Section 7 provides employees with the right "to engage in other concerted activities for the purpose of collective bargaining..." It has been determined that the wearing of union buttons and insignia falls under the heading of "other concerted activities," but the wearing of union buttons is a qualified right. That is, under certain circumstances the employer may refuse to permit his employees to wear such buttons during working time. The key question is whether the employer's rule is for efficiency or safety purposes, falls under a well-established and long-standing policy prohibiting the wearing of any emblems or other adornment, and is nondiscriminatory in nature.

Two interesting cases have been decided by the courts on this issue. One was the NLRB v. Harrah's Club (U.S. Court of Appeals, 9th Circuit, 19177, September 28, 1964) and the other, Caterpillar Tractor v. NLRB (U.S. Court of Appeals, Chicago, 11560, March 2, 1956). In NLRB v. Harrah's Club, the employer had a rule which prohibited the wearing of any jewelry or other personal adornment on the uniform of employees. There were daily inspections conducted by management in advance of employees going on duty. The rule had been enforced in the past against badges, pins and buttons showing religious, political or social affiliations. The court of appeals ruled in favor of the management's position in prohibiting the wearing of the buttons because it was established as fact that the employees had decided to wear their union buttons after having for many years respected the company's policy against such display.

In Caterpillar Tractor, after a period of time under a collective bargaining agreement which provided an open shop arrangement, the union made an all-out membership drive. Buttons were worn by members of the union while at work. Many of the buttons had the slogan "DON'T BE A SCAB." The company objected to these inflammatory buttons, but the members persisted in wearing them. Employees were warned and then sent home after refusing to remove such badges. The appeals court ruled in favor of the company on the basis that such activities and inflammatory slogans disrupt or tend to disrupt production and to break down employee discipline. The Court held:

> In its application to organizational activities, the protective mantle of Section 7 is tempered by the employer's right to exact a day's work for a day's pay and to maintain discipline and does not reach activities which inherently carry with them a tendency toward or likelihood of disturbing efficient operation of the employer's business. Perhaps no greater disruptive force can be found in the field of labor relations than that innate in the application of the term "scab" to one employee by his fellow workmen. The term when applied to one embraced in a labor group bears an inescapable connotation of opprobriousness and

vileness commonly recognized by all members of modern American society.

In another case, Republic Aviation Corporation v. NLRB (324 US 793, 16 LRRM 620, 1945), the employer discharged employees for wearing union insignia in the factory area while the union was not the designated representative of the employees. The Supreme Court held that the employer's action was a violation of Section 7. Other cases supporting the wearing of union buttons as a right guaranteed by Section 7 are: NLRB v. The Floridian Hotel of Tampa, Inc. (318 F.2d 545, 53 LRRM 2420, 5th Circuit, 1957); Kimball Wire Corporation (245 F.2d 484, 37 LRRM 2697, 6th Circuit).

In Fabri-Tek, Inc. v. NLRB (352 F.2d 577, 8th Circuit, 1965), the court held that the right to wear union insignia does not encompass the wearing of oversized and unusual emblems by employees whose work required a high degree of concentration. In applying a rule prohibiting workers from wearing union buttons, it is well for management to be aware of prior history on this issue. Has the employer permitted the wearing of any emblems or adornments on uniforms during working hours? If not, and the employer's rule was for efficiency or safety purposes and was nondiscriminatory and well established, the rule in all probability would be upheld by the courts when an institution requires its employees to remove union buttons during an organizational campaign.

NO-DISTRIBUTION AND NO-SOLICITATION RULES

The National Labor Relations Board has upheld the right of institutions to implement a broad no-distribution rule on the basis of "need for keeping the plant clean and orderly or the need to maintain discipline" (United Steelworkers v. NLRB, 243 F.2d dc, CIR, 1956). Such rules are normally upheld if they refer to working hours and working areas, but have been declared invalid if the distribution of literature takes place in nonworking areas or during nonworking hours (U.S.: Republic Aviation Corporation v. NLRB, 324 US, 1945). Institutions will have a difficult time in obtaining Board approval of rules that broadly prohibit solicitation on the institution's premises without limitation as to time or place. Employees generally have the right to solicit on institution premises after working hours. Nonworking time has been construed by the Board to include lunch hours, rest periods and after-work hours. Nonworking areas have been held to include lunch rooms, locker rooms, rest areas and parking lots.

The key to a valid no-solicitation rule is the employer's right to maintain production and discipline. A landmark case in the area of access to the employer's premises by nonemployees is NLRB v. Babcock and Wilcox Company. In this case, the Court ruled that

"An employer may validly post his property against nonemployee distribution of union literature if reasonable efforts by the union through other available channels of communication will enable it to reach the employees with its message and if the employer's notice or order does not discriminate against the union by allowing other distribution." The meaning of this court decision is that non-employee organizers can enter the property of an employer only if the employees are so inaccessible as to make reasonable attempts to reach them through usual channels ineffective or practically impossible.

The NLRB has differentiated between solicitation and distribution. The Board will normally rule against institutions that prohibit employees from distributing or soliciting on institution property during nonworking time unless there are special circumstances making such rules necessary in order to maintain production or discipline. The Board set the following ground rules in such cases:

> 1. An institution may prohibit union solicitation during working time in any area of the institution.
> 2. An institution may prohibit the distribution of union literature in working areas during both working and nonworking time.
> 3. The handing out of union authorization cards (membership cards) whether or not accompanied by conversation is considered solicitation, not distribution, and therefore cannot be prohibited anywhere on the institution's premises during nonworking time in the absence of unusual circumstances.
> 4. An institution may not prohibit its employees from distributing union literature in nonworking areas during nonworking time.
> 5. An institution may not prohibit employees from union solicitation during their own time even in working areas.

In Guyan Valley Hospital, Inc. and National Union of Hospitals and Nursing Home Employees, Local 1199 (198 NLRB 1972), the Board ruled that the hospital did not violate the Act when it enforced the rule against solicitation during working hours where 1) the rule was adopted before the union's organizing campaign began; 2) the rule prohibits solicitation only in the hospital's working area; and 3) evidence does not support the contention that the rule was disparately enforced. Portions of working areas of health care facilities are necessarily open to the use of patients and to visitors. The Board stated in its decision that patients may be upset by employees' arguments concerning a union.

In Summit Nursing and Convalescent Home, Inc. and National

Union of Hospital and Nursing Home Employees, Local 1199, (196 NLRB 1972), the Board ruled that the hospital had violated the Act by promulgating and maintaining a rule which prohibited employees from soliciting for unions during nonworking time and from distributing union literature in nonworking areas during nonworking time. The Board in its decision stated:

> While we recognize that a broad, no-soliciation rule such as that promulgated by the Respondent may be lawful where extraordinary circumstances are shown to exist, we are unable to agree with the Trial Examiner that the records support such a finding here.... We find significant that employees were previously solicited during working hours and in work areas for gifts for departing employees with the Respondent's knowledge.... We conclude that the Respondent has failed to come forward with any showing that unusual circumstances or special needs justify the limitations upon the rights to self-organization imposed on the employees by Respondent's no-solicitation rule.

In Forbes Pavilion Nursing Home, Inc. and National Union of Hospital and Nursing Home Employees (198 NLRB 1972), the Board ruled that the nursing home had violated the Act by prohibiting employees from engaging in union activities at any time on its premises and threatening them with discharge if they failed to comply with this prohibition. In this case, prior to the union's organizing campaign, the nursing home permitted the employees to sell cosmetics, raffle tickets and other items. Shortly after the union began its organizing campaign, an employee who had solicited union card signatures from other employees was summoned before a supervisor and told that the home did not want the employee to solicit for the union at any time on the employer's premises. The employee was warned that if he did not comply with this prohibition he would be discharged on the spot. The Board found that the administrator prohibited the employee from engaging in union activities at any time on the employer's premises and threatened the employee with discharge.

In Extendicare of Kentucky, Inc. and Service Employees International Union, Local 557 (199 NLRB 1972), the Board found that the hospital violated the Act by maintaining an unlawfully broad rule forbidding solicitation by employees on behalf of the union on hospital premises during nonwork time and forbidding employees to distribute union literature in nonwork areas during nonwork time. The hospital's personnel manual distributed by the employer contained a no-solicitation and a no-distribution rule. These rules prohibited "any person" from engaging in "soliciation or distribution for any purpose...on the premises of the infirmary." This rule was later rescinded. The Board ruled that during the period of organization the rule was inoperative and indeed illegal, since it was a broad rule and did not allow for such activity during non-working time and in nonworking areas.

The Supreme Court ruled in February 1974 that a union cannot bargain away the right of its members to distribute union leaflets during off hours and outside the working area. In writing the majority opinion, Justice William Douglas said that "a ban on the distribution of union literature or the solicitation of union support by employees at the plant during non-working time may constitute an interference" with the basic right of labor to organize (NLRB v. Magnavox Co., Case No. 72-1637).

CONTRACT NEGOTIATIONS

> However much specific unions may differ in their exact structures, governments and general operations, virtually all labor organizations share at least the same primary objective. Whatever in the way of concrete demands may be sought from the employer, the union's major goal is to negotiate with him a written agreement covering both employment conditions and the union-management relationship itself on terms which are "acceptable" to the union. But the employer, too, must be able to "live with" these terms and it is because of this second requirement that bargaining sessions almost unavoidably contain stresses and strains.[4]

The law requires an employer to recognize and bargain in good faith with a certified union, but it does not force the employer to agree with the union. Management is free to yield to union's persuasions, but it does not have to be persuaded, provided always that management has given the union opportunity--in good faith--to persuade.

Dunlop and Healy[5] have described collective bargaining as 1) a poker game with the largest pots going to those who combine deception, bluff and luck or ability to come up with a strong hand on the occasions on which they are challenged or "seen" by the other side; 2) an exercise in power politics with the relative strengths of the parties being decisive; 3) a debating society marked by both rhetoric and name-calling; and 4) a "rational process" with both sides remaining completely flexible and willing to be persuaded only when all the facts have been dispassionately presented. It may well be that all of these characteristics come into play and at times overlap. There are many ingredients which affect the bargaining milieu. The actual approach that will succeed in any given negotiation depends upon many factors, such as the following:

1. personalities involved in bargaining
2. the past history of management-labor relations in the institution
3. the character of the union and its hold on the rank and file
4. the general economic conditions
5. the personal characteristics of the institution's bargaining unit

Of these the personalities and training of the negotiators may well play the most important role in the outcome of negotiations. Noted below are several principles upon which a successful bargaining effort should be constructed.

1. The strategy must be planned in advance. Negotiators who play by the seat of their pants end up on the seat of their pants.
2. Experienced labor relations personnel should supervise the strategic planning and actual conduct of negotiations.
3. Management's principal negotiators should have a clear and thorough understanding of trade union principles.
4. Management's key spokesmen should be respected by the union.
5. One or more of the negotiators should come from the line organization in the institution--e.g., the assistant director or associate director of the institution.
6. Technicalities and legalisms should be minimized.
7. Management's negotiators should have the power to bind management.
8. Management's principal negotiators should be in complete charge and control of their temper and demeanor. It is not unusual for the negotiator to involve themselves in play-acting in order to convince extreme hotheads in the union group. Calculated emotionalism can sometimes serve a useful purpose.
9. Management's chief negotiator should keep control of negotiations.

Management must arrive at certain basic decisions before selecting the members of its negotiating team. One of the first and most important decisions is the character of the approach to the union at the bargaining table. Will the institution take a hard-nosed approach? Will it attempt to contain the union at each turn?

Will it attempt to discredit the union during the bargaining process? Will it attempt to "win" where it has lost the certification election? Will it accept that the union is here to stay now, no matter what its feelings were during the union's organizing campaign, and therefore will it take a softer approach? Will it be guided by the levels established at other similar institutions or will it have to take a leadership role in terms of wages, benefits and working conditions?

Benjamin Selekman lists some principal structures of union-management relationships of which four follow:[6]

1. The structure of containment aggression. Here the employer assumes a firm defensive position in an attempt to "contain" a militant aggressive union. Between bitter contract negotiations there are wildcat stoppages and armed truces. In the administration of the contract, management seeks the narrowest possible interpretation of a contract, while the union aggressively attempts to get all it can from the contract.

2. The structure of power bargaining. Here both parties respect each other and accept the legitimacy of relative economic strengths as the prime determinant of the terms of the agreement. In such a pattern, both parties are usually strong and well established and are likely to be fairly evenly matched in bargaining ability and economic power.

3. The structure of deal bargaining. This involves a semi-secretive type of negotiation between top management and top union leadership. A substantial number of contracts are indeed negotiated in virtual privacy by top leadership on both sides.

4. The structure of accommodation. This involves a relationship in which the employer and the union work cooperatively within the conventional framework of collective bargaining. The employer accepts the union as the integral part of the industrial relations scene, but will negotiate only on the conventional subjects of wages, hours and other conditions of employment.

Union negotiators are skilled practitioners of the bargaining art. Collective bargaining is indeed an art where personalities play a far more important role than any theoretical or academic formats which are suggested as a successful approach to bargaining. The average union negotiator is thoroughly schooled in negotiating techniques and often appears to be better informed on the institutional working conditions, policies, wage scales and benefit schedules than his counterpart across the table. More often than not, they are also equipped with information on an industry-wide basis. They know what they are there for and they invariably come to the bargaining session with a specific program and specific demands. Their approach is programmed; their alternatives are identified in advance; their tactical program provides for clear lines of compromise and clear lines of no compromise.

Contract negotiation is indeed more an art than a science. It is not carried out according to fixed laws easily applicable by anyone who happens to play the role of management negotiator, but rather depends upon the personal skills and judgment brought forth by the individual negotiator. Most of the experts in the field agree on one aspect of the negotiation: there is no universal approach to the successful culmination of collective bargaining.

Davey makes these general observations:[7]

1. No matter how adept in human relations an individual negotiator may be, he is unlikely to be successful unless he has the facts and a basic economic strength working with him.

2. There is no substitute for personal integrity and courage. A successful negotiator must have these attributes in abundance.

3. Success in negotiations, as in other aspects of human management relationships, involves an informed awareness and understanding of the compulsions that are operating upon the other party.

He goes on to list suggested negotiating procedures. Among them are the following:

1. Both the union and management negotiating committees should be kept reasonably small. If the union or company committee is too large and everyone insists on participating, much time will be consumed, tempers will become frayed and much that is irrelevant will be introduced.

2. One person should be in charge of conducting negotiations for each side. Division of authority in negotiations is fatal to orderly procedure and usually impedes the agreement-making process.

3. Company and union negotiators should have the authority to make decisive commitments in the course of negotiations. Company negotiators should have the power to bind their principals.

4. Negotiators should begin with a well-planned agenda that includes a complete statement of all disputed issues together with a listing of proposals and counterproposals on disputed points.

5. The negotiators should first eliminate the least controversial issues and put the agreement on these in writing before proceeding to negotiate on the tougher issues.

6. The difficult issues may be divided into those that involve money outlays and those that are non-economic demands.

7. Use of the basket approach on economic issues is recommended.

TAFT-HARTLEY ACT
DEFINITION OF COLLECTIVE BARGAINING

Section 8(d) of the Act defines collective bargaining as follows:

> To bargain collectively is the performance of the mutual obligation of the employer and the representative of the employees to meet at reasonable times and confer in good faith with respect to wages, hours and terms and conditions of employ-

> ment or the negotiation of an agreement for any question arising thereunder and the executing of a written contract incorporating any agreement reached requested by either party, but such obligation does not compel either party to agree to a proposal or require the making of a concession.

The Act further states that where there is in effect a collective bargaining contract covering health care facility employees, the duty to bargain collectively shall also mean that no party to such contract shall terminate or modify such contract unless the party desiring such termination or modification serves a written notice on the other party to the contract of the proposed termination or modification ninety days prior to the expiration date thereof. At the onset of bargaining, management must set its bargaining goals clearly, precisely and ideally, in three categories:

1. those issues which cannot be compromised, no matter what;
2. those issues which can be compromised--to what degree and in exchange for what concession from the union; and
3. those issues which are counters to excessive union demands and will be dropped when and if the union does the same with its demands.

SAMPLE CONTRACT CLAUSES

Provided below are several model collective bargaining clauses, the subject matter of which is addressed in nearly every contract. The clauses presented here are meant to be merely indicative of how selected topics can be addressed in the contract. They should be considered only as suggestions for constructing contract language rather than as models to be strictly followed.

Severance Pay. Except for part-time employees, severance pay shall be paid by the health care facility to employees on the seniority list in cases where layoffs occur for periods of two weeks or more in accordance with the following provisions: (a) if the period of most recent employment is one year, but less than five years, five days' severance pay; (b) if the period of most recent employment is five years or more, ten days' severance pay.

Job Posting and Bidding. When a new department or job is created or when a present job is vacant, the institution agrees to post notice of same on bulletin boards. Employees who are interested may make application stating why they want to change and why they are qualified. The institution agrees to give such application careful consideration and to make such transfers based on the employee's seniority rights, fitness and ability.

Seniority. In cases of layoff, recall, promotion or demotion, the following factors shall be considered: (1) ability to work; (2) seniority. Where factor (1) is relatively equal, factor (2) shall be the governing factor.

Discipline and Discharge. Employees are entitled to retain their jobs on the basis of good behavior, efficiency and honesty. The institution shall have the right to discipline or discharge any employee who fails to meet the foregoing conditions and particularly, but without limitation, may discharge an employee because of the use of intoxicating liquors during working hours, violation of safety rules, absent without leave, dishonesty, insubordination, habitual neglect or carelessness resulting in damage to property or equipment, sleeping while on duty or for any other just cause.

No Strike. The union, its officers, agents, members and employees covered by this agreement agree that so long as this agreement is in effect, there shall be no strikes, sit-downs, sit-ins, slow-downs, stoppages of work or any unlawful acts that interfere with the institution's operations. It further agrees that it will take affirmative action to prevent and stop any such action that occurs in disregard of this commitment. Fulfilling this obligation, the union shall within 12 hours of a request by the health care facility (1) notify employees of its disapproval of such action and instruct such employees to cease such action and return to work immediately; (2) publicly disavow such action by the employee.

Waiver Clause. The institution and the union for the life of this agreement each voluntarily waives the right and agrees to suspend collective bargaining with respect to any subject or matter not specifically referred to or covered in this agreement.

Grievance Procedure. 1. A grievance shall be defined as a dispute or complaint arising between the parties hereto under or out of this agreement or the interpretation, application, performance, termination, or any alleged breach thereof, and shall be processed and disposed of in the following manner:

Step 1. Within a reasonable time, an employee having a grievance and/or his union delegate or other representative within five (5) working days after the presentation of the grievance in Step 1.

Step 2. If the grievance is not settled in Step 1, the grievance may, within five (5) working days after the answer in Step 1, be presented in Step 2. When grievances are presented in Step 2, they shall be reduced to writing, signed by the grievant and his union representative, and presented to the grievant's department head or his designee. A grievance so presented in Step 2 shall be answered by the health care facility in writing within five (5) working days after its presentation.

Step 3. If the grievance is not settled in Step 2, the grievance may, within five (5) working days after the answer in Step 2, be presented in Step 3. A grievance shall be presented in this step to the personnel director or administrator of the health care facility or his designee; and he or his designee shall render a decision in writing within five (5) working days after the presentation of the grievance in this step.

Failure on the part of the health care facility to answer a grievance at any step shall not be deemed acquiescence thereto, and the union may proceed to the next step.

Anything to the contrary herein notwithstanding, a grievance concerning a discharge or suspension may be presented initially at Step 3 by notice in writing addressed to the union at its offices.

2. All time limits herein specified shall be deemed to be exclusive of Saturdays, Sundays and holidays.

3. Any disposition of a grievance from which no appeal is taken within the time limits specified herein shall be deemed resolved and shall not thereafter be considered subject to the grievance and arbitration provisions of this agreement.

4. A grievance which affects a substantial number or class of employees, and which the health care facility representative designated in Steps 1 and 2 lacks authority to settle, may initially be presented at Step 3 by the union representative.

<u>Arbitration</u>. 1. A grievance which has not been resolved under the grievance procedure clause may, within ten (10) working days after completion of Step 3 of the grievance procedure, be referred for arbitration by the health care facility or the union to an arbitrator selected in accordance with the procedures of the American Arbitration Association. The arbitration shall be conducted under the Voluntary Labor Arbitration Rules then prevailing of the American Arbitration Association.

2. The fees and expenses of the American Arbitration Association and the arbitrator shall be borne equally by the parties.

3. The award of an arbitrator hereunder shall be final, conclusive and binding upon the health care facility, the union and the employees.

4. The arbitrator shall have jurisdiction only over disputes arising out of grievances, as defined in the grievance procedure clause, and he shall have no power to add to, subtract from, or modify in any way any of the terms of this agreement.

<u>Management Rights</u>. 1. Except as in this agreement otherwise provided, the health care facility retains the exclusive right to hire, direct and schedule the working force; to plan, direct and to control operations; to discontinue, or reorganize or combine any depart-

ment or branch of operations with any consequent reduction or other changes in the working force; to hire and lay off employees; to promulgate rules and regulations; to introduce new or improved methods or facilities regardless of whether or not the same cause a reduction in the working force and in all respects to carry out, in addition, the ordinary and customary functions of management. None of these rights shall be exercised in a capricious or arbitrary manner.

2. The union, on behalf of the employees, agrees to cooperate with the health care facility to attain and maintain full efficiency and maximum patient care, and the health care facility agrees to receive and consider constructive suggestions submitted by the union toward these objectives.

Subcontracting. 1. Health care facilities that are presently subcontracting all or any part of their present services of whatever nature or description to other health care facilities that are covered by a current collective bargaining agreement with the union may continue to do so without restriction provided that such work is performed by members of the union in the bargaining unit of the health care facility performing such work.

2. Health care facilities which are now subcontracting all or any part of their present services to another health care facility but which are not covered by a current collective bargaining agreement with the union may continue to do so, provided that the total amount of such services presently so subcontracted shall remain at the current existing level. In the event, however, that the present level of such subcontracted services shall, at any time in the future, be increased by a figure in excess of twenty percent (20%) of the present total amount of such subcontracted services, then and in that event the parties shall attempt to negotiate a solution concerning such increase. Partial increases in the level of such subcontracted services are not to be considered until the totality of such increases reach or exceed the aforesaid twenty percent (20%) figure. Upon failure to arrive at an adjustment within twenty (20) days after such increase, the matter shall be to determine (a) the ability or inability of the health care facility to accommodate itself (because of a manpower shortage or any other legitimate reason) to the increased services without the need to subcontract to a health care facility which is not covered by a collective bargaining agreement; (b) the health, safety and welfare of the health care facility patients who might be affected by the alleged inability of the health care facility to accommodate itself to the required increase in services. This factor (b) shall be deemed and considered as the prime objective. (c) the purpose and function of the subcontracted work must be given first consideration and not the nature of the job duties or skills of the individual employees.

3. In the event that two or more health facilities covered by a collective bargaining agreement with the union shall at any time in

the future desire to combine for the purpose of creating a centralized agency to perform services of any kind, nature or description theretofore required by the health care facility participating in centralized agency shall not be deemed nor considered as subcontracting provided that the services are performed by members of the union and that such centralized agency enter into a collective bargaining agreement with the union, which shall contain the same terms and conditions as are presently contained in the current collective bargaining agreement, or as such terms and conditions shall be amended by any subsequent collective bargaining agreement.

4. Except insofar as it is limited by item (2) hereof, the health care facility shall not hereafter subcontract to any profit or non-profit organization any of its (a) services and/or maintenance work, (b) clerical and/or office work, (c) licensed practical nurse work of any kind, nature or description. If the health care facility is presently subcontracting any part of the above listed work, it may continue to do so but in the event that the level of such presently subcontracted services shall, at any time in the future, be increased by a figure in excess of twenty percent (20%) of the total amount of such presently subcontracted service, then and in that event the procedures for adjustment and the criteria outlined in Section (2) hereof shall become applicable. The itemization of (a), (b), and (c) above listed shall be deemed to include but shall not be limited to kitchen operations, laundry services, dietary service and maintenance frequently recurring, rather than unusual or infrequent, janitorial work, porter work, clerical, office accounting work, etc.

5. In the event of any emergency such as fire, epidemic, power failure, machine breakdown, war, major catastrophe and the like, the health care facility may subcontract part or all of any of its services for the duration of the emergency. This itemization shall not be deemed or construed as being limited solely to the above listed emergencies.

6. The health care facility may, if it desires, subcontract any and all technical and/or laboratory services which, in the health facility's opinion and judgment, it cannot properly, adequately or fully perform so as to protect the health, safety and welfare of its patients. In the event, however, that the union shall claim an abuse of such judgment, then the procedures for adjustment of that claim shall be resolved in accordance with the method and tests set forth in item (2) hereof. This section shall not be deemed or considered as applying to those employees who may be attached to the laboratory or technical staff and classified as laboratory or technical employees but who are performing maintenance, porter, cleaning or upkeep services for the laboratory and/or technical department.

7. The health care facility may subcontract any and all diagnostic and/or specialized medical services which would improve its diagnostic abilities and/or specialized medical services involving the health and welfare of its patients whenever such member is

unequipped, because of a manpower shortage or absence of appropriate mechanical, electrical or electronic equipment to provide its patients with such care. If at any time in the future any one or more of these elements are substantially reduced or the member acquires the appropriate mechanical, electric or electronic equipment, then and in that event the question of whether or not such member shall thereafter itself perform such services shall be submitted to negotiation and failing adjustment the procedures and tests outlined in Section (2) hereof shall become applicable.

CONCLUSION

In preparing this introduction to health facility labor law, the authors have presented a panoramic view of the National Labor Relations Act. A summary of the 1974 amendments to the Act brought to the reader the intent and history of the legislation as well as its actual application. In reviewing the Act, special attention was directed to the duty to bargain, the determination of bargaining units, the way in which representation elections are conducted, and a view of unfair labor practices of both employers and unions. Becoming familiar with the organization and function of the National Labor Relations Board is an essential ingredient of preparing for organizational activity in the health services industry. But beyond that, we have expanded our discussion from labor law to labor relations. In an earlier book the authors stated, "The need for enforceable, workable, uniform and equitable procedures of employee-employer relations in what is soon to be the nation's largest industry is critical. What is at stake is not only the internal viability of the health services industry, but certain availability of good medical care to the citizenry."[8] Whether the Act as amended now provides "workable, uniform and equitable procedures of employee-employer relations" remains to be seen.

The health care industry faces a challenge. Amendment of the National Labor Relations Act now requires that health care facility administrators operate under an exhaustive and complex body of statutory law, administrative rulings and court decisions. This is new territory for administrators, but familiar ground for labor organizers. It has been the objective of this book to provide those who may face the problems of dealing with unions with an introductory tour of the legal terrain on which they will be required to operate.

Footnotes

1. Matthew Goodfellow, "How the Union Organizes or Rates Your Hospital: A Check-List," Administration Briefs, American College of Hospital Administrators, Vol. VII, No. 1, January 1973.
2. Louis Jackson and Robert Lewis, Winning NLRB Elections: Management's Strategy and Preventive Programs, Corporate Law and Practice, Practice Handbook Series No. 6 (New York: Practicing Law Institute, 1972), pp. 53-56.
3. Chicopee Manufacturing Company, 197 NLRB 106, 107, 33 LRRM 1064 (1953).
4. Arthur A. Sloane and Fred Witney, Labor Relations (Englewood Cliffs, N.J.: Prentice-Hall, Inc., 1967), p. 167.
5. John P. Dunlop and James J. Healy, Collective Bargaining (Homewood, Ill., Richard D. Irwin, Inc., 1955), p. 53.
6. Benjamin M. Selekman, "Varieties of Labor Relations," Harvard Business Review, Vol. XXXII (March 1949), pp. 175-199.
7. Howard W. Davey, Contemporary Collective Bargaining (Englewood Cliffs, N.J.: Prentice-Hall, Inc., 1959), pp. 110-111.
8. Norman Metzger and Dennis Pointer, Labor-Management Relations in the Health Services Industry: Theory and Practice (Washington, D.C.: Science and Health Publications, 1972), p. 248.

Appendix A. The National Labor Relations Act, as amended 1974 by P.L. 93-360

Authors' Note: Changes in existing law made by P.L. 93-360 are shown as follows: 1) deletions from existing law are enclosed in bold face brackets; 2) new provisions are printed in italic; and 3) existing law, in which no changes made, are in roman.

LABOR MANAGEMENT RELATIONS ACT, 1947, AS AMENDED

AN ACT

To amend the National Labor Relations Act, to provide additional facilities for the mediation of labor disputes affecting commerce, to equalize legal responsibilities of labor organizations and employers, and for other purposes

Be it enacted by the Senate and House of Representatives of the United States of America in Congress assembled,

SHORT TITLE AND DECLARATION OF POLICY

SECTION 1. (a) This Act may be cited as the "Labor Management Relations Act, 1947."

(b) Industrial strife which interferes with the normal flow of commerce and with the full production of articles and commodities for commerce, can be avoided or substantially minimized if employers, employees, and labor organizations each recognize under law one another's legitimate rights in their relations with each other, and above all recognize under law that neither party has any right in its relations with any other to engage in acts or practices which jeopardize the public health, safety, or interest.

It is the purpose and policy of this Act, in order to promote the full flow of commerce, to prescribe the legitimate rights of both employees and employers in their relations affecting commerce, to provide orderly and peaceful procedures for preventing the interference by either with the legitimate rights of the other, to protect the rights of individual employees in their relations with labor organizations whose activities affect commerce, to define and proscribe practices on the part of labor and management which affect commerce and are inimical to the general welfare, and to protect the rights of the public in connection with labor disputes affecting commerce.

TITLE I—AMENDMENT OF NATIONAL LABOR RELATIONS ACT

SEC. 101. The National Labor Relations Act is hereby amended to read as follows:

FINDINGS AND POLICIES

SECTION 1. The denial by some employers of the right of employees to organize and the refusal by some employers to accept the procedure of collective bargaining lead to strikes and other forms of industrial strife or unrest, which have the intent or the necessary effect of burdening or obstructing commerce by (a) impairing the efficiency, safety, or operation of the instrumentalities of commerce; (b) occurring in the current of commerce; (c) materially affecting, restraining, or controlling the flow of raw materials or manufactured or processed goods from or into the channels of commerce, or the prices of such materials or goods in commerce; or (d) causing diminution of employment and wages in such volume as substantially to impair or disrupt the market for goods flowing from or into the channels of commerce.

The inequality of bargaining power between employees who do not possess full freedom of association or actual liberty of contract, and employers who are organized in the corporate or other forms of ownership association substantially burdens and affects the flow of commerce, and tends to aggravate recurrent business depressions, by depressing wage rates and the purchasing power of wage earners in industry and by preventing the stabilization of competitive wage rates and working conditions within and between industries.

Experience has proved that protection by law of the right of employees to organize and bargain collectively safeguards commerce from injury, impairment, or interruption, and promotes the flow of commerce by removing certain recognized sources of industrial strife and unrest, by encouraging practices fundamental to the friendly adjustment of industrial disputes arising out of differences as to wages, hours, or other working conditions, and by restoring equality of bargaining power between employers and employees.

Experience has further demonstrated that certain practices by some labor organizations, their officers, and members have the intent or the necessary effect of burdening or obstructing commerce by preventing the free flow of goods in such commerce through strikes and other forms of industrial unrest or through concerted activities which impair the interest of the public in the free flow of such commerce. The elimination of such practices is a necessary condition to the assurance of the rights herein guaranteed.

It hereby declared to the policy of the United States to eliminate the causes of certain substantial obstructions to the free flow of commerce and to mitigate and eliminate these obstructions when they have occurred by encouraging the practice and procedure of collective bargaining and by protecting the exercise by workers of full freedom of association, self-organization, and designation of representatives of their own choosing, or the purpose of negotiating the terms and conditions of their employment or other mutual aid or protection.

DEFINITIONS

SEC. 2. When used in this Act—

(1) The term "person" includes one or more individuals, labor organizations, partnerships, associations, corporations, legal representatives, trustees, trustees in bankruptcy, or receivers.

(2) The term "employer" includes any person acting as an agent of an employer, directly or indirectly, but shall not include the United States or any wholly owned Government corporation, or any Federal Reserve Bank, or any State or political subdivision thereof, [or any corporation or association operating a hospital, if no part of the net earnings inures to the benefit of any private shareholder or individual,] or any person subject to the Railway Labor Act, as amended from time to time, or any labor organization (other than when acting as an employer), or anyone acting in the capacity of officer or agent of such labor organization.

(3) The term "employee" shall include any employee, and shall not be limited to the employees of a particular employer, unless the Act explicitly states otherwise, and shall include any individual whose work has ceased as a consequence of, or in connection with, any current labor dispute or because of any unfair labor practice, and who has not obtained any other regular and substantially equivalent employment, but shall not include any individual employed as an agricultural laborer, or in the domestic service of any family or person at his home, or any individual employed by his parent or spouse, or any individual having the status of an independent contractor, or any individual employed as a supervisor, or any individual employed by an employer subject to the Railway Labor Act, as amended from time to time, or by any other person who is not an employer as herein defined.

(4) The term "representatives" includes any individual or labor organization.

(5) The term "labor organization" means any organization of any kind, or any agency or employee representation committee or plan, in which employees participate and which exists for the purpose, in whole or in part, of dealing with employers concerning grievances, labor disputes, wages, rates of pay, hours of employment, or conditions of work.

(6) The term "commerce" means trade, traffic, commerce, transportation, or communication among the several States, or between the District of Columbia or any Territory of the United States and any State or other Territory, or between any foreign country and any State, Territory, or the District of Columbia, or within the District of Columbia or any Territory, or between points in the same State but through any other State or any Territory or the District of Columbia or any foreign country.

(7) The term "affecting commerce" means in commerce, or burdening or obstructing commerce or the free flow of commerce, or having led or tending to lead to a labor dispute burdening or obstructing commerce or the free flow of commerce.

(8) The term "unfair labor practice" means any unfair labor practice listed in section 8.

(9) The term "labor dispute" includes any controversy concerning terms, tenure or conditions of employment, or concerning the association or representation of persons in negotiating, fixing, maintaining, changing, or seeking to arrange terms or conditions of employment, regardless of whether the disputants stand in the proximate relation of employer and employee.

(10) The term "National Labor Relations Board" means the National Labor Relations Board provided for in section 3 of this Act.

(11) The term "supervisor" means any individual having authority, in the interest of the employer, to hire, transfer, suspend, lay off, recall, promote, discharge, assign, reward, or discipline other employees, or responsibly to direct them, or to adjust their grievances, or effectively to recommend such action, if in connection with the foregoing the exercise of such authority is not of a merely routine or clerical nature, but requires the use of independent judgment.

(12) The term "professional employee" means—

(a) any employee engaged in work (i) predominantly intellectual and varied in character as opposed to routine mental, manual, mechanical, or physical work; (ii) involving the consistent exercise of discretion and judgment in its performance; (iii) of such a character that the output produced or the result accomplished cannot be standardized in relation to a given period of time; (iv) requiring knowledge of an advanced type in a field of science or learning customarily acquired by a prolonged course of specialized intellectual instruction and study in an institution of higher learning or a hospital, as distinguished from a general academic education or from an apprenticeship or from training in the performance of routine mental, manual, or physical processes; or

(b) any employee, who (i) has completed the courses of specialized intellectual instruction and study described in clause (iv) of paragraph (a), and (ii) is performing related work under the supervision of a professional person to qualify himself to become a professional employee as defined in paragraph (a).

(13) In determining whether any person is acting as an "agent" of another person so as to make such other person responsible for his acts, the question of whether the specific acts performed were actually authorized or subsequently ratified shall not be controlling.

(14) The term "health care institution" shall include any hospital, convalescent hospital, health maintenance organization, health clinic, nursing home, extended care facility, or other institution devoted to the care of sick, infirm or aged persons.

NATIONAL LABOR RELATIONS BOARD

Sec. 3. (a) The National Labor Relations Board (hereinafter called the "Board") created by this Act prior to its amendment by the Labor Management Relations Act, 1947, is hereby continued as an agency of the United States, except that the Board shall consist of five instead of three members, appointed by the President by and with the advice and consent of the Senate. Of the two additional members so provided for, one shall be appointed for a term of five years and the other for a term of two years. Their successors, and the successors of the other members, shall be appointed for terms of five years each, excepting that any individual chosen to fill a vacancy shall be appointed only for the unexpired term of the member whom he shall succeed. The President shall designate one member to serve as Chairman of the Board. Any member of the Board may be removed by the President, upon notice and hearing, for neglect of duty or malfeasance in office, but for no other cause.

(b) The Board is authorized to delegate to any group of three or more members any or all of the powers which it may itself exercise. The Board is also authorized to delegate to its regional directors its powers under section 9 to determine the unit appropriate for the purpose of collective bargaining, to investigate and provide for hearings, and determine whether a question of representation exists, and to direct an election or take a secret ballot under subsection (c) or (e) of section 9 and certify the results thereof, except that upon the filing of a request therefor with the Board by any interested person, the Board may review any action of a regional director delegated to him under this paragraph, but such a review shall not, unless specifically ordered by the Board, operate as a stay of any action taken by the regional director. A vacancy in the Board shall not impair the right of the remaining members to exercise all of the powers of the Board, and three members of the Board shall, at all times, constitute a quorum of the Board, except that two members shall constitute a quorum of any group designated pursuant to the first sentence hereof. The Board shall have an official seal which shall be judicially noticed.

(c) The Board shall at the close of each fiscal year make a report in writing to Congress and to the President stating in detail the cases it has heard, the decisions it has rendered, the names, salaries, and duties of all employees and officers in the employ or under the supervision of the Board, and an account of all moneys it has disbursed.

(d) There shall be a General Counsel of the Board who shall be appointed by the President, by and with the advice and consent of the Senate, for a term of four years. The General Counsel of the Board shall exercise general supervision over all attorneys employed by the Board (other than trial examiners and legal assistants to Board members) and over the officers and employees in the regional offices. He shall have final authority, on behalf of the Board, in respect to the investigation of charges and issuance of complaints under section 10, and in respect of the prosecution of such complaints before the Board, and shall have such other duties as the Board may prescribe or as may be provided by law. In case of a vacancy in the office of the General Counsel the President is authorized to designate the officer or employee who shall act as General Counsel during such vacancy, but no person or persons so designated shall so act (1) for more than forty days when the Congress is in session unless a nomination to fill such vacancy shall have been submitted to the Senate, or (2) after the adjournment *sine die* of the session of the Senate in which such nomination was submitted.

SEC. 4. (a) Each member of the Board and the General Counsel of the Board shall receive a salary of $12,000 a year, shall be eligible for reappointment, and shall not engage in any other business, vocation, or employment. The Board shall appoint an executive secretary, and such attorneys, examiners, and regional directors, and such other employees as it may from time to time find necessary for the proper performance of its duties. The Board may not employ any attorneys for the purpose of reviewing transcripts of hearings or preparing drafts of opinions except that any attorney employed for assignment as a legal assistant to any Board member may for such Board member review such transcripts and prepare such drafts. No trial examiner's report shall be reviewed, either before or after its publication, by any person other than a member of the Board or his legal assistant, and no trial examiner shall advise or consult with the Board with respect to exceptions taken to his findings, rulings, or recommendations. The Board may establish or utilize such regional, local, or other agencies, and utilize such voluntary and uncompensated services, as may from time to time be needed. Attorneys appointed under this section may, at the direction of the Board, appear for and represent the Board in any case in court. Nothing in this Act shall be construed to authorize the Board to appoint individuals for the purpose of conciliation or mediation, or for economic analysis.

(b) All of the expenses of the Board, including all necessary traveling and subsistence expenses outside the District of Columbia incurred by the members or employees of the Board under its orders, shall be allowed and paid on the presentation of itemized vouchers therefor approved by the Board or by any individual it designates for that purpose.

Sec. 5. The principal office of the Board shall be in the District of Columbia, but it may meet and exercise any or all of its powers at any other place. The Board may, by one or more of its members or by such agents or agencies as it may designate, prosecute any inquiry necessary to its functions in any part of the United States. A member who participates in such an inquiry shall not be disqualified from subsequently participating in a decision of the Board in the same case.

Sec. 6. The Board shall have authority from time to time to make, amend, and rescind, in the manner prescribed by the Administrative Procedure Act, such rules and regulations as may be necessary to carry out the provisions of this Act.

RIGHTS OF EMPLOYEES

Sec. 7. Employees shall have the right to self-organization, to form, join, or assist labor organizations, to bargain collectively through representatives of their own choosing, and to engage in other concerted activities for the purpose of collective bargaining or other mutual aid or protection, and shall also have the right to refrain from any or all of such activities except to the extent that such right may be affected by an agreement requiring membership in a labor organization as a condition of employment as authorized in section 8(a)(3).

UNFAIR LABOR PRACTICES

Sec. 8. (a) It shall be an unfair labor practice for an employer—

(1) to interfere with, restrain, or coerce employees in the exercise of the rights guaranteed in section 7;

(2) to dominate or interfere with the formation or administration of any labor organization or contribute financial or other support to it: *Provided*, That subject to rules and regulations made and published by the Board pursuant to section 6, an employer shall not be prohibited from permitting employees to confer with him during working hours without loss of time or pay;

(3) by discrimination in regard to hire or tenure of employment or any term or condition of employment to encourage or discour-

age membership in any labor organization: *Provided*, That nothing in this Act, or in any other statute of the United States, shall preclude an employer from making an agreement with a labor organization (not established, maintained, or assisted by any action defined in section 8(a) of this Act as an unfair labor practice) to require as a condition of employment membership therein on or after the thirtieth day following the beginning of such employment or the effective date of such agreement, whichever is the later, (i) if such labor organization is the representative of the employees as provided in section 9(a), in the appropriate collective-bargaining unit covered by such agreement when made, and (ii) unless following an election held as provided in section 9(e) within one year preceding the effective date of such agreement, the Board shall have certified that at least a majority of the employees eligible to vote in such election have voted to rescind the authority of such labor organization to make such an agreement: *Provided further*, That no employer shall justify any discrimination against an employee for nonmembership in a labor organization (A) if he has reasonable grounds for believing that such membership was not available to the employee on the same terms and conditions generally applicable to other members, or (B) if he has reasonable grounds for believing that membership was denied or terminated for reasons other than the failure of the employee to tender the periodic dues and the initiation fees uniformly required as a condition of acquiring or retaining membership;

(4) to discharge or otherwise discriminate against an employee because he has filed charges or given testimony under this Act;

(5) to refuse to bargain collectively with the representatives of his employees, subject to the provisions of section 9(a).

(b) It shall be an unfair labor practice for a labor organization or its agents—

(1) to restrain or coerce (A) employees in the exercise of the rights guaranteed in section 7: *Provided*, That this paragraph shall not impair the right of a labor organization to prescribe its own rules with respect to the acquisition or retention of membership therein; or (B) an employer in the selection of his representatives for the purposes of collective bargaining or the adjustment of grievances;

(2) to cause or attempt to cause an employer to discriminate against an employee in violation of subsection (a)(3) or to discriminate against an employee with respect to whom membership in such organization has been denied or terminated on some ground other than his failure to tender the periodic dues and the initiation fees uniformly required as a condition of acquiring or retaining membership;

(3) to refuse to bargain collectively with an employer, provided it is the representative of his employees subject to the provisions of section 9(a);

(4) (i) to engage in, or to induce or encourage any individual employed by any person engaged in commerce or in an industry affecting commerce to engage in, a strike or a refusal in the course of his employment to use, manufacture, process, transport, or otherwise handle or work on any goods, articles, materials,

or commodities or to perform any services; or (ii) to threaten, coerce, or restrain any person engaged in commerce or in an industry affecting commerce, where in either case an object thereof is:

(A) forcing or requiring any employer or self-employed person to join any labor or employer organization or to enter into any agreement which is prohibited by section 8(e);

(B) forcing or requiring any person to cease using, selling, handling, transporting, or otherwise dealing in the products of any other producer, processor, or manufacturer, or to cease doing business with any other person, or forcing or requiring any other employer to recognize or bargain with a labor organization as the representative of his employees unless such labor organization has been certified as the representative of such employees under the provisions of section 9: *Provided,* That nothing contained in this clause (B) shall be construed to make unlawful, where not otherwise unlawful, any primary strike or primary picketing;

(C) forcing or requiring any employer to recognize or bargain with a particular labor organization as the representative of his employees if another labor organization has been certified as the representative of such employees under the provisions of section 9;

(D) forcing or requiring any employer to assign particular work to employees in a particular labor organization or in a particular trade, craft, or class rather than to employees in another labor organization or in another trade, craft, or class, unless such employer is failing to conform to an order or certification of the Board determining the bargaining representative for employees performing such work:

Provided, That nothing contained in this subsection (b) shall be construed to make unlawful a refusal by an person to enter upon the premises of any employer (other than his own employer), if the employees of such employer are engaged in a strike ratified or approved by a representative of such employees whom such employer is required to recognize under this Act: *Provided further,* That for the purposes of this paragraph (4) only, nothing contained in such paragraph shall be construed to prohibit publicity, other than picketing, for the purpose of truthfully advising the public, including consumers and members of a labor organization, that a product or products are produced by an employer with whom the labor organization has a primary dispute and are distributed by another employer, as long as such publicity does not have an effect of inducing any individual employed by any person other than the primary employer in the course of his employment to refuse to pick up, deliver, or transport any goods, or not to perform any services, at the establishment of the employer engaged in such distribution;

(5) to require of employees covered by an agreement authorized under subsection (a)(3) the payment, as a condition precedent to becoming a member of such organization, of a fee in an amount which the Board finds excessive or discriminatory under all the circumstances. In making such a finding, the Board shall consider,

among other relevant factors, the practices and customs of labor organizations in the particular industry, and the wages currently paid to the employees affected;

(6) to cause or attempt to cause an employer to pay or deliver or agree to pay or deliver any money or other thing of value, in the nature of an exaction, for services which are not performed or not to be performed; and

(7) to picket or cause to be picketed, or threaten to picket or cause to be picketed, any employer where an object thereof is forcing or requiring an employer to recognize or bargain with a labor organization as the representative of his employees, or forcing or requiring the employees of an employer to accept or select such labor organization as their collective bargaining representative, unless such labor organization is currently certified as the representative of such employees:

(A) where the employer has lawfully recognized in accordance with this Act any other labor organization and a question concerning representation may not appropriately be raised under section 9(c) of this Act,

(B) where within the preceding twelve months a valid election under section 9(c) of this Act has been conducted, or

(C) where such picketing has been conducted without a petition under section 9(c) being filed within a reasonable period of time not to exceed thirty days from the commencement of such picketing: *Provided*, That when such a petition has been filed the Board shall forthwith, without regard to the provisions of section 9(c)(1) or the absence of a showing of a substantial interest on the part of the labor organization, direct an election in such unit as the Board finds to be appropriate and shall certify the results thereof: *Provided further*, That nothing in this subparagraph (C) shall be construed to prohibit any picketing or other publicity for the purpose of truthfully advising the public (including consumers) that an employer does not employ members of, or have a contract with, a labor organization, unless an effect of such picketing is to induce any individual employed by any other person in the course of his employment, not to pick up, deliver or transport any goods or not to perform any services.

Nothing in this paragraph (7) shall be construed to permit any act which would otherwise be an unfair labor practice under this section 8(b).

(c) The expressing of any views, argument, or opinion, or the dissemination thereof, whether in written, printed, graphic, or visual form, shall not constitute or be evidence of an unfair labor practice under any of the provisions of this Act, if such expression contains no threat of reprisal or force or promise of benefit.

(d) For the purposes of this section, to bargain collectively is the performance of the mutual obligation of the employer and the representative of the employees to meet at reasonable times and confer in good faith with respect to wages, hours, and other terms and conditions of employment, or the negotiation of an agreement, or any question arising thereunder, and the execution of a written contract incorporating any agreement reached if requested by either party, but such obligation does not compel either party to agree to a proposal or require the making of a concession: *Provided,* That where there is in effect a collective-bargaining contract covering employees in an industry affecting commerce, the duty to bargain collectively shall also mean that no party to such contract shall terminate or modify such contract, unless the party desiring such termination or modification—

(1) serves a written notice upon the other party to the contract of the proposed termination or modification sixty days prior to the expiration date thereof, or in the event such contract contains no expiration date, sixty days prior to the time it is proposed to make such termination or modification;

(2) offers to meet and confer with the other party for the purpose of negotiating a new contract or a contract containing the proposed modifications;

(3) notifies the Federal Mediation and Conciliation Service within thirty days after such notice of the existence of a dispute, and simultaneously therewith notifies any State or Territorial agency established to mediate and conciliate disputes within the State or Territory where the dispute occurred, provided no agreement has been reached by that time; and

(4) continues in full force and effect, without resorting to strike or lockout, all the terms and conditions of the existing contract for a period of sixty days after such notice is given or until the expiration date of such contract, whichever occurs later:

The duties imposed upon employers, employees, and labor organizations by paragraphs (2), (3), and (4) shall become inapplicable upon an intervening certification of the Board, under which the labor organization or individual, which is a party to the contract, has been superseded as or ceased to be the representative of the employees subject to the provisions of section 9(a), and the duties so imposed shall not be construed as requiring either party to discuss or agree to any modification of the terms and conditions contained in a contract for a fixed period, if such modification is to become effective before such terms and conditions can be reopened under the provisions of the contract. Any employee who engages in a strike within ⟦the sixty-day⟧ *any notice* period specified in this subsection, *or who engages in any strike within the appropriate period specified in subsection (g) of this section,* shall lose his status as an employee of the employer engaged in the particular labor dispute, for the purposes of sections 8, 9, and 10 of this Act, as amended, but such loss of status for such employee shall terminate if and when he is reemployed by such employer. *Whenever the collective bargaining involves employees of a health care institution, the provisions of this section 8(d) shall be modified as follows:*

(A) The notice period of section 8(d)(1) shall be ninety days; the notice period of section 8(d)(3) shall be sixty days; and the contract period of section 8(d)(4) shall be ninety days.

(B) Where the bargaining is for an initial agreement following certification or recognition, at least thirty days' notice of the existence of a dispute shall be given by the labor organization to the agencies set forth in section 8(d)(3).

(C) After notice is given to the Federal Mediation and Conciliation Service under either clause (A) or (B) of this sentence, the Service shall promptly communicate with the parties and use its best efforts, by mediation and conciliation, to bring them to agreement. The parties shall participate fully and promptly in such meetings as may be undertaken by the Service for the purpose of aiding in a settlement of the dispute.

(e) It shall be an unfair labor practice for any labor organization and any employer to enter into any contract or agreement, express or implied, whereby such employer ceases or refrains or agrees to cease or refrain from handling, using, selling, transporting or otherwise dealing in any of the products of any other employer, or to cease doing business with any other person, and any contract or agreement entered into heretofore or hereafter containing such an agreement shall be to such extent unenforceable and void: *Provided*, That nothing in this subsection (e) shall apply to an agreement between a labor organization and an employer in the construction industry relating to the contracting or subcontracting of work to be done at the site of the construction, alteration, painting, or repair of a building, structure, or other work: *Provided further*, That for the purposes of this subsection (e) and section 8(b)(4)(B) the terms "any employer", "any person engaged in commerce or in industry affecting commerce", and "any person" when used in relation to the terms "any other producer, processor, or manufacturer", "any other employer", or "any other person" shall not include persons in the relation of a jobber, manufacturer, contractor, or subcontractor working on the goods or premises of the jobber or manufacturer or performing parts of an integrated process of production in the apparel and clothing industry: *Provided further*, That nothing in this Act shall prohibit the enforcement of any agreement which is within the foregoing exception.

(f) It shall not be an unfair labor practice under subsections (a) and (b) of this section for an employer engaged primarily in the building and construction industry to make an agreement covering employees engaged (or who, upon their employment, will be engaged) in the building and construction industry with a labor organization of which building and construction employees are members (not established, maintained, or assisted by any action defined in section 8(a) of this Act as an unfair labor practice) because (1) the majority status of such labor organization has not been established under the provisions of section 9 of this Act prior to the making of such agreement, or (2) such agreement requires as a condition of employment, membership in such labor organization after the seventh day following the begining of such employment or the effective date of the agreement, whichever is later, or (3) such agreement requires the employer to notify such labor organization of opportunities for employment with such employer, or gives such labor organization an opportunity to refer qualified applicants for such employment, or (4) such agreement specifies minimum training or experience qualifications for employment or provides for priority in opportunities for employment based upon length of service with such employer, in the industry or in the particular geographical area: *Provided*, That nothing in this subsection shall set aside the final proviso to section 8(a)(3) of this Act: *Provided further*, That any agreement which would be invalid, but for clause (1) of this subsection, shall not be a bar to a petition filed pursuant to section 9(c) or 9(e).

(g) A labor organization before engaging in any picketing, striking, or other concerted refusal to work at any health care institution shall, not less than ten days prior to such action notify the institution in writing and the Federal Mediation and Conciliation Service of that intention, except that in the case of bargaining for an initial agreement following certification or recognition the notice required by this sentence shall not be given until the expiration of the period specified in clause (B) of the last sentence of section 8(d) of this Act. The notice shall state the date and time that such action will commence. The notice, once given, may be extended by the written agreement of both parties.

REPRESENTATIVES AND ELECTIONS

SEC. 9. (a) Representatives designated or selected for the purposes of collective bargaining by the majority of the employees in a unit appropriate for such purposes, shall be the exclusive representatives of all the employees in such unit for the purposes of collective bargaining in respect to rates of pay, wages, hours of employment, or other conditions of employment: *Provided,* That any individual employee or a group of employees shall have the right at any time to present grievances to their employer and to have such grievances adjusted, without the intervention of the bargaining representative, as long as the adjustment is not inconsistent with the terms of a collective-bargaining contract or agreement then in effect: *Provided further,* That the bargaining representative has been given opportunity to be present at such adjustment.

(b) The Board shall decide in each case whether, in order to assure to employees the fullest freedom in exercising the rights guaranteed by this Act, the unit appropriate for the purposes of collective bargaining shall be the employer unit, craft unit, plant unit, or subdivision thereof: *Provided,* That the Board shall not (1) decide that any unit is appropriate for such purposes if such unit includes both professional employees and employees who are not professional employees unless a majority of such professional employees vote for inclusion in such unit; or (2) decide that any craft unit is inappropriate for such purposes on the ground that a different unit has been established by a prior Board determination, unless a majority of the employees in the proposed craft unit vote against separate representation or (3) decide that any unit is appropriate for such purposes if it includes, together with other employees, any individual employed as a guard to enforce against employees and other persons rules to protect property of the employer or to protect the safety of persons on the employer's premises; but no labor organization shall be certified as the representative of employees in a bargaining unit of guards if such organization admits to membership, or is affiliated directly or indirectly with an organization which admits to membership, employees other than guards.

(c)(1) Wherever a petition shall have been filed, in accordance with such regulations as may be prescribed by the Board—

(A) by an employee or group of employees or any individual or labor organization acting in their behalf alleging that a substantial number of employees (i) wish to be represented for collective bargaining and that their employer declines to recognize their representative as the representative defined in section 9(a), or (ii) assert that the individual or labor organization, which has been certified or is being currently recognized by their employer as the bargaining representative, is no longer a representative as defined in section 9(a); or

(B) by an employer, alleging that one or more individuals or labor organizations have presented to him a claim to be recognized as the representative defined in section 9(a);

the Board shall investigate such petition and if it has reasonable cause to believe that a question of representation affecting commerce exists shall provide for an appropriate hearing upon due notice. Such hearing may be conducted by an officer or employee of the regional office, who shall not make any recommendations with respect thereto. If the Board finds upon the record of such hearing that such a question of representation exists, it shall direct an election by secret ballot and shall certify the results thereof.

(2) In determining whether or not a question of representation affecting commerce exists, the same regulations and rules of decision shall apply irrespective of the identity of the persons filing the petition or the kind of relief sought and in no case shall the Board deny a labor organization a place on the ballot by reason of an order with respect to such labor organization or its predecessor not issued in conformity with section 10(c).

(3) No election shall be directed in any bargaining unit or any subdivision within which, in the preceding twelve-month period, a valid election shall have been held. Employees engaged in an economic strike who are not entitled to reinstatement shall be eligible to vote under such regulations as the Board shall find are consistent with the purposes and provisions of this Act in any election conducted within twelve months after the commencement of the strike. In any election where none of the choices on the ballot receives a majority, a run-off shall be conducted, the ballot providing for a selection between the two choices receiving the largest and second largest number of valid votes cast in the election.

(4) Nothing in this section shall be construed to prohibit the waiving of hearings by stipulation for the purpose of a consent election in conformity with regulations and rules of decision of the Board.

(5) In determining whether a unit is appropriate for the purposes specified in subsection (b) the extent to which the employees have organized shall not be controlling.

(d) Whenever an order of the Board made pursuant to section 10(c) is based in whole or in part upon facts certified following an investigation pursuant to subsection (c) of this section and there is a petition for the enforcement or review of such order, such certification and the record of such investigation shall be included in the transcript of the entire record required to be filed under section 10(e) or 10(f), and thereupon the decree of the court enforcing, modifying, or setting aside in whole or in part the order of the Board shall be made and entered upon the pleadings, testimony, and proceedings set forth in such transcript.

(e)(1) Upon the filing with the Board, by 30 per centum or more of the employees in a bargaining unit covered by an agreement between their employer and a labor organization made pursuant to section 8(a)(3), of a petition alleging they desire that such authority be rescinded, the Board shall take a secret ballot of the employees in such unit and certify the results thereof to such labor organization and to the employer.

(2) No election shall be conducted pursuant to this subsection in any bargaining unit or any subdivision within which, in the preceding twelve-month period, a valid election shall have been held.

PREVENTION OF UNFAIR LABOR PRACTICES

SEC. 10. (a) The Board is empowered, as hereinafter provided, to prevent any person from engaging in any unfair labor practice (listed in section 8) affecting commerce. This power shall not be affected by any other means of adjustment or prevention that has been or may be established by agreement, law, or otherwise: *Provided*, That the Board is empowered by agreement with any agency of any State or Territory to cede to such agency jurisdiction over any cases in any industry (other than mining, manufacturing, communications, and transportation except where predominantly local in character) even though such cases may involve labor disputes affecting commerce, unless the provision of the State or Territorial statute applicable to the determination of such cases by such agency is inconsistent with the corresponding provision of this Act or has received a construction inconsistent therewith.

(b) Whenever it is charged that any person has engaged in or is engaging in any such unfair labor practice, the Board, or any agent or agency designated by the Board for such purposes, shall have power to issue and cause to be served upon such person a complaint stating the charges in that respect, and containing a notice of hearing before the Board or a member thereof, or before a designated agent or agency, at a place therein fixed, not less than five days after the serving of said complaint: *Provided*, That no complaint shall issue based upon any unfair labor practice occurring more than six months prior to the filing of the charge with the Board and the service of a copy thereof upon the person against whom such charge is made, unless the person aggrieved thereby was prevented from filing such charge by reason of service in the armed forces, in which event the six-month period shall be computed from the day of his discharge. Any such complaint may be amended by the member, agent, or agency conducting the hearing or the Board in its discretion at any time prior to the issuance of an order based thereon. The person so complained of shall have the right to file an answer to the original or amended complaint and to appear in person or otherwise and give testimony at the place and time fixed in the complaint. In the discretion of the member, agent, or agency conducting the hearing or the Board, any other person may be allowed to intervene in the said proceeding and to present testimony. Any such proceeding shall, so far as practicable, be conducted in accordance with the rules of evidence applicable in the district courts of the United States under the rules of civil procedure for the district courts of the United States, adopted by the Supreme Court of the United States pursuant to the Act of June 19, 1934 (U.S.C., title 28, secs. 723–B, 723–C).

(c) The testimony taken by such member, agent, or agency or the Board shall be reduced to writing and filed with the Board. Thereafter, in its discretion, the Board upon notice may take further testimony or hear argument. If upon the preponderance of the testimony taken the Board shall be of the opinion that any person named in the complaint has engaged in or is engaging in any such unfair labor practice, then the Board shall state its findings of fact and shall issue and cause to be served on such person an order requiring such person to cease and desist from such unfair labor practice, and to take such affirmative action including reinstatement of employees with or without back pay, as will effectuate the policies of this Act: *Provided,* That where an order directs reinstatement of an employee, back pay may be required of the employer or labor organization, as the case may be, responsible for the discrimination suffered by him: *And provided further,* That in determining whether a complaint shall issue alleging a violation of section 8(a)(1) or section 8(a)(2), and in deciding such cases, the same regulations and rules of decision shall apply irrespective of whether or not the labor organization affected is affiliated with a labor organization national or international in scope. Such order may further require such person to make reports from time to time showing the extent to which it has complied with the order. If upon the preponderance of the testimony taken the Board shall not be of the opinion that the person named in the complaint has engaged in or is engaging in any such unfair labor practice, then the Board shall state its findings of fact and shall issue an order dismissing the said complaint. No order of the Board shall require the reinstatement of any individual as an employee who has been suspended or discharged, or the payment to him of any back pay, if such individual was suspended or discharged for cause. In case the evidence is presented before a member of the Board, or before an examiner or examiners thereof, such member, or such examiner or examiners, as the case may be, shall issue and cause to be served on the parties to the proceeding a proposed report, together with a recommended order, which shall be filed with the Board, and if no exceptions are filed within twenty days after service thereof upon such parties, or within such further period as the Board may authorize, such recommended order shall become the order of the Board and become effective as therein prescribed.

(d) Until the record in a case shall have been filed in a court, as hereinafter provided, the Board may at any time, upon reasonable notice and in such manner as it shall deem proper, modify or set aside, in whole or in part, any finding or order made or issued by it.

(e) The Board shall have power to petition any court of appeals of the United States, or if all the courts of appeals to which application may be made are in vacation, any district court of the United States, within any circuit or district, respectively, wherein the unfair labor practice in question occurred or wherein such person resides or transacts business, for the enforcement of such order and for appropriate temporary relief or restraining order, and shall file in the court the record in the proceedings, as provided in section 2112 of title 28, United States Code. Upon the filing of such petition, the court shall cause notice thereof to be served upon such person, and thereupon shall have jurisdiction of the proceeding and of the question determined therein, and shall have power to grant such temporary relief or restraining order as it deems just and proper, and to make and enter a decree enforcing, modifying, and enforcing as so modified, or setting aside in whole or in part the order of the Board. No objection that has not been urged before the Board, its member, agent, or agency, shall be considered by the court, unless the failure or neglect to urge such objection shall be excused because of extraordinary circumstances. The findings of the Board with respect to questions of fact if supported by substantial evidence on the record considered as a whole shall be conclusive. If either party shall apply to the court for leave to adduce additional evidence and shall show to the satisfaction of the court that such additional evidence is material and that there were reasonable grounds for the failure to adduce such evidence in the hearing before the Board, its member, agent, or agency, the court may order such additional evidence to be taken before the Board, its member, agent, or agency, and to be made a part of the record. The Board may modify its findings as to the facts, or make new findings, by reason of additional evidence so taken and filed, and it shall file such modified or new findings, which findings with respect to questions of fact if supported by substantial evidence on the record considered as a whole shall be conclusive, and shall file its recommendations, if any, for the modification or setting aside of its original order. Upon the filing of the record with it the jurisdiction of the court shall be exclusive and its judgment and decree shall be final, except that the same shall be subject to review by the appropriate United States court of appeals if application was made to the district court as hereinabove provided, and by the Supreme Court of the United States upon writ of certiorari or certification as provided in section 1254 of title 28.

(f) Any person aggrieved by a final order of the Board granting or denying in whole or in part the relief sought may obtain a review of such order in any circuit court of appeals of the United States in the circuit wherein the unfair labor practice in question was alleged to have been engaged in or wherein such person resides or transacts business, or in the United States Court of Appeals for the District of Columbia, by filing in such court a written petition praying that the order of the Board be modified or set aside. A copy of such petition shall be forthwith transmitted by the clerk of the court to the Board, and thereupon the aggrieved party shall file in the court the record in the proceeding, certified by the Board, as provided in section 2112 of title 28, United States Code. Upon the filing of such petition, the court shall proceed in the same manner as in the case of an application by the Board under subsection (e) of this section, and shall have the same jurisdiction to grant to the Board such temporary relief of restraining order as it deems just and proper, and in like manner to make and enter a decree enforcing, modifying, and enforcing as so modified, or setting aside in whole or in part the order of the Board; the findings of the Board with respect to questions of fact if supported by substantial evidence on the record considered as a whole shall in like manner be conclusive.

(g) The commencement of proceedings under subsection (e) or (f) of this section shall not, unless specifically ordered by the court, operate as a stay of the Board's order.

(h) When granting appropriate temporary relief or a restraining order, or making and entering a decree enforcing, modifying, and enforcing as so modified, or setting aside in whole or in part an order of the Board, as provided in this section, the jurisdiction of courts sitting in equity shall not be limited by the Act entitled "An Act to amend the Judicial Code and to define and limit the jurisdiction of courts sitting in equity, and for other purposes," approved March 23, 1932 (U.S.C., Supp. VII, title 29, secs. 101–115).

(i) Petitions filed under this Act shall be heard expeditiously, and if possible within ten days after they have been docketed.

(j) The Board shall have power, upon issuance of a complaint as provided in subsection (b) charging that any person has engaged in or is engaging in an unfair labor practice, to petition any district court of the United States (including the District Court of the United States for the District of Columbia), within any district wherein the unfair labor practice in question is alleged to have occurred or wherein such person resides or transacts business, for appropriate temporary relief or restraining order. Upon the filing of any such petition the court shall cause notice thereof to be served upon such person, and thereupon shall have jurisdiction to grant to the Board such temporary relief or restraining order as it deems just and proper.

(k) Whenever it is charged that any person has engaged in an unfair labor practice within the meaning of paragraph (4)(D) of section 8(b), the Board is empowered and directed to hear and determine the dispute out of which such unfair labor practice shall have arisen, unless, within ten days after notice that such charge has been filed, the parties to such dispute submit to the Board satisfactory evidence that they have adjusted, or agreed upon methods for the voluntary adjustment of, the dispute. Upon compliance by the parties to the dispute with the decision of the Board or upon such voluntary adjustment of the dispute, such charge shall be dismissed.

(l) Whenever it is charged that any person has engaged in an unfair labor practice within the meaning of paragraph (4) (A), (B), or (C) of section 8(b), or section 8(e) or section 8(b)(7), the preliminary investigation of such charge shall be made forthwith and given priority over all other cases except cases of like character in the office where it is filed or to which it is referred. If, after such investigation, the officer or regional attorney to whom the matter may be referred has reasonable cause to believe such charge is true and that a com plaint should issue, he shall on behalf of the Board, petition any district court of the United States (including the District Court of the United States for the District of Columbia) within any district where the unfair labor practice in question has occurred, is alleged to have occurred, or wherein such person resides or transacts business, for appropriate injunctive relief pending the final adjudication of the Board with respect to such matter. Upon the filing of any such petition the district court shall have jurisdiction to grant such injunctive relief or temporary restraining order as it deems just and proper, notwithstanding any other provision of law: *Provided further,* That no temporary restraining order shall be issued without notice unless a petition alleges that substantial and irreparable injury to the charging party will be unavoidable and such temporary restraining order shall be effective for no longer than five days and will become void at the expiration of such period: *Provided further,* That such officer or regional attorney shall not apply for any restraining order under section 8(b)(7) if a charge against the employer under section 8(a)(2) has been filed and after the preliminary investigation, he has reasonable cause to believe that such charge is true and that a complaint should issue. Upon filing of any such petition the courts shall cause notice thereof to be served upon any person involved in the charge and such person, including the charging party, shall be given an opportunity to appear by counsel and present any relevant testimony: *Provided further,* That for the purposes of this subsection district courts shall be deemed to have jurisdiction of a labor organization (1) in the district in which such organization maintains its principal office, or (2) in any district in which its duly authorized officers or agents are engaged in promoting or protecting the interests of employee members. The service of legal process upon such officer or agent shall constitute service upon the labor organization and make such organizations a party to the suit. In situations where such relief is appropriate the procedure specified herein shall apply to charges with respect to section 8(b)(4)(D).

(m) Whenever it is charged that any person has engaged in an unfair labor practice within the meaning of subsection (a)(3) or (b)(2) of section 8, such charge shall be given priority over all other cases except cases of like character in the office where it is filed or to which it is referred and cases given priority under subsection (l).

INVESTIGATORY POWERS

SEC. 11. For the purpose of all hearings and investigations, which, in the opinion of the Board, are necessary and proper for the exercise of the powers vested in it by section 9 and section 10—

(5) The Board, or its duly authorized agents or agencies, shall at all reasonable times have access to, for the purpose of examination, and the right to copy any evidence of any person being investigated or proceeded against that relates to any matter under investigation or in question. The Board, or any member thereof, shall upon application of any party to such proceedings, forthwith issue to such party subpenas requiring the attendance and testimony of witnesses or the production of any evidence in such proceeding or investigation requested in such application. Within five days after the service of a subpena on any person requiring the production of any evidence in his possession or under his control, such person may petition the Board to revoke, and the Board shall revoke, such subpena if in its opinion the evidence whose production is required does not relate to any matter under investigation, or any matter in question in such proceedings, or if in its opinion such subpena does not describe with sufficient particularity the evidence whose production is required. Any member of the Board, or any agent or agency designed by the Board for such purposes, may administer oaths and affirmations, examine witnesses, and receive evidence. Such attendance of witnesses and the production of such evidence may be required from any place in the United States or any Territory or possession thereof, at any designated place of hearing.

(2) In case of contumacy or refusal to obey a subpena issued to any person, any district court of the United States or the United States courts of any Territory or possession, or the District Court of the United States for the District of Columbia, within the jurisdiction of which the inquiry is carried on or within the jurisdiction of which said person guilty of contumacy or refusal to obey is found or resides or transacts business, upon application by the Board shall have jurisdiction to issue to such person an order requiring such person to appear before the Board, its member, agent, or agency, there to produce evidence if so ordered, or there to give testimony touching the matter under investigation or in question; and any failure to obey such order of the court may be punished by said court as a contempt thereof.

(3)*

*Section 11(3) is repealed by Sec. 234, Public Law 91-452, 91st Congress, S. 30, 84 Stat. 926, October 15, 1970. See Title 18, U.S.C. Sec. 6001, et seq.

(4) Complaints, orders, and other process and papers of the Board, its member, agent, or agency, may be served either personally or by registered mail or by telegraph or by leaving a copy thereof at the principal office or place of business of the person required to be served. The verified return by the individual so serving the same setting forth the manner of such service shall be proof of the same, and the return post office receipt or telegraph receipt therefor when registered and mailed or telegraphed as aforesaid shall be proof of service of the same. Witnesses summoned before the Board, its member, agent, or agency, shall be paid the same fees and mileage that are paid witnesses in the courts of the United States, and witnesses whose depositions are taken and the persons taking the same shall severally be entitled to the same fees as are paid for like services in the courts of the United States.

(5) All process of any court to which application may be made under this Act may be served in the judicial district wherein the defendant or other person required to be served resides or may be found.

(6) The several departments and agencies of the Government, when directed by the President, shall furnish the Board, upon its request, all records, papers, and information in their possession relating to any matter before the Board.

SEC. 12. Any person who shall willfully resist, prevent, impede, or interfere with any member of the Board or any of its agents or agencies in the performance of duties pursuant to this Act shall be punished by a fine of not more than $5,000 or by imprisonment for not more than one year, or both.

LIMITATIONS

SEC. 13. Nothing in this Act, except as specifically provided for herein, shall be construed so as either to interfere with or impede or diminish in any way the right to strike, or to affect the limitations or qualifications on that right.

SEC. 14. (a) Nothing herein shall prohibit any individual employed as a supervisor from becoming or remaining a member of a labor organization, but no employer subject to this Act shall be compelled to deem individuals defined herein as supervisors as employees for the purpose of any law, either national or local, relating to collective bargaining.

(b) Nothing in this Act shall be construed as authorizing the execution or application of agreements requiring membership in a labor organization as a condition of employment in any State or Territory in which such execution or application is prohibited by State or Territorial law.

(c)(1) The Board, in its discretion, may, by rule of decision or by published rules adopted pursuant to the Administrative Procedure Act, decline to assert jurisdiction over any labor dispute involving any class or category of employers, where, in the opinion of the Board, the effect of such labor dispute on commerce is not sufficiently substantial to warrant the exercise of its jurisdiction: *Provided*, That the Board shall not decline to assert jurisdiction over any labor dispute over which it would assert jurisdiction under the standards prevailing upon August 5, 1959.

(2) Nothing in this Act shall be deemed to prevent or bar any agency or the courts of any State or Territory (including the Commonwealth of Puerto Rico, Guam, and the Virgin Islands), from

assuming and asserting jurisdiction over labor disputes over which the Board declines, pursuant to paragraph (1) of this subsection, to assert jurisdiction.

SEC. 15. Wherever the application of the provisions of section 272 of chapter 10 of the Act entitled "An Act to establish a uniform system of bankruptcy throughout the United States," approved July 1, 1898, and Acts amendatory thereof and supplementary thereto (U.S.C., title 11, sec. 672), conflicts with the application of the provisions of this Act, this Act shall prevail: *Provided*, That in any situation where the provisions of this Act cannot be validly enforced, the provisions of such other Acts shall remain in full force and effect.

SEC. 16. If any provision of this Act, or the application of such provision to any person or circumstances, shall be held invalid, the remainder of this Act, or the application of such provision to persons or circumstances other than those as to which it is held invalid, shall not be affected thereby.

SEC. 17. This Act may be cited as the "National Labor Relations Act."

SEC. 18. No petition entertained, no investigation made, no election held, and no certification issued by the National Labor Relations Board, under any of the provisions of section 9 of the National Labor Relations Act, as amended, shall be invalid by reason of the failure of the Congress of Industrial Organizations to have complied with the requirements of section 9(f), (g), or (h) of the aforesaid Act prior to December 22, 1949, or by reason of the failure of the American Federation of Labor to have complied with the provisions of section 9(f), (g), or (h) of the aforesaid Act prior to November 7, 1947: *Provided*, That no liability shall be imposed under any provision of this Act upon any person for failure to honor any election of certificate referred to above, prior to the effective date of this amendment: *Provided, however*, That this proviso shall not have the effect of setting aside or in any way affecting judgments or decrees heretofore entered under section 10(e) or (f) and which have become final.

SEC. 19. Any employee of a health care institution who is a member of and adheres to established and traditional tenets or teachings of a bona fide religion, body, or sect which has historically held conscientious objections to joining or financially supporting labor organizations shall not be required to join or financially support any labor organization as a condition of employment; except that such employee may be required, in lieu of periodic dues and initiation fees, to pay sums equal to such dues and initiation fees to a nonreligious charitable fund exempt from taxation under section 501(c)(3) of the Internal Revenue Code, chosen by such employee from a list of at least three such funds, designated in a contract between such institution and a labor organization, or if the contract fails to designate such funds, then to any such fund chosen by the employee.

EFFECTIVE DATE OF CERTAIN CHANGES

SEC. 102. No provision of this title shall be deemed to make an unfair labor practice any act which was performed prior to the date of the enactment of this Act which did not constitute an unfair labor practice prior thereto, and the provisions of section 8(a)(3) and section 8(b)(2) of the National Labor Relations Act as amended by this title shall not make an unfair labor practice the performance of any obligation under a collective-bargaining agreement entered into prior to the date of the enactment of this Act, or (in the case of an agreement for a period of not more than one year) entered into on or after such date of enactment, but prior to the effective date of this title, if the performance of such obligation would not have constituted an unfair labor practice under section 8(3) of the National Labor Relations Act prior to the effective date of this title, unless such agreement was renewed or extended subsequent thereto.

SEC. 103. No provisions of this title shall affect any certification of representatives or any determination as to the appropriate collective-bargaining unit, which was made under section 9 of the National Labor Relations Act prior to the effective date of this title until one year after the date of such certification or if, in respect of any such certification, a collective-bargaining contract was entered into prior to the effective date of this title, until the end of the contract period or until one year after such date, whichever first occurs.

SEC. 104. The amendments made by this title shall take effect sixty days after the date of the enactment of this Act, except that the authority of the President to appoint certain officers conferred upon him by section 3 of the National Labor Relations Act as amended by this title may be exercised forthwith.

TITLE II—CONCILIATION OF LABOR DISPUTES IN INDUSTRIES AFFECTING COMMERCE; NATIONAL EMERGENCIES

SEC. 201. That it is the policy of the United States that—

(a) sound and stable industrial peace and the advancement of the general welfare, health, and safety of the Nation and of the best interest of employers and employees can most satisfactorily be secured by the settlement of issues between employers and employees through the processes of conference and collective bargaining between employers and the representatives of their employees;

(b) the settlement of issues between employers and employees through collective bargaining may be advanced by making available full and adequate governmental facilities for conciliation, mediation, and voluntary arbitration to aid and encourage employers and the representatives of their employees to reach and maintain agreements concerning rates of pay, hours, and working conditions, and to make all reasonable efforts to settle their differences by mutual agreement reached through conferences and collective bargaining or by such methods as may be provided for in any applicable agreement for the settlement of disputes; and

(c) certain controversies which arise between parties to collective-bargaining agreements may be avoided or minimized by making available full and adequate governmental facilities for furnishing assistance to employers and the representatives of their employees in formulating for inclusion within such agreements provision for adequate notice of any proposed changes in the terms of such agreements, for the final adjustment of grievances or questions regarding the application or interpretation of such agreements, and other provisions designed to prevent the subsequent arising of such controversies.

SEC. 202. (a) There is hereby created an independent agency to be known as the Federal Mediation and Conciliation Service (herein referred to as the "Service," except that for sixty days after the date of the enactment of this Act such term shall refer to the Conciliation Service of the Department of Labor). The Service shall be under the direction of a Federal Mediation and Conciliation Director (hereinafter referred to as the "Director"), who shall be appointed by the President by and with the advice and consent of the Senate. The Director shall receive compensation at the rate of $12,000 per annum. The Director shall not engage in any other business, vocation, or employment.

(b) The Director is authorized, subject to the civil-service laws; to appoint such clerical and other personnel as may be necessary for the execution of the functions of the Service, and shall fix their compensation in accordance with the Classification Act of 1923,• as amended, and may, without regard to the provisions of the civil service laws and the Classification Act of 1923, as amended, appoint and fix the compensation of such conciliators and mediators as may be necessary to carry out the functions of the Service. The Director is authorized to make such expenditures for supplies, facilities, and services as he deems necessary. Such expenditures shall be allowed and paid upon presentation of itemized vouchers therefor approved by the Director or by any employee designated by him for that purpose.

(c) The principal office of the Service shall be in the District of Columbia, but the Director may establish regional offices convenient to localities in which labor controversies are likely to arise. The Director may by order, subject to revocation at any time, delegate any authority and discretion conferred upon him by this Act to any regional director, or other officer or employee of the Service. The Director may establish suitable procedures for cooperation with State and local mediation agencies. The Director shall make an annual report in writing to Congress at the end of the fiscal year.

(d) All mediation and conciliation functions of the Secretary of Labor or the United States Conciliation Service under section 8 of the Act entitled "An Act to create a Department of Labor," approved March 4, 1913 (U.S.C., title 29, sec. 51), and all functions of the United States Conciliation Service under any other law are hereby transferred to the Federal Mediation and Conciliation Service, together with the personnel and records of the United States Conciliation Service. Such transfer shall take effect upon the sixtieth day after the date of enactment of this Act. Such transfer shall not affect any proceedings pending before the United States Conciliation Service or any certification, order, rule, or regulation theretofore made by it or by the Secretary of Labor. The Director and the Service shall not be subject in any way to the jurisdiction or authority of the Secretary of Labor or any official or division of the Department of Labor.

FUNCTIONS OF THE SERVICE

SEC. 203. (a) It shall be the duty of the Service, in order to prevent or minimize interruptions of the free flow of commerce growing out of labor disputes to assist parties to labor disputes in industries affecting commerce to settle such disputes through conciliation and mediation.

(b) The Service may proffer its services in any labor dispute in any industry affecting commerce, either upon its own motion or upon the request of one or more of the parties to the dispute, whenever in its judgment such dispute threatens to cause a substantial interruption of commerce. The Director and the Service are directed to avoid attempting to mediate disputes which would have only a minor effect on interstate commerce if State or other conciliation services are available to the parties. Whenever the Service does proffer its services in any dispute, it shall be the duty of the Service promptly to put itself in communication with the parties and to use its best efforts, by mediation and conciliation, to bring them to agreement.

(c) If the Director is not able to bring the parties to agreement by conciliation within a reasonable time, he shall seek to induce the parties voluntarily to seek other means of settling the dispute without resort to strike, lock-out, or other coercion, including submission to the employees in the bargaining unit of the employer's last offer of settlement for approval or rejection in a secret ballot. The failure or refusal of either party to agree to any procedure suggested by the Director shall not be deemed a violation of any duty or obligation imposed by this Act.

(d) Final adjustment by a method agreed upon by the parties is hereby declared to be the desirable method for settlement of grievance disputes arising over the application or interpretation of an existing collective-bargaining agreement. The Service is directed to make its conciliation and mediation services available in the settlement of such grievance disputes only as a last resort and in exceptional cases.

SEC. 204. (a) In order to prevent or minimize interruptions of the free flow of commerce growing out of labor disputes, employers and employees and their representatives, in any industry affecting commerce, shall—

(1) exert every reasonable effort to make and maintain agreements concerning rates of pay, hours, and working conditions, including provision for adequate notice of any proposed change in the terms of such agreements;

(2) whenever a dispute arises over the terms or application of a collective-bargaining agreement and a conference is requested by a party or prospective party thereto, arrange promptly for such a conference to be held and endeavor in such conference to settle such dispute expeditiously; and

(3) in case such dispute is not settled by conference, participate fully and promptly in such meetings as may be undertaken by the Service under this Act for the purpose of aiding in a settlement of the dispute.

SEC. 205. (a) There is hereby created a National Labor-Management Panel which shall be composed of twelve members appointed by the President, six of whom shall be selected from among persons outstanding in the field of management and six of whom shall be selected from among persons outstanding in the field of labor. Each member shall hold office for a term of three years, except that any member appointed to fill a vacancy occurring prior to the expiration of the term for which his predecessor was appointed shall be appointed for the remainder of such term, and the terms of office of the members first taking office shall expire, as designated by the President at the time of appointment, four at the end of the first year, four at the end of the second year, and four at the end of the third year after the date of appointment. Members of the panel, when serving on business of the panel, shall be paid compensation at the rate of $25 per day, and shall also be entitled to receive an allowance for actual and necessary travel and subsistence expenses while so serving away from their places of residence.

(b) It shall be the duty of the panel, at the request of the Director, to advise in the avoidance of industrial controversies and the manner in which mediation and voluntary adjustment shall be administered, particularly with reference to controversies affecting the general welfare of the country.

NATIONAL EMERGENCIES

Sec. 206. Whenever in the opinion of the President of the United States, a threatened or actual strike or lock-out affecting an entire industry or a substantial part thereof engaged in trade, commerce, transportation, transmission, or communication among the several States or with foreign nations, or engaged in the production of goods for commerce, will, if permitted to occur or to continue, imperil the national health or safety, he may appoint a board of inquiry to inquire into the issues involved in the dispute and to make a written report to him within such time as he shall prescribe. Such report shall include a statement of the facts with respect to the dispute, including each party's statement of its position but shall not contain any recommendations. The President shall file a copy of such report with the Service and shall make its contents available to the public.

Sec. 207. (a) A board of inquiry shall be composed of a chairman and such other members as the President shall determine, and shall have power to sit and act in any place within the United States and to conduct such hearings either in public or in private, as it may deem necessary or proper, to ascertain the facts with respect to the causes and circumstances of the dispute.

(b) Members of a board of inquiry shall receive compensation at the rate of $50 for each day actually spent by them in the work of the board, together with necessary travel and subsistence expenses.

(c) For the purpose of any hearing or inquiry conducted by any board appointed under this title, the provisions of sections 9 and 10 (relating to the attendance of witnesses and the production of books, papers, and documents) of the Federal Trade Commission Act of September 16, 1914, as amended (U.S.C. 19, title 15, secs. 49 and 50, as amended), are hereby made applicable to the powers and duties of such board.

Sec. 208. (a) Upon receiving a report from a board of inquiry the President may direct the Attorney General to petition any district court of the United States having jurisdiction of the parties to enjoin such strike or lock-out or the continuing thereof, and if the court finds that such threatened or actual strike or lock-out—

(i) affects an entire industry or a substantial part therof engaged in trade, commerce, transportation, transmission, or communication among the several States or with foreign nations, or engaged in the production of goods for commerce; and

(ii) if permitted to occur or to continue, will imperil the national health or safety, it shall have jurisdiction to enjoin any such strike or lock-out, or the continuing thereof, and to make such other orders as may be appropriate.

(b) In any case, the provisions of the Act of March 23, 1932, entitled "An Act to amend the Judicial Code and to define and limit the jurisdiction of courts sitting in equity, and for other purposes," shall not be applicable.

(c) The order or orders of the court shall be subject to review by the appropriate circuit court of appeals and by the Supreme Court upon writ of certiorari or certification as provided in section 239 and 240 of the Judicial Code, as amended (U.S.C., title 29, secs, 346 and 347).

SEC. 209. (a) Whenever a district court has issued an order under section 208 enjoining acts or practices which imperil or threaten to imperil the national health or safety, it shall be the duty of the parties to the labor dispute giving rise to such order to make every effort to adjust and settle their differences, with the assistance of the Service created by this Act. Neither party shall be under any duty to accept, in whole or in part, any proposal of settlement made by the Service.

(b) Upon the issuance of such order, the President shall reconvene the board of inquiry which has previously reported with respect to the dispute. At the end of a sixty-day period (unless the dispute has been settled by that time), the board of inquiry shall report to the President the current position of the parties and the efforts which has been made for settlement, and shall include a statement by each party of its position and a statement of the employer's last offer of settlement. The President shall made such report available to the public. The National Labor Relations Board, within the succeeding fifteen days, shall take a secret ballot of the employees of each employer involved in the dispute on the question of whether they wish to accept the final offer of settlement made by their employer as stated by him and shall certify the results thereof to the Attorney General within five days thereafter.

SEC. 210. Upon the certification of the results of such ballot or upon a settlement being reached, whichever happens sooner, the Attorney General shall move the court to discharge the injunction, which motion shall then be granted and the injunction discharged. When such motion is granted, the President shall submit to the Congress a full and comprehensive report of the proceedings, including the findings of the board of inquiry and the ballot taken by the National Labor Relations Board, together with such recommendations as he may see fit to make for consideration and appropriate action.

COMPILATION OF COLLECTIVE-BARGAINING AGREEMENTS, ETC.

SEC. 211. (a) For the guidance and information of interested representatives of employers, employees, and the general public, the Bureau of Labor Statistics of the Department of Labor shall maintain a file of copies of all available collective-bargaining agreements and other available agreements and actions thereunder settling or adjusting labor disputes. Such file shall be open to inspection under appropriate conditions prescribed by the Secretary of Labor, except that no specific information submitted in confidence shall be disclosed.

(b) The Bureau of Labor Statistics in the Department of Labor is authorized to furnish upon request of the Service, or employers, employees, or their representatives, all available data and factual information which may aid in the settlement of any labor dispute, except that no specific information submitted in confidence shall be disclosed.

EXEMPTION OF RAILWAY LABOR ACT

Sec. 212. The provisions of this title shall not be applicable with respect to any matter which is subject to the provisions of the Railway Labor Act, as amended from time to time.

CONCILIATION OF LABOR DISPUTES IN THE HEALTH CARE INDUSTRY

"Sec. 213. (a) If, in the opinion of the Director of the Federal Mediation and Conciliation Service a threatened or actual strike or lockout affecting a health care institution will, if permitted to occur or to continue, substantially interrupt the delivery of health care in the locality concerned, the Director may further assist in the resolution of the impasse by establishing within 30 days after the notice to the Federal Mediation and Conciliation Service under clause (A) of the last sentence of section 8(d) (which is required by clause (3) of such section 8(d)), or within 10 days after the notice under clause (B), an impartial Board of Inquiry to investigate the issues involved in the dispute and to make a written report thereon to the parties within fifteen (15) days after the establishment of such a Board. The written report shall contain the findings of fact together with the Board's recommendations for settling the dispute, with the objective of achieving a prompt, peaceful and just settlement of the dispute. Each such Board shall be composed of such number of individuals as the Director may deem desirable. No member appointed under this section shall have any interest or involvement in the health care institutions or the employee organizations involved in the dispute.

(b)(1) Members of any board established under this section who are otherwise employed by the Federal Government shall serve without compensation but shall be reimbursed for travel, subsistence, and other necessary expenses incurred by them in carrying out its duties under this section.

(2) Members of any board established under this section who are not subject to paragraph (1) shall receive compensation at a rate prescribed by the Director but not to exceed the daily rate prescribed for GS-18

TITLE III—SUITS BY AND AGAINST LABOR ORGANIZATIONS

Sec. 301. (a) Suits for violation of contracts between an employer and a labor organization representing employees in an industry affecting commerce as defined in this Act, or between any such labor organizations, may be brought in any district court of the United States having jurisdiction of the parties, without respect to the amount in controversy or without regard to the citizenship of the parties.

(b) Any labor organization which represents employees in an industry affecting commerce as defined in this Act and any employer whose activities affect commerce as defined in this Act shall be bound by the acts of its agents. Any such labor organization may sue or be sued as an entity and in behalf of the employees whom it represents in the courts of the United States. Any money judgment against a labor organization in a district court of the United States shall be enforceable only against the organization as an entity and against its assets, and shall not be enforceable against any individual member or his assets.

(c) For the purposes of actions and proceedings by or against labor organizations in the district courts of the United States, district courts shall be deemed to have jurisdiction of a labor organization (1) in the district in which such organization maintains its principal offices, or (2) in any district in which its duly authorized officers or agents are engaged in representing or acting for employee members.

(d) The service of summons, subpena, or other legal process of any court of the United States upon an officer or agent of a labor organization, in his capacity as such, shall constitute service upon the labor organization.

(e) For the purposes of this section, in determining whether any person is acting as an "agent" of another person so as to make such other person responsible for his acts, the question of whether the specific acts performed were actually authorized or subsequently ratified shall not be controlling.

RESTRICTIONS ON PAYMENTS TO EMPLOYEE REPRESENTATIVES

SEC. 302. (a) It shall be unlawful for any employer or association of employers or any person who acts as a labor relations expert, adviser, or consultant to an employer or who acts in the interest of an employer to pay, lend, or deliver, or agree to pay, lend, or deliver, any money or other thing of value—

(1) to any representative of any of his employees who are employed in an industry affecting commerce; or

(2) to any labor organization, or any officer or employee thereof, which represents, seeks to represent, or would admit to membership, any of the employees of such employer who are employed in an industry affecting commerce; or

(3) to any employee or group or committee of employees of such employer employed in an industry affecting commerce in excess of their normal compensation for the purpose of causing such employee or group or committee directly or indirectly to influence any other employees in the exercise of the right to organize and bargain collectively through representatives of their own choosing; or

(4) to any officer or employee of a labor organization engaged in an industry affecting commerce with intent to influence him in respect to any of his actions, decisions, or duties as a representative of employees or as such officer or employee of such labor organization.

(b)(1) It shall be unlawful for any person to request, demand, receive, or accept, or agree to receive or accept, any payment, loan, or delivery of any money or other thing of value prohibited by subsection (a).

(2) It shall be unlawful for any labor organization, or for any person acting as an officer, agent, representative, or employee of such labor organization, to demand or accept from the operator of any motor vehicle (as defined in part II of the Interstate Commerce Act) employed in the transportation of property in commerce, or the employer of any such operator, any money or other thing of value payable to such organization or to an officer, agent, representative or employee thereof as a fee or charge for the unloading, or the connection with the unloading, of the cargo of such vehicle: *Provided*, That nothing in this paragraph shall be construed to make unlawful any payment by an employer to any of his employees as compensation for their services as employees.

(c) The provisions of this section shall not be applicable (1) in respect to any money or other thing of value payable by an employer to any of his employees whose established duties include acting openly for such employer in matters of labor relations or personnel administration or to any representative of his employees, or to any officer or employee of a labor organization, who is also an employee or former employee of such employer, as compensation for, or by reason of, his service as an employee of such employer; (2) with respect to the payment or delivery of any money or other thing of value in satisfaction of a judgment of any court or a decision or award of an arbitrator or impartial chairman or in compromise, adjustment, settlement, or release of any claim, complaint, grievance, or dispute in the absence of fraud or duress; (3) with respect to the sale or purchase of an article or commodity at the prevailing market price in the regular course of business; (4) with respect to money deducted from the wages of employees in payment of membership dues in a labor organization: *Provided,* That the employer has received from each employee, on whose account such deductions are made, a written assignment which shall not be irrevocable for a period of more than one year, or beyond the termination date of the applicable collective agreement, whichever occurs sooner; (5) with respect to money or other thing of value paid to a trust fund established by such representative, for the sole and exclusive benefit of employees of such employer, and their families and dependents (or of such employees, families, and dependents jointly with the employees of other employers making similar payments, and their families and dependents): *Provided,* That (A) such payments are held in trust for the purpose of paying, either from principal or income or both, for the benefit of employees, their families and dependents, for medical or hospital care, pensions on retirement or death of employees, compensation for injuries or illness resulting from occupational activity or insurance to provide any of the foregoing, or unemployment benefits or life insurance, disability and sickness insurance, or accident insurance; (B) the detailed basis on which such payments are to be made is specified in a written agreement with the employer, and employees and employers are equally represented in the administration of such fund, together with such neutral persons as the representatives of the employers and the representatives of employees may agree upon and in the event the employer and employee groups deadlock on the administration of such fund and there are no neutral persons empowered to break such deadlock, such agreement provides that the two groups shall agree on an impartial umpire to decide such dispute, or in event of their failure to agree within a reasonable length of time, an impartial umpire to decide such dispute shall, on petition of either group, be appointed by the district court of the United States for the district where the trust fund has its principal office, and shall also contain provisions for an annual audit of the trust fund, a statement of the results of which shall be available for inspection by interested persons at the principal office of the trust fund and at such other places as may be designated in such written agreement; and (C) such payments as are intended to be used for the purpose of providing pensions or annuities for employees are made to a separate trust which provides that the funds held therein cannot be used for any purpose other than paying such pensions or annuities; (6) with respect to money or other thing of value paid by any employer to a trust fund established by such representative for the purpose of pooled vacation, holiday, severance or similar benefits, or defraying costs of apprenticeship or other training program; *Provided,* That the requirements of clause (B) of the proviso to clause (5) of this subsection shall apply to such trust funds; or (7) with respect to money or other thing of value paid by any employer to a pooled or individual trust fund established by such representative for the purpose of (A) scholarships for the benefit of employees, their families, and dependents for study at educational institutions, or (B) child care centers for preschool and school age dependents of employees: *Provided,* That no labor organization or employer shall be required to bargain on the establishment of any such trust fund, and refusal to do so shall not constitute an unfair labor practice: *Provided further,* That the requirements of clause (B) of the proviso to clause (5) of this subsection shall apply to such trust funds; or (8) with respect to money or any other thing of value paid by any employer to a trust fund established by such representative for the purpose of defraying the costs of legal services for employees, their families, and dependents for counsel or plan of their choice: *Provided,* That the requirements of clause (B) of the proviso to clause (5) of this subsection shall apply to such trust funds: *Provided further,* That no such legal services shall be furnished: (A) to initiate any proceeding directed (i) against any such employer or its officers or agents except in workman's compensation cases, or (ii) against such labor organization, or its parent or subordinate bodies, or their officers or agents, or (iii) against any other employer or labor organization, or their officers or agents, in any matter arising under the National Labor Relations Act, as amended, or this Act; and (B) in any proceeding where a labor organization would be prohibited from defraying the costs of legal services by the provisions of the Labor-Management Reporting and Disclosure Act of 1959.

(d) Any person who willfully violates any of the provisions of this section shall, upon conviction thereof, be guilty of a misdemeanor and be subject to a fine of not more than $10,000 or to imprisonment for not more than one year, or both.

(e) The district courts of the United States and the United States courts of the Territories and possessions shall have jurisdiction, for cause shown, and subject to the provisions of section 17 (relating to notice to opposite party) of the Act entitled "An Act to supplement existing laws against unlawful restraints and monopolies, and for other purposes," approved October 15, 1914, as amended (U.S.C., title 28, sec. 381), to restrain violations of this section, without regard to the provisions of sections 6 and 20 of such Act of October 15, 1914, as amended (U.S.C., title 15, sec. 17, and title 29, sec. 52), and the provisions of the Act entitled "An Act to amend the Judicial Code and to define and limit the jurisdiction of courts sitting in equity, and for other purposes," approved March 23, 1932 (U.S.C., title 29, secs. 101–115).

(f) This section shall not apply to any contract in force on the date of enactment of this Act, until the expiration of such contract, or until July 1, 1948, whichever first occurs.

(g) Compliance with the restrictions contained in subsection (c)(5)(B) upon contributions to truse funds, otherwise lawful, shall not be applicable to contributions to such trust funds established by collective agreement prior to January 1, 1946, nor shall subsection (c)(5)(A) be construed as prohibiting contributions to such trust funds if prior to January 1, 1947, such funds contained provisions for pooled vacation benefits.

BOYCOTTS AND OTHER UNLAWFUL COMBINATIONS

SEC. 303. (a) It shall be unlawful, for the purpose of this section only, in an industry or activity affecting commerce, for any labor organization to engage in any activity or conduct defined as an unfair labor practice in section 8(b)(4) *or 8(g)* of the National Labor Relations Act, as amended.

(b) Whoever shall be injured in his business or property by reason of any violation of subsection (a) may sue therefore in any district court of the United States subject to the limitations and provisions of section 301 hereof without respect to the amount in controversy, or in any other court having jurisdiction of the parties, and shall recover the damages by him sustained and the cost of the suit.

RESTRICTION ON POLITICAL CONTRIBUTIONS

SEC. 304. Section 313 of the Federal Corrupt Practices Act, 1925 (U.S.C., 1940 edition, title 2, sec. 251; Supp. V, title 50, App., sec. 1509), as amended, is amended to read as follows:

SEC. 353. It is unlawful for any national bank, or any corporation organized by authority of any law of Congress to make a contribution or expenditure in connection with any election to any political office, or in connection with any primary election or political convention or caucus held to select candidates for any political office, or for any corporation whatever, or any labor organization to make a contribution or expenditure in connection with any election at which Presidential and Vice Presidential electors or a Senator or Representative in, or a Delegate or Resident Commissioner to Congress are to be voted for, or in connection with any primary election or political convention or caucus held to select candidates for any of the foregoing offices, or for any candidate, political committee, or other person to accept or receive any contribution prohibited by this section. Every corporation or labor organization which makes any contribution or expenditure in violation of this section shall be fined not more than $5,000; and every officer or director of any corporation, or officer of any labor organization, who consents to any contribution or expenditure by the corporation or labor organization, as the case may be, in violation of this section shall be fined not more than $1,000 or imprisoned for not more than one year, or both. For the purposes of this section "labor organization" means any organization of any kind, or any agency or employee representation committee or plan, in which employees participate and which exists for the purpose, in whole or in part, of dealing with employers concerning grievances, labor disputes, wages, rates of pay, hours of employment, or conditions of work.

TITLE IV

CREATION OF JOINT COMMITTEE TO STUDY AND REPORT ON BASIC PROBLEMS AFFECTING FRIENDLY LABOR RELATIONS AND PRODUCTIVITY

* * * * * * *

TITLE V

DEFINITIONS

SEC. 501. When used in this Act—

(1) The term "industry affecting commerce" means any industry or activity in commerce or in which a labor dispute would burden or obstruct commerce or tend to burden or obstruct commerce or the free flow of commerce.

(2) The term "strike" includes any strike or other concerted stoppage of work by employees (including a stoppage by reason of the expiration of a collective-bargaining agreement) and any concerted slow-down or other concerted interruption of operations by employees.

(3) The terms "commerce," "labor disputes,". "employer," "employee," "labor organization," "representative," "person," and "supervisor" shall have the same meaning as when used in the National Labor Relations Act as amended by this Act.

SAVING PROVISION

SEC. 502. Nothing in this Act shall be construed to require an individual employee to render labor or service without his consent, nor shall anything in this Act be construed to make the quitting of his labor by an individual employee an illegal act; nor shall any court issue any process to compel the performance by an individual employee of such labor or service, without his consent; nor shall the quitting of labor by an employee or employees in good faith because of abnormally dangerous conditions for work at the place of employment of such employee or employees be deemed a strike under this Act.

SEPARABILITY

SEC. 503. If any provision of this Act, or the application of such provision to any person or circumstance, shall be held invalid, the remainder of this Act, or the application of such provision to persons or circumstances other than those as to which it is held invalid, shall not be affected thereby.

Appendix B. P.L. 93-360: The 1974 Amendments to the National Labor Relations Act

Public Law 93-360
93rd Congress, S. 3203
July 26, 1974

An Act

To amend the National Labor Relations Act to extend its coverage and protection to employees of nonprofit hospitals, and for other purposes.

Be it enacted by the Senate and House of Representatives of the United States of America in Congress assembled, That (a) section 2(2) of the National Labor Relations Act is amended by striking out "or any corporation or association operating a hospital, if no part of the net earnings inures to the benefit of any private shareholder or individual,".

National Labor Relations Act, amendments. 61 Stat. 137. 29 USC 152.

(b) Section 2 of such Act is amended by adding at the end thereof the following new subsection:

"Health care institution."

"(14) The term 'health care institution' shall include any hospital, convalescent hospital, health maintenance organization, health clinic, nursing home, extended care facility, or other institution devoted to the care of sick, infirm, or aged person.".

(c) The last sentence of section 8(d) of such Act is amended by striking out the words "the sixty-day" and inserting in lieu thereof "any notice" and by inserting before the words "shall lose" a comma and the following: "or who engages in any strike within the appropriate period specified in subsection (g) of this section,".

29 USC 158.

Infra.

(d)(1) The last paragraph of section 8(d) of such Act is amended by adding at the end thereof the following new sentence: "Whenever the collective bargaining involves employees of a health care institution, the provisions of this section 8(d) shall be modified as follows:

Notices.

88 STAT. 395

88 STAT. 396

"(A) The notice of section 8(d)(1) shall be ninety days; the notice of section 8(d)(3) shall be sixty days; and the contract period of section 8(d)(4) shall be ninety days.

"(B) Where the bargaining is for an initial agreement following certification or recognition, at least thirty days' notice of the existence of a dispute shall be given by the labor organization to the agencies set forth in section 8(d)(3).

"(C) After notice is given to the Federal Mediation and Conciliation Service under either clause (A) or (B) of this sentence, the Service shall promptly communicate with the parties and use its best efforts, by mediation and conciliation, to bring them to agreement. The parties shall participate fully and promptly in such meetings as may be undertaken by the Service for the purpose of aiding in a settlement of the dispute."

(e) Section 8 of such Act is amended by adding at the end thereof the following new subsection.

Notification preceding strikes.

"(g) A labor organization before engaging in any strike, picketing, or other concerted refusal to work at any health care institution shall, not less than ten days prior to such action, notify the institution in writing and the Federal Mediation and Conciliation Service of that intention, except that in the case of bargaining for an initial agreement following certification or recognition the notice required by this subsection shall not be given until the expiration of the period specified in clause (B) of the last sentence of section 8(d) of this Act. The notice shall state the date and time that such action will commence. The notice, once given, may be extended by the written agreement of both parties."

SEC. 2. Title II of the Labor Management Relations Act, 1947, is amended by adding at the end thereof the following new section: Board of Inquiry. 61 Stat. 152. 29 USC 171.

"CONCILIATION OF LABOR DISPUTES IN THE HEALTH CARE INDUSTRY

"SEC. 213. (a) If, in the opinion of the Director of the Federal Mediation and Conciliation Service a threatened or actual strike or lockout affecting a health care institution will, if permitted to occur or to continue, substantially interrupt the delivery of health care in the locality concerned, the Director may further assist in the resolution of the impasse by establishing within 30 days after the notice to the Federal Mediation and Conciliation Service under clause (A) of the last sentence of section 8(d) (which is required by clause (3) of such section 8(d)), or within 10 days after the notice under clause (B), an impartial Board of Inquiry to investigate the issues involved in the dispute and to make a written report thereon to the parties within fifteen (15) days after the establishment of such a Board. The written report shall contain the findings of fact together with the Board's recommendations for settling the dispute, with the objective of achieving a prompt, peaceful and just settlement of the dispute. Each such Board shall be composed of such number of individuals as the Director may deem desirable. No member appointed under this section shall have any interest or involvement in the health care institutions or the employee organizations involved in the dispute.

29 USC 183. *Ante*, p. 395. Report. Membership.

"(b)(1) Members of any board established under this section who are otherwise employed by the Federal Government shall serve without compensation but shall be reimbursed for travel, subsistence, and other necessary expenses incurred by them in carrying out its duties under this section.

88 STAT. 396
88 STAT. 397

"(2) Members of any board established under this section who are not subject to paragraph (1) shall receive compensation at a rate prescribed by the Director but not to exceed the daily rate prescribed for GS-18 of the General Schedule under section 5332 of title 5, United States Code, including travel for each day they are engaged in the performance of their duties under this section and shall be entitled to reimbursement for travel, subsistence, and other necessary expenses incurred by them in carrying out their duties under this section.

Compensation. 5 USC 5332 note.

"(c) After the establishment of a board under subsection (a) of this section and for 15 days after any such board has issued its report, no change in the status quo in effect prior to the expiration of the contract in the case of negotiations for a contract renewal, or in effect prior to the time of the impasse in the case of an initial bargaining negotiation, except by agreement, shall be made by the parties to the controversy.

"(d) There are authorized to be appropriated such sums as may be necessary to carry out the provisions of this section." Appropriation.

SEC. 3. The National Labor Relations Act is amended by adding immediately after section 18 thereof the following new section: 65 Stat. 601. 29 USC 168.

"INDIVIDUALS WITH RELIGIOUS CONVICTIONS

"SEC. 19. Any employee of a health care institution who is a member of and adheres to established and traditional tenets or teachings of a bona fide religion, body, or sect which has historically held conscientious objections to joining or financially supporting labor organiza- 29 USC 169.

July 26, 1974 - 3 - Pub. Law 93-360

88 STAT. 397

tions shall not be required to join or financially support any labor organization as a condition of employment; except that such employee may be required, in lieu of periodic dues and initiation fees, to pay sums equal to such dues and initiation fees to a nonreligious charitable fund exempt from taxation under section 501(c)(3) of the Internal Revenue Code, chosen by such employee from a list of at least three such funds, designated in a contract between such institution and a labor organization, or if the contract fails to designate such funds, then to any such fund chosen by the employee."

68A Stat. 163.
26 USC 501.

SEC. 4. The amendments made by this Act shall become effective on the thirtieth day after its date of enactment.

Effective date.
29 USC 169 note.

Approved July 26, 1974.

LEGISLATIVE HISTORY:

HOUSE REPORTS: No. 93-1051 accompanying H.R. 13678 (Comm. on Education and Labor) and No. 93-1175 (Comm. of Conference).

SENATE REPORTS: No. 93-766 (Comm. on Labor and Public Welfare) and No. 93-988 (Comm. of Conference).

CONGRESSIONAL RECORD, Vol. 120 (1974):

May 2,3,7, considered and passed Senate.

May 30, considered and passed House, amended, in lieu of H.R. 13678.

July 10, Senate agreed to conference report.

July 11, House agreed to conference report.

Calendar No. 738

93D CONGRESS 2d Session } SENATE { REPORT No. 93-766

COVERAGE OF NONPROFIT HOSPITALS UNDER THE NATIONAL LABOR RELATIONS ACT

APRIL 2, 1974—Ordered to be printed

Mr. CRANSTON, from the Committee on Labor and Public Welfare, submitted the following

REPORT

together with

INDIVIDUAL VIEWS

[To accompany S. 3203]

The Committee on Labor and Public Welfare to which was referred the bill (S. 3203) to amend the National Labor Relations Act to extend its coverage and protection to employees of nonprofit hospitals, and for other purposes, having considered the same, reports favorably thereon and recommends that the bill do pass.

SUMMARY

The National Labor Relations Act governs the collective bargaining relationship of millions of workers including employees of proprietary hospitals, proprietary nursing homes and nonprofit nursing homes. It specifically exempts from coverage employees of private nonprofit hospitals. This bill repeals the present exemption, establishes certain new procedures governing labor relations in health care institutions, and creates a new definition of health care institution to include hospitals, nursing homes, health maintenance organizations, extended care facilities, health and medical clinics and other similar institutions caring for the sick, infirm or aged. The bill also contains several additional special provisions designed to facilitate collective bargaining settlements and to provide advance notice of any strike or picketing involving a health care institution, as follows:

1. The requirement for notice of termination or expiration of a contract will be 90 days;

99-010—74——1

2. The Federal Mediation and Conciliation Service [FMCS] must be given 60 days notice of such termination or expiration;

3. In initial contract negotiations a 30 day notice of a dispute to FMCS will be required;

3. In initial contract negotiation a 30 day notice of a dispute to FMCS will be required;

4. The health care institution and labor organization will be required to participate in mediation at the direction of the FMCS.

5. The health care institution must be given a 10 day notice by a labor organization before any picketing or strike (whether or not related to bargaining) can take place.

On February 7, 1973, S. 794 was introduced by Senators Cranston and Javits and on July 31, 1973, S. 2292 was introduced by Senator Taft. The Subcommittee on Labor conducted hearings on these bills on July 31, August 1, 2 and October 4, 1973.

During the course of these hearings testimony was received from a number of interested groups, including the U.S. Department of Labor; AFL–CIO; the Service Employees International Union, AFL–CIO; American Hospital Association; Industrial Union Department, AFL–CIO; Local 1199, Drug and Hospital Workers Union; American Nurses Association; Communication Workers of America, AFL–CIO; General Conference of Seventh-day Adventists; American Federation of State, County, and Municipal Employees, AFL–CIO; New Jersey Hospital Association; Committee of Interns and Residents of New York City; Colorado Hospital Association; Federation of American Hospitals; Catholic Hospital Association Board of Trustees; Commission on Economic and General Welfare of the American Nurses' Association; Hospital Association of Pennsylvania; Texas Hospital Association; Iowa Hospital Association; International Union of Operating Engineers; Ohio Hospital Association; Minnesota Hospital Association; National Right to Work Committee; Mt. Sinai Hospital; National Federation of Licensed Practical Nurses; Physicians National Housestaff Association; United States Industrial Council; California Hospital Association; New York University Medical Center; and Mount Sinai Medical Center.

On February 28, 1973, S. 3088 was introduced by Senator Taft and on March 13, 1973, the full Committee discharged the Subcommittee from further consideration of S. 794, S. 2292 and S. 3088. On March 20, 1973, S. 3203 was introduced by Senators Williams, Cranston, Javits, Taft, Stafford, Pell, Kennedy, Eagleton, Hughes, and Schweiker. The Committee considered the legislation in executive session on March 20, 1973, and ordered S. 3203 reported by voice vote.

During the executive session an amendment proposed by Senator Mondale was offered. It would have required the NLRB to cede jurisdiction to certain state agencies covering nonprofit hospitals where the state law was in existence prior to 1947. The amendment was defeated by voice vote.

Background

Section 2(2) of the National Labor Relations Act defines the term "employer" as not to include "any corporation or association operating a hospital, if no part of the net earnings inures to the benefit of any private shareholder or individual."

The original Wagner Act of 1935 did not contain this exemption and in the only reported case relating to coverage of nonprofit hospitals, the NLRB and the Court of Appeals upheld the coverage.[1]

In 1947, the Wagner Act was amended by the Taft-Hartley Act. Included in these amendments was a provision, added as a floor amendment in the Senate, to exempt nonprofit hospitals. This amendment was retained in conference.

In 1972, the House passed H.R. 11357 which would have repealed the exemption. No action was taken by the Senate beyond hearings on the bill.

Need for the Bill

The bill removes the existing exemption in section 2(2) of the NLRA for employees of non-profit hospitals and extends the protections of the Act to such employees to the same extent as currently applicable to employees of nursing homes and proprietary hospitals.

The Committee could find no acceptable reason why 1,427,012 employees of these non-profit, non-public hospitals, representing 56% of all hospital employees, should continue to be excluded from the coverage and protections of the Act. In the Committee's deliberations on this measure, it was recognized that the needs of patients in health care institutions required special consideration in the Act including a provision requiring hospitals to have sufficient notice of any strike or picketing to allow for appropriate arrangements to be made for the continuance of patient care in the event of a work stoppage. In this respect the Committee believed that the special notice requirements should be extended to all proprietary and nonprofit hospitals, convalescent hospitals, health maintenance organizations, health or medical clinics, nursing homes, extended care facilities or other institutions devoted to the care of sick, infirm or aged persons. Accordingly this bill will provide the same procedures for employees of all health care institutions.

The Committee was also impressed with the fact, emphasized by many witnesses, that the exemption of nonprofit hospitals from the Act had resulted in numerous instances of recognition strikes and picketing. Coverage under the Act should completely eliminate the need for any such activity, since the procedures of the Act will be available to resolve organizational and recognition disputes.

Provisions of the Bill

REPEAL OF EXISTING EXEMPTION

The present exemption in Section 2(2) of the National Labor Relations Act for "any corporation or association operating a hospital, if no part of the net earnings inures to the benefit of any private shareholder or individual" is removed from the Act by this bill.

DEFINITION OF HEALTH CARE INSTITUTION

The bill adds to the Act a definition of health care institution which includes any hospital, convalescent hospital, health maintenance organization, health clinic, nursing home, extended care facility, or other institution devoted to the care of sick, infirm, or aged persons.

[1] *Central Dispensary and Emergency Hospital* 44 NLRB 533 (1942), 145 F.2d 852 (1944), cert. den. 655 ct. 684.

By so defining a health care institution the Committee does not intend to affect the exemption for "the United States or any wholly owned Government corporation * * * or any State or political subdivision thereof" as set forth in Section 2(2) of the Act.

TEN DAY NOTICE

It is in the public interest to insure the continuity of health care to the community and the care and well being of patients by providing for a statutory advance notice of any anticipated strike or picketing. For this reason, the Committee approved an amendment adding a new Section 8(g) which generally prohibits a labor organization from striking or picketing a health care institution without first giving 10 days' notice. Violation of this provision will constitute an unfair labor practice. The failure to give the statutory notice will be remedial under Section 10(j) of the Act. This notice period will also give the National Labor Relations Board the opportunity, when charges are filed, to make a determination as to the legality of any strike or picketing before it occurs.[1]

The 10-day notice is intended to give health care institutions sufficient advance notice of a strike or picketing to permit them to make arrangements for the continuity of patient care. It is not the intention of the Committee that a labor organization shall be required to commence a strike or picketing at the precise time specified in the notice; on the other hand, it would be inconsistent with the Committee's intent if a labor organization failed to act within a reasonable time after the time specified in the notice. Thus, it would be unreasonable, in the Committee's judgment, if a strike or picketing commenced more than 72 hours after the time specified in the notice. In addition, since the purpose of the notice is to give a health care institution advance notice of the actual commencement of a strike or picketing, if a labor organization does not strike at the time specified in the notice, at least 12 hours notice should be given of the actual time for commencement of the action.

Repeatedly serving such ten day notices upon the employer is to be construed as constituting evidence of a refusal to bargain in good faith by the labor organization.

Likewise, the public interest demands that employees of health care institutions be accorded the same type of treatment under the law as other employees in our society, and that the notice not be utilized to deprive employees of their statutory rights. It is clear, therefore, that a labor organization will not be required to serve a ten day notice or to wait until the expiration of the ten day notice when the employer has committed unfair labor practices as in *Mastro Plastics Corp.* v. *NLRB*, 350 U.S. 270, 37 L.R.R.M. 2587 (1956).

Moreover, it is the sense of the Committee that during the ten-day notice period the employer should remain free to take whatever action is necessary to maintain health care, but not to use the ten-day period to undermine the bargaining relationship that would otherwise exist. For example, the employer would not be free to bring in large numbers of supervisory help, nurses, staff and other personnel from other facilities for replacement purposes. It would clearly be free to receive supplies, but it would not be free to take extraordinary steps to stock

[1] For example, the picketing may be a violation of Section 8(b)(4).

up on ordinary supplies for an unduly extended period. While not necessarily a violation of the Act, violation of these principles would serve to release the labor organization from its obligation not to engage in economic action during the course of the ten-day notice period.

The Committee is aware that a work interruption at particular hospitals, such as those in rural areas, could pose special problems of continuation of patient care. It is the Committee's hope that parties to a dispute in such an institution would be cognizant of such special problems and take steps, either in advance of any dispute, or during its resolution, to mitigate the effects of a scarcity of alternative local resources.

CONTRACT NOTICE REQUIREMENTS

Under the existing provisions of the National Labor Relations Act, an employer or a labor organization is required, where a collective bargaining agreement is in effect, to provide written notice to the other party before termination or modification of the agreement. This notice of termination or modification must be given at least 60 days prior to the termination or modification date. In addition, present law requires the Federal Mediation and Conciliation Service to receive 30 days notice.

The bill extends the 60 day notice to 90 days and requires the FMCS to receive 60 days notice instead of 30 days, in the case of health care institutions.

Under existing law there is no obligation on either party to engage in mediation. The bill provides for mandatory mediation by the parties with the FMCS in the case of collective bargaining involving health care institutions.

Under present law there is no notification requirement to any party with regard to initial contract negotiations. The bill requires 30 days notice to the FMCS, in the case of collective bargaining involving health care institutions.

Effect on Existing Law

BARGAINING UNITS

Due consideration should be given by the Board to preventing proliferation of bargaining units in the health care industry. In this connection, the Committee notes with approval the recent Board decisions in *Four Seasons Nursing Center*, 208 NLRB No. 50, 85 LRRM 1093 (1974), and *Woodland Park Hospital*, 205 NLRB No. 144, 84 LRRM 1075 (1973), as well as the trend toward broader units enunciated in *Extendicare of West Virginia*, 203 NLRB No. 170 83 LRRM 1242 (1973).[1]

ALLY DOCTRINE

It has been held that where during the course of a labor dispute, a secondary employer performs work that, but for the existence of such labor dispute, would have been performed by the striking employees of the primary employer, the secondary employer loses his status as a neutral, and the labor organization is entitled to extend its economic activity to the secondary employer.

[1] By our reference to *Extendicare*, we do not necessarily approve all of the holdings of that decision.

It is the sense of the Committee that where such secondary institutions accept the patients of a primary employer or otherwise provide life-sustaining services to the primary employer, by providing the primary employer with an employee or employees who possess critical skills, such as an EKG technician, such conduct shall not be sufficient to cause the secondary employer to lose its neutral status. It should be clear, however, that where a secondary employer enmeshes itself into the primary dispute by providing supervisors, nurses or staff other than those described, it loses its status of neutrality.

SUPERVISORS

Various organizations representing health care professionals have urged an amendment to Section 2(11) of the Act so as to exclude such professionals from the definition of "supervisor". The Committee has studied this definition with particular reference to health care professionals, such as registered nurses, interns, residents, fellows, and salaried physicians and concludes that the proposed amendment is unnecessary because of existing Board decisions. The Committee notes that the Board has carefully avoided applying the definition of "supervisor" to a health care professional who gives direction to other employees in the exercise of professional judgment, which direction is incidental to the professional's treatment of patients and thus is not the exercise of supervisory authority in the interest of the employer.

The Committee expects the Board to continue evaluating the facts of each case in this manner when making its determinations.

RECOGNITION PICKETING

In recognition picketing cases under Section 8(b)(7)(C), the National Labor Relations Board has ruled that a reasonable period of time is thirty days absent unusual circumstances such as violence or intimidation. It is the sense of the Committee that picketing of a health care institution would in itself constitute an unusual circumstance justifying the application of a period of time less than thirty days.

PRIORITY CASE HANDLING

Many of the witnesses before the Committee, including both employee and employer witnesses, stressed the uniqueness of health care institutions. There was a recognized concern for the need to avoid disruption of patient care wherever possible.

It was this sensitivity to the need for continuity of patient care that led the Committee to adopt amendments with regard to notice requirements and other procedures related to potential strikes and picketing.

The Board's priorities for handling various types of cases were carefully considered by the Committee and some observations and directions to the Board are reflected in the following commentary.

The Committee notes the present existence of priority case handling directives to the Board under Section 10(l) of the Act with respect to charges filed under Sections 8(b)(4), 8(b)(7) or 8(e) and other priority directives under 10 (m).

Because of the need for continuity of patient care, the Committee expects the NLRB to give special attention and priority to all charges of employer, employee and labor organization unfair labor practices involving health care institutions consistent with the existing statutory priority requirements for particular classes of cases. The General Counsel and Chairman are directed to take such steps as necessary to provide appropriate investigatory and other resources needed to give this requisite priority to unfair labor practice cases involving health care institutions.

COST ESTIMATE

The estimated cost of this legislation is $1.2 million in each of the five years following enactment.

Section-by-Section Analysis

Subsection (a) repeals the existing exemption for non-profit hospitals in Section 2(2) of the Act.

Subsection (b) amends Section 2 of the Act by adding a definition "health care institution" to include any hospital, convalescent hospital, health maintenance organization, health clinic, nursing home, extended care facility, or other institution devoted to the care of sick, infirm, or aged persons.

Subsection (c) amends Section 8(d) relating to loss of status when an employee strikes in violation of the section's notice requirements. The Amendment substitutes "any notice" in lieu of the "sixty-day notice" in existing law to allow for the additional notice requirements placed on representations of employees of health care institutions. The loss of status is also extended to violations of the newly created ten-day notice period of section 8(g).

Subsection (d) amends Section 8(d) by modifying the notice provisions of that Section as follows:

1. The requirement for notice of termination or expiration of a contract will be 90 days;
2. The Federal Mediation and Conciliation Service must be given a 60 day notice of such termination or expiration:
3. In initial contract negotiations a 30 day notice to FMCS will be required;
4. The health care institution and labor organization will be required to participate in mediation at the direction of the FMCS.

Subsection (c) amends Section 8 by adding a new Subsection (g) which provides that labor organizations give a 10 day written notice to the health care institution and the FMCS before engaging in any picketing, strike or other concerted refusal to work.

Appendix D. Joint House-Senate Conference Committee Report on S. 3203

93D CONGRESS } HOUSE OF REPRESENTATIVES { REPORT
2d Session } { No. 93-1175

COVERAGE OF NONPROFIT HOSPITALS UNDER THE NATIONAL LABOR RELATIONS ACT

JULY 3, 1974.—Ordered to be printed

Mr. PERKINS from the committee of conference, submitted the following

CONFERENCE REPORT

[To accompany S. 3203]

The committee of conference on the disagreeing votes of the two Houses on the amendment of the House to the bill (S. 3203) to amend the National Labor Relations Act to extend its coverage and protection to employees of nonprofit hospitals, and for other purposes, having met, after full and free conference, have agreed to recommend and do recommend to their respective Houses as follows:

That the Senate recede from its disagreement to the amendment of the House and agree to the same with an amendment as follows:

In lieu of the matter proposed to be inserted by the Senate amendment insert the following:

That (a) section 2(2) of the National Labor Relations Act is amended by striking out "or any corporation or association operating a hospital, if no part of the net earnings inures to the benefit of any private shareholder or individual,".

(b) Section 2 of such Act is amended by adding at the end thereof the following new subsection:

"(14) The term 'health care institution' shall include any hospital, convalescent hospital, health maintenance organization, health clinic, nursing home, extended care facility, or other institution devoted to the care of sick, infirm, or aged person.".

(c) The last sentence of section 8(d) of such Act is amended by striking out the words "the sixty-day" and inserting in lieu thereof "any notice" and by inserting before the words "shall lose" a comma and the following: "or who engages in any strike within the appropriate period specified in subsection (g) of this section,".

(d)(1) The last paragraph of section 8(d) of such Act is amended by adding at the end thereof the following new sentence: "Whenever the collective bargaining involves employees of a health care institution, the provisions of this section 8(d) shall be modified as follows:

"(A) The notice of section 8(d)(1) shall be ninety days; the notice of section 8(d)(3) shall be sixty days; and the contract period of section 8(d)(4) shall be ninety days.

★38–006

"(B) Where the bargaining is for an initial agreement following certification or recognition, at least thirty days' notice of the existence of a dispute shall be given by the labor organization to the agencies set forth in section 8(d)(3).

"(C) After notice is given to the Federal Mediation and Conciliation Service under either clause (A) or (B) of this sentence, the Service shall promptly communicate with the parties and use its best efforts, by mediation and conciliation, to bring them to agreement. The parties shall participate fully and promptly in such meetings as may be undertaken by the Service for the purpose of aiding in a settlement of the dispute."

(e) Section 8 of such Act is amended by adding at the end thereof the following new subsection.

"(g) A labor organization before engaging in any strike, picketing, or other concerted refusal to work at any health care institution shall, not less than ten days prior to such action, notify the institution in writing and the Federal Mediation and Conciliation Service of that intention, except that in the case of bargaining for an initial agreement following certification or recognition the notice required by this subsection shall not be given until the expiration of the period specified in clause (B) of the last sentence of section 8(d) of this Act. The notice shall state the date and time that such action will commence. The notice, once given, may be extended by the written agreement of both parties."

SEC. 2. Title II of the Labor Management Relations Act, 1947, is amended by adding at the end thereof the following new section:

CONCILIATION OF LABOR DISPUTES IN THE HEALTH CARE INDUSTRY

"SEC. 213. (a) If, in the opinion of the Director of the Federal Mediation and Conciliation Service a threatened or actual strike or lockout affecting a health care institution will, if permitted to occur or to continue, substantially interrupt the delivery of health care in the locality concerned, the Director may further assist in the resolution of the impasse by establishing within 30 days after the notice to the Federal Mediation and Conciliation Service under clause (A) of the last sentence of section 8(d) (which is required by clause (3) of such section 8(d)), or within 10 days after the notice under clause (B), an impartial Board of Inquiry to investigate the issues involved in the dispute and to make a written report thereon to the parties within fifteen (15) days after the establishment of such a Board. The written report shall contain the findings of fact together with the Board's recommendations for settling the dispute, with the objective of achieving a prompt, peaceful and just settlement of the dispute. Each such Board shall be composed of such number of individuals as the Director may deem desirable. No member appointed under this section shall have any interest or involvement in the health care institutions or the employee organizations involved in the dispute.

(b)(1) Members of any board established under this section who are otherwise employed by the Federal Government shall serve without compensation but shall be reimbursed for travel, subsistence, and other necessary expenses incurred by them in carrying out its duties under this section.

(2) Members of any board established under this section who are not subject to paragraph (1) shall receive compensation at a rate prescribed by the Director but not to exceed the daily rate prescribed for GS-18 of the

General Schedule under section 5332 of title 5, United States Code, including travel for each day they are engaged in the performance of their duties under this section and shall be entitled to reimbursement for travel, subsistence, and other necessary expenses incurred by them in carrying out their duties under this section.

(c) After the establishment of a board under subsection (a) of this section and for 15 days after any such board has issued its report, no change in the status quo in effect prior to the expiration of the contract in the case of negotiations for a contract renewal, or in effect prior to the time of the impasse in the case of an initial bargaining negotiation, except by agreement, shall be made by the parties to the controversy.

(d) There are authorized to be appropriated such sums as may be necessary to carry out the provisions of this section.

SEC. 3. The National Labor Relations Act is amended by adding immediately after Section 18 thereof the following new section:

"INDIVIDUALS WITH RELIGIOUS CONVICTIONS

SEC. 19. Any employee of a health care institution who is a member of and adheres to established and traditional tenets or teachings of a bona fide religion, body, or sect which has historically held conscientious objections to joining or financially supporting labor organizations shall not be required to join or financially support any labor organization as a condition of employment; except that such employee may be required, in lieu of periodic dues and initiation fees, to pay sums equal to such dues and initiation fees to a nonreligious charitable fund exempt from taxation under section 501(c)(3) of the Internal Revenue Code, chosen by such employee from a list of at least three such funds, designated in a contract between such institution and a labor organization, or if the contract fails to designate such funds, then to any such fund chosen by the employee.

SEC. 4. The amendments made by this Act shall become effective on the thirtieth day after its date of enactment.

And the House agree to the same.

CARL D. PERKINS,
FRANK THOMPSON, Jr.,
WILLIAM D. FORD,
W. L. CLAY,
ALBERT H. QUIE,
JOHN M. ASHBROOK,
Managers on the Part of the House.

And the Senate agree to the same.

HARRISON WILLIAMS,
JENNINGS RANDOLPH,
CLAIBORNE PELL,
GAYLORD NELSON,
THOMAS F. EAGLETON,
HAROLD E. HUGHES,
W. D. HATHAWAY,
ALAN CRANSTON,
J. JAVITS,
RICHARD S. SCHWEIKER,
ROBERT TAFT,
ROBERT STAFFORD,
Managers on the Part of the Senate.

JOINT EXPLANATORY STATEMENT OF THE COMMITTEE OF CONFERENCE

The managers on the part of the House and the Senate at the conference on the disagreeing votes of the two Houses on the amendment of the House to the bill (S. 3203) to amend the National Labor Relations Act to extend its coverage and protection to employees of nonprofit hospitals, and for other purposes, submit the following joint statement to the House and the Senate in explanation of the effect of the action agreed upon by the managers and recommended in the accompanying conference report:

The House amendment struck out all of the Senate bill after the enacting clause and inserted a substitute text.

The Senate recedes from its disagreement to the amendment of the House with an amendment which is a substitute for the Senate bill and the House amendment. The differences between the Senate bill, the House amendment, and the substitute agreed to in conference are noted below, except for clerical corrections, conforming changes made necessary by agreements reached by the conferees, and minor drafting and clarifying changes.

BASIC PURPOSE OF THE SENATE BILL AND THE HOUSE AMENDMENT

Both Senate bill and the House amendment amended the National Labor Relations Act to remove the exemption for employees of nonprofit hospitals. Both the Senate bill and the House amendment establishes additional mediation and conciliation procedures for employees of all health care institutions including requirements for mandatory mediation and that a 10 day notice of any strike or picketing be given to a health care institution.

The language of the House amendment is identical to the Senate bill except in the following two respects:

INDIVIDUALS WITH RELIGIOUS CONVICTIONS

Subsection (g) of the first section of the House amendment amended the Act by adding at the end thereof a new section 19 (relating to individuals with religious convictions). The new section 19 provided that employees of health care institutions who object to joining or financially supporting labor organizations on religious grounds shall not be required to do so as a condition of employment. The Senate receded with a clarifying amendment under which, in recognition of the special humanitarian character of health care institutions, an employee may be required to make payments to a nonreligious charitable fund in lieu of periodic dues and initiation fees designated from among at least three funds pursuant to the collective bargaining agreement between the employer and the labor organization, or if the labor-management agreement fails to make such designation, to any nonreligious charitable fund selected by the employee.

MEDIATION, CONCILIATION AND BOARD OF INQUIRY

Subsection (f) of the first section of the House amendment amended title II of the Labor Management Relations Act, 1947, by adding at the end thereof a new section 213 (relating to conciliation of labor disputes in the health care industry; interruptions). This section proposed that in the event a labor dispute between a health care institution and its employees is not settled and the Director of the Federal Mediation and Conciliation Service determined that the dispute threatened substantially to interrupt the delivery of health care, he would create a Board of Inquiry to investigate and report with respect to such dispute. For a period of 30 days pending the Board of Inquiry report and for an additional 30 days thereafter the parties would be required to maintain the status quo. The Senate bill contained no comparable provisions.

The Senate receded with an amendment under which in the event that the labor dispute by the health care institution and its employees is not settled and the Director of the FMCS determines that the dispute substantially threatens to interrupt health care in the affected locality the Director may create a board of inquiry to investigate and report with respect to such dispute. The Board must be appointed within 30 days after the FMCS is notified of the intention of either or both of the parties to terminate the contract as required under section 8(d) of the NLRA, as amended by this legislation, or 10 days after the FMCS is notified in the case of an initial contract. The report of the Board of Inquiry will be issued within 15 days of its appointment and the parties to the dispute are required to maintain the status quo for 15 days after the issuance of the Board's report. The Board's report shall contain findings of fact, together with the Board's public recommendations for the settlement of the dispute. The notification as provided in section 8(g) of the National Labor Relations Act may be given on or after the commencement of the final 10 days of the conciliation period.

The Conferees intend that the appointment of a Board of Inquiry shall not operate to interrupt mediation by the FMCS which is made mandatory under other provisions of this legislation, and that the service will pursue these parallel procedures to bring about a fair, prompt and just settlement of any dispute. The Conferees further intend that the Board of Inquiry, in formulating its recommendations for settlement of a dispute shall take into account all those factors normally considered by similar tribunals in formulating recommendations for the settlement of labor disputes.

The Committee, in adding special mediation and conciliation procedures, including the Board of Inquiry, for the health care industry, recognizes the need for continuity of health services during labor-management disputes and that the labor organizations representing health care workers have publicly pledged their best efforts to persuade their affiliates voluntarily to avoid work stoppages through acceptance of arbitration in the event of an impasse in negotiations. Under these new procedures, it is anticipated that, in the event of such an impasse, the findings of fact and recommendations of the Board of Inquiry would provide the framework of the arbitrator's decision.

And the House agree to the same.

CARL D. PERKINS,
FRANK THOMPSON, Jr.,
WILLIAM D. FORD,
W. L. CLAY,
ALBERT H. QUIE,
JOHN M. ASHBROOK,
Managers on the Part of the House.

And the Senate agree to the same.

HARRISON WILLIAMS,
JENNINGS RANDOLPH,
CLAIBORNE PELL,
GAYLORD NELSON,
THOMAS F. EAGLETON,
HAROLD E. HUGHES,
W. D. HATHAWAY,
ALAN CRANSTON,
J. JAVITS,
RICHARD S. SCHWEIKER,
ROBERT TAFT,
ROBERT STAFFORD,
Managers on the Part of the Senate.

○

Appendix E. Delineation of Bargaining Units in Health Care Facilities: Foundational Rulings of the National Labor Relations Board

205 NLRB No. 144

D--7776
Portland, Oreg.

UNITED STATES OF AMERICA

BEFORE THE NATIONAL LABOR RELATIONS BOARD

WOODLAND PARK HOSPITAL, INC.

Employer

and

Case 36--RC--3018

HOSPITAL EMPLOYEES OF SERVICE EMPLOYEES UNION LOCAL NO. 49, AFL--CIO

Petitioner[1]

and

Case 36--RC--3025

OREGON SOCIETY OF RADIOLOGIC TECHNOLOGISTS

Petitioner[2]

DECISION ON REVIEW

On February 12, 1973, the Regional Director for Region 19 issued a Decision and Direction of Election in the above-entitled proceeding in which he found appropriate Hospital Employees' originally requested broad unit of hospital employees, and directed a self-determination election among the radiologic technologists (X-ray technicians), as requested by OSORT, to determine whether or not they wished to constitute a separate appropriate unit. Thereafter, in accordance with National Labor Relations Board Rules and Regulations, the Employer filed a timely request for review of the Regional Director's Decision on the grounds that in establishing a separate unit for the X-ray technicians herein, he departed from officially reported precedent and that there are compelling reasons for reconsideration of the policy enunciated in the decision.

By telegraphic order dated March 13, the National Labor Relations Board granted the request for review and stayed the election pending decision on review. Thereafter, the Employer filed a brief on review, and Hospital Employees filed a statement in sup-

1. Referred to herein as Hospital Employees.
2. Referred to herein as OSORT.

port of the Regional Director's decision.

The Board has considered the entire record in this case with respect to the issue under review, including the brief and statement on review, and makes the following findings:

The Employer is engaged in the operation of a proprietary general hospital in Portland, Oregon. Hospital Employees, as indicated, petitioned for a broad unit of hospital employees. It was willing to consent to an election in that unit. However, when OSORT filed a petition for a unit confined to X-ray technicians at the hospital and the Regional Director consolidated the cases for hearing, Hospital Employees changed its unit position. As aforesaid, the Regional Director found a broad unit of hospital employees may be appropriate[3] and, deeming himself bound by Ochsner Clinic, 192 NLRB No. 156, directed a self-determination election to determine whether or not the X-ray technicians wished to be represented separately by OSORT. He noted, however, that while, in his view, Ochsner was factually similar to the instant case, that no other union sought a broader unit.

The X-ray technicians sought by OSORT in the instant case work in a separate radiology department, also described as the X-ray department. The majority of the X-ray technicians are registered by the American Registry of Radiological Technologists. The registered X-ray technicians perform substantially the same work as those not registered, except that the former generally will be called upon to handle certain special procedures involving the use of more expensive equipment. This department also contains clerical employees and an orderly. All employees in the department are supervised by the chief radiological technologist who does not supervise any other employees. While the chief radiological technologist is the administrative supervisor of the radiology department and actually does the hiring and firing of the employees in that department, the department is also staffed by a radiologist who is a medical doctor and who is in overall supervision of the department. The X-ray technicians perform the work of taking X-ray pictures through the use of X-ray machines. It is their responsibility to obtain a clear picture so that the doctor can make a proper diagnosis. This involves, in addition to the operation of the machine, the proper

3. Subsequent to the hearing, Hospital Employees took the position that an all employee unit was inappropriate and suggested instead three separate units: (1) a unit of all clericals; (2) a unit of all technicals including X-ray technicians; and (3) a unit for the remaining employees. However, it stated that it would participate in an election in any unit found appropriate. The Regional Director found that the employees in each of the proposed separate units do not possess a sufficiently separate distinguishable community of interest to warrant finding the suggested units appropriate. Hospital Employees filed no request for review of the Regional Director's unit findings.

of the patient and the use of safety procedures to avoid injury to both the technician and the patient. The radiology department is centrally located in the hospital and occupies the same floor as the laboratory, operating room, and emergency room. However, the X-ray technicians also are required to perform their duties in many other areas of the hospital such as the operating room, emergency department, intensive care unit, or the patient's room. At these locations, they work with the nurses, licensed practical nurses (LPN's), other technicians, and doctors there involved to coordinate the procedures. Thus, for example, when X-rays are taken in the intensive care unit, the X-ray technician must work with the head nurse, charge nurse, or RN in that area or the LPN to accomplish the X-ray. In the operating room, the X-ray technician must work with the supervisor in that department, the circulating nurse, operating room technicians, and the doctor involved. On these occasions, they use a portable X-ray machine which can be moved from area to area or X-ray equipment available in the operating room. As is the case with other technicians in the hospital,[4] their work brings them into regular contact with doctors, nurses, orderlies, clericals, and other hospital personnel.

The X-ray technicians enjoy the same fringe benefits as other hospital personnel and share the same working conditions. They have a separate wage scale, and the amount they receive is somewhere in the middle between the highest and lowest rates received by other technicians. All the X-ray technicians are required to complete a 2-year formal education in their field before being eligible for hire. Except in an emergency, other hospital personnel do not perform the work of the X-ray technicians, nor do the latter perform the work of other hospital employees. All employees work an 8-hour day and receive a half hour for lunch and two 15-minute rest breaks. All training is centrally located in the office of the director of staff development who provides in-service training for all departments in the hospital. All employees are covered by a hospital-wide grievance procedure. All employees are hourly paid and are paid on the same day each 2 weeks. The wage rates vary between departments, with the technical departments generally receiving higher wages.

Upon the foregoing, it does not appear that the X-ray technicians involved herein have a community of interest that is any more separately identifiable than that of certain other employees in other

4. Including, aside from the 10 to 12 X-ray technicians in question, 4 to 5 emergency room technicians, 3 inhalation therapy technicians, 1 electrocardiagram technician (EKG), 1 electroencephalogram technician (EEG), 10 to 12 laboratory technicians, 10 to 12 operating room technicians, and 2 medical records technicians, all of whom are departmentalized in accordance with their various skills.

technical departments. In this regard, we note particularly the frequent contacts of X-ray technicians with other hospital employees, the fact that they perform their work at various locations throughout the hospital, and the functional integration of their work with that of other technical employees. To establish a separate unit for X-ray technicians, in circumstances such as these, would in our opinion lead to severe fragmentation of units in the health care industry.[5] As we see no basis for concluding that the X-ray technicians here involved, although separately supervised, constitute a separate appropriate unit, we shall dismiss the petition in Case 36--RC--3025. We therefore find, in Case 36--RC--3018, that the following employees constitute an appropriate unit for the purpose of collective bargaining:

> All employees employed at the Employer's Portland, Oregon, hospital, excluding all professional employees, confidential employees, registered nurses, dieticians, pharmacists, guards, and supervisors as defined in the Act.

Accordingly, we shall remand the case to the Regional Director in order that he may conduct an election pursuant to his Decision and Direction of Election as modified herein, except that the eligibility payroll period therefore shall be the one immediately preceding the issuance date of this decision.[6]

ORDER

It is hereby ordered that the petition filed in Case 36--RC--3025,

---

5. The case of Ochsner Clinic, 192 NLRB No. 156, to the extent inconsistent herewith, is hereby overruled.

6. In order to assure that all eligible voters may have the opportunity to be informed of the issues in the exercise of their statutory right to vote, all parties to the election should have access to a list of voters and their addresses which may be used to communicate with them. Excelsior Underwear Inc., 156 NLRB 1236; N.L.R.B. v. Wyman-Gordon Co., 394 U.S. 759. Accordingly, it is hereby directed that a corrected election eligibility list, containing the names and addresses of all the eligible voters, must be filed by the Employer with the Regional Director for Region 19 within 7 days of the date of this Decision on Review. The Regional Director shall make the list available to all parties to the election. No extension of time to file this list shall be granted by the Regional Director except in extraordinary circumstances. Failure to comply with this requirement shall be grounds for setting aside the election whenever proper objections are filed.

be, and it hereby is, dismissed.

Dated, Washington, D.C.

Edward B. Miller, Chairman

Ralph E. Kennedy, Member

John A. Penello, Member

NATIONAL LABOR RELATIONS BOARD

(SEAL)

MEMBER JENKINS, dissenting:

My colleagues, in overruling Ochsner Clinic, 192 NLRB No. 156, apparently are deciding that a unit of X-ray technicians is per se inappropriate. I would adhere to Ochsner and, under the principles applied there, find the unit of X-ray technicians sought here to be appropriate.

Howard Jenkins, Jr., Member

NATIONAL LABOR RELATIONS BOARD

208 NLRB No. 50

D--8291
Joliet, Ill.

UNITED STATES OF AMERICA

BEFORE THE NATIONAL LABOR RELATIONS BOARD

FOUR SEASONS NURSING
CENTER OF JOLIET

Employer

and

Case 13--RC--13149

INTERNATIONAL UNION OF
OPERATING ENGINEERS,
LOCAL 399, AFL--CIO

Petitioner

DECISION ON REVIEW AND ORDER

On September 28, 1973, the Acting Regional Director for Region 13 issued a Decision and Direction of Election in the above-entitled proceeding in which he directed an election in a unit of "all maintenance men and helpers...," comprised of two employees at the Employer's nursing center. In rendering that unit determination the Acting Regional Director rejected the Employer's contention that a unit composed solely of maintenance employees is not appropriate. Thereafter, in accordance with Section 102.67 of the National Labor Relations Board's Rules and Regulations, Series 8, as amended, the Employer filed a timely request for review of the Acting Regional Director's decision and brief, asserting, inter alia, that in finding a unit of maintenance employees without a determination that the two maintenance men had special skills or interests distinct from the other employees, the Acting Regional Director's findings were clearly erroneous and departed from officially reported precedent.

By telegraphic order dated October 29, 1973, the National Labor Relations Board granted the request for review and stayed the election pending decision on review. Pursuant to the provisions of Section 3(b) of the National Labor Relations Act, as amended, the National Labor Relations Board has delegated its authority in this proceeding to a three-member panel.

The Board has considered the entire record in this case with respect to the issues under review and makes the following findings:

The Employer operates a nursing home in Joliet, Illinois, where it employs approximately 143 employees in seven distinct departments: activities, administration, dietary, housekeeping, laundy, nursing, and maintenance.

Three men are employed in the maintenance department, including a supervisor. The duties of maintenance employees include cleaning, emptying trash, moving furniture, replacing light bulbs, keeping up the outer grounds, and minor functions of carpentry, painting, and plumbing. They also perform minor repair work; major repair work is contracted out to specially skilled workers from outside the nursing home.

All employees of the nursing home work throughout the home, are hourly paid, punch the same timeclock, and share common dining and locker areas. Although there is virtually no interchange of duties between the maintenance department and the other departments, both maintenance and housekeeping employees perform basically a cleaning function. Moreover, when the maintenance supervisor is absent, his duties are taken over by the housekeeping supervisor.

On the basis of the foregoing, and especially the fact that the maintenance employees primarily perform duties not requiring a high degree of skill or specialized training, we find, contrary to the Acting Regional Director, that the maintenance unit sought herein is not composed of a distinct and homogeneous group of employees with interests separate from those of other employees, and therefore is not an appropriate unit.[1] Accordingly, we shall dismiss the petition.

ORDER

It is hereby ordered that the petition herein be, and it hereby is, dismissed.

Dated, Washington, D.C.

Edward B. Miller, Chairman

Howard Jenkins, Jr., Member

Ralph E. Kennedy, Member

NATIONAL LABOR RELATIONS BOARD

(SEAL)

1. See Monsanto Company, 183 NLRB No. 53.

203 NLRB No. 170

D--7258
Bluefield, W. Va.

UNITED STATES OF AMERICA

BEFORE THE NATIONAL LABOR RELATIONS BOARD

EXTENDICARE OF WEST VIRGINIA, INC., d/b/a ST. LUKE'S HOSPITAL

Employer

and

Cases 9--RC--9709
9--RC--9710
9--RC--9711

LOCAL 1199--W. VA., NATIONAL UNION OF HOSPITAL AND NURSING HOME EMPLOYEES, RETAIL, WHOLESALE AND DEPARTMENT STORE UNION, AFL--CIO

Petitioner

DECISION AND DIRECTION OF ELECTIONS

Upon petitions duly filed under Section 9(c) of the National Labor Relations Act, as amended, a hearing was held before Hearing Officer Andrew L. Lang of the National Labor Relations Board. Following the close of the hearing, the Regional Director for Region 9 transferred this case to the Board for decision. Thereafter, the Employer and the Petitioner each filed briefs and supplemental briefs.[1]

The Board has reviewed the Hearing Officer's rulings made at the hearing and finds that they are free from prejudicial error. They are hereby affirmed.

Upon the entire record in this proceeding, the Board finds:

1. The Employer is engaged in commerce within the meaning of the Act, and it will effectuate the purposes of the Act to assert jurisdiction herein. The parties stipulated that the Employer, which operates an acute care general hospital for profit in Bluefield, West Virginia, and employs 140 people, has a gross annual income in excess of $500,000 per year, and during the past year has purchased supplies directly from outside the State of West Virginia valued in excess of $50,000. While the Employer questioned the Board's

---

1. The Employer has requested oral argument. This request is hereby denied as the record and the briefs adequately set forth the issues and the positions of the parties.

jurisdiction over it, it is clear that the Board's jurisdictional requirements have been satisfied.[2]

2. The labor organization involved claims to represent certain employees of the Employer. While the Employer questioned the Petitioner's status as a labor organization and its ability to adequately represent the employees in the units sought, the record discloses that the Petitioner admits employees to membership and represents employees concerning wages, hours, and working conditions. In addition, the Petitioner is actively engaged in organizational activities throughout West Virginia and surrounding States.

3. A question affecting commerce exists concerning the representation of certain employees of the Employer within the meaning of Sections 9(c)(1) and 2(6) and (7) of the Act.

4. The Petitioner seeks to represent three separate units of the Employer's employees (licensed practical nurses, technical employees, and service and maintenance employees). The Employer, however, contends that the only appropriate unit would be an all-employee unit containing the employees sought to be excluded by the Petitioner as office clericals should be included in the all-employee unit.

The 23 licensed practical nurses (LPN's) employed by the Employer work in the nursing department and are supervised by registered nurses (RN's), who are in charge on the various shifts, or by the shift supervisor. LPN's requisition and administer medicines and drugs, chart patients, and sometimes confer with doctors. The duties performed by the LPN's are not performed by any of the 34 nurses aides and 6 orderlies employed by the Employer (whom the Petitioner seeks to include in a service and maintenance unit). The record also establishes that while the LPN's are paid hourly, their wage rate is 40 percent higher than the rate for nurses aides or orderlies. The LPN's possess a high school diploma and, in addition, must complete 1 year of formal training and be licensed by the State of West Virginia. No such requirements are imposed on nurses aides and orderlies or any of the other categories of employees sought to be represented in the service and maintenance unit. Thus the record shows that the LPN's have a community of interest separate and distinct from the other employees and we therefore find appropriate a separate unit of LPN's as requested by the Petitioner.[3]

---

2. Butte Medical Properties, d/b/a Medical Center Hospital, 168 NLRB 266.

3. See Madeira Nursing Center, Inc., 203 NLRB No. 42, where we decided not to preclude exclusion of LPN's from a unit of nursing home employees when the LPN's enjoyed a substantial community of interest among themselves which was separate and distinct from the interests shared with other employees of the nursing home.

The Employer employs four X-ray technicians, two laboratory technicians, and an inhalation therapist. As noted above, the Petitioner seeks a unit of technical employees which would include these employees, while the Employer would include them in an all-employee unit. The Petitioner also seeks to represent a unit of approximately 62 service and maintenance employees including nurses aides, orderlies, housekeepers, dietary employees, and maintenance employees. The Employer again would include these employees in an all-employee unit. Alternatively, the Petitioner indicated a willingness to represent a single unit of technical employees and service and maintenance employees, as well as the separate unit of LPN's discussed above.

The record discloses that the X-ray technicians take and develop X-rays and transcribe physicians' findings. Their skills are developed by attending a 2-year postsecondary school course in radiology. The laboratory technicians perform laboratory-associated work such as blood and urine tests. In addition to possessing a high school diploma, they must complete a 1-year formal education program. The lone inhalation therapist employed at the hospital administers oxygen, operates oxygen tanks, and gives breathing treatments. She is required to possess a high school diploma or its equivalent and to complete 6 months of formal training. Thus, in view of the training received and the work performed by the X-ray technicians, laboratory technicians, and inhalation therapist, we find that they are technical employees. We also note, however, that these technical employees work under conditions substantially similar to those of the service and maintenance employees. For example, all such employees are paid on an hourly basis, punch a timeclock, and share the same fringe benefits. Additionally, they share a common dining room and generally intermingle in their work. The laboratory technicians perform at least some of their work outside the laboratory, and when in the laboratory they also have contact with the service and maintenance employees. The inhalation therapist spends most of her time on the hospital floors. She is under the supervision of the nursing department, which also supervises some of the service and maintenance people (nurses aides and orderlies).

We further note that the Petitioner primarily seeks to represent in separate units a total of approximately 62 service and maintenance employees and only 7 technical employees. In this situation, given the appropriateness of a separate unit of LPN's where the technical employees and service and maintenance employees share a community of interest, and the technical employees are relatively few in number, a finding that two separate units are appropriate for bargaining would create unwarranted unit fragmentation. Accordingly, and as the Petitioner has indicated a willingness to represent the technical employees and service and maintenance employees in one unit, we find that the technical employees service and maintenance employees together constitute a unit appropriate for bargaining.

The units requested by the Petitioner would exclude office

clericals, among others. Thus, it would exclude employees in Employer's medical records department and business office. The Employer, however, contends that employees in those departments share a community of interest with the service and maintenance employees and should be included in the unit.

The medical records section is located in a building separate from the main hospital building and, while the record indicates that the employees in the section do have contact with other employees, they spend 90 percent of their time in the medical records office. Their duties include preparing medical records, sorting, filing and retrieving old charts, organizing final charts, and compiling statistics. The business office employees, who are located in the main hospital building, spend only minimal time outside the business office. Their duties include switchboard operations, cashier and billing functions, and the handling of admissions. As the employees in both sections are essentially office workers who have little contact with other employees, they will be excluded from the technical, service, and maintenance unit.[4]

Accordingly, upon the entire record, we find that the following employees of the Employer constitute units appropriate for the purposes of collective bargaining within the meaning of Section 9(b) of the Act:

> All service and maintenance employees including nurses aides, orderlies, housekeeping employees, dietary employees, and maintenance employees, and all technical employees including X-ray technicians, laboratory technicians, and inhalation therapist; but excluding all office clerical employees, licensed practical nurses, registered nurses, professional employees, guards and supervisors as defined in the Act.
>
> All licensed practical nurses, but excluding service and maintenance employees, office clerical employees, technical employees, registered nurses, professional employees, guards and supervisors as defined in the Act.

DIRECTION OF ELECTIONS

Elections by secret ballot shall be conducted among the employees in the units found appropriate, as early as possible, but not later than 30 days from the date below. The Regional Director for Region 9 shall direct and supervise the elections, subject to the National Labor Relations Board Rules, Series 8, as amended. Eligible to

4. The Swanholm, An Operation of the Martin Luther Foundation, Inc., 186 NLRB 45.

vote are those in the units who were employed during the payroll period immediately preceding the date below, including employees who did not work during that period because they were ill, on vacation, or temporarily laid off. Also eligible are employees engaged in an economic strike which commenced less than 12 months before the election date and who retained their status as such during the eligibility period and their replacements. Those in the military services of the United States may vote if they appear in person at the polls. Ineligible to vote are employees who have quit or been discharged for cause since the designated payroll period; employees engaged in a strike who have been discharged for cause since the commencement thereof and who have not been rehired or reinstated before the election date; and employees engaged in an economic strike which commenced more than 12 months before the election date and who have been permanently replaced.[5] Those eligible shall vote whether or not they desire to be represented for collective-bargaining purposes by Local 1199--W. Va., National Union of Hospital and Nursing Home Employees, Retail, Wholesale and Department Store Union, AFL--CIO.

Dated, Washington, D.C.

Edward B. Miller, Chairman

John H. Fanning, Member

Howard Jenkins, Jr., Member

5. In order to assure that all eligible voters may have the opportunity to be informed of the issues in the exercise of their statutory right to vote, all parties to the elections should have access to lists of voters and their addresses which may be used to communicate with them. Excelsior Underwear Inc., 156 NLRB 1236; N.L.R.B. v. Wyman-Gordon Co., 394 U.S. 759. Accordingly, it is hereby directed that election eligibility lists, containing the names and addresses of all the eligible voters, must be filed by the Employer with the Regional Director for Region 9 within 7 days of the date of this Decision and Direction of Elections. The Regional Director shall make the lists available to all parties to the elections. No extension of time to file these lists shall be granted by the Regional Director except in extraordinary circumstances. Failure to comply with this requirement shall be grounds for setting aside the elections whenever proper objections are filed.

John A. Penello, Member

NATIONAL LABOR RELATIONS BOARD

(SEAL)

MEMBER KENNEDY, dissenting:

Contrary to my colleagues, I would find an overall unit of all employees sought to be represented by the Petitioner to be the appropriate unit, and I would direct a single election.

The Petitioner seeks to represent all employees except office clericals and the standard exclusions. This constitutes an appropriate overall unit.[6] The majority, however, permits the Petitioner to divide this comprehensive unit into two units, one consisting of the LPN's and the other consisting of the service and maintenance employees, X-ray and laboratory technicians, and the inhalation therapist. I know of no precedent for splintering a comprehensive unit into separate units when there is a single union involved and no prior history of collective bargaining.[7] The basis for this action is the asserted separate and distinct interest of the LPN's from the other employees. Such expressions as "distinct and separate interest" are words of art of a mere conclusionary assertion. Factually, there appears little to distinguish the duties and functions of the LPN's in this case from those in other cases in which the Board included the LPN's in an overall unit sought by a union even though their inclusion may have been opposed by the employer.[8] They work under the same supervision and in close contact with the aides and orderlies. The educational and formal training for an LPN is less than that required of some of the employees (X-ray technicians) in the other unit. Seemingly, the quantum of the LPN's mutuality of interest increases or decreases depending on the desires of the union as to their inclusion or exclusion.

Further, I cannot see what useful purpose is accomplished by establishing the LPN's as a separate unit. There is no showing that the Petitioner has a special interest in the LPN's apart from other employees or that it has devoted itself to serving their special

6. Butte Medical Properties, d/b/a Medical Center Hospital, supra.

7. Seemingly, this precedent would permit a union seeking to represent the production and maintenance employees to obtain one certification for the production employees and another for the maintenance employees; a union seeking to represent all the employees of a retail food store to obtain a certification for the meat department employees and another for the remainder of the store employees, etc.

8. Leisure Hill Health Centers, Inc., 203 NLRB No. 46.

interest by historically representing them on the basis of a separate unit. Under such circumstances, I believe that the fragmentation of the comprehensive unit into two separate units for the purpose of representation by the Petitioner would serve only to impede collective bargaining and is not in the best interest of all employees involved.[9]

Dated, Washington, D.C.

Ralph E. Kennedy, Member

NATIONAL LABOR RELATIONS BOARD

9. See F.N. Burt Company, Inc., 130 NLRB 1115.

Subject Index